WHAT PEOPLE ARE SAYING ABOUT THE FIGHT FOR JUSTICE

The first thing I did after I finished reading Ruth Kreindler's compelling saga of the 1988 bombing of Pan Am Flight 103 was give the book to an acquaintance of mine who produces movies. "It's the next blockbuster," I told him. A true crime, legal drama peppered with sex, drugs, thievery, lies and plain old bad manners. There's no let up in action when all this winds up in court. It's a fact-filled, highly detailed story that is both sweeping and intimate and capped with a stunning conclusion. I know a good story when I read one.
 — *Christine Negroni*
 aviation journalist, public speaker and broadcaster
 author of The Crash Detectives.

An impressive book. Not only is it a clear presentation of an enormous enormously complex story, it moves forward with great momentum like a spy thriller.
 — *David E.K. Hunter*
 author of Working Hard and Working Well.

The Fight for Justice: Lee Kreindler and Lockerbie chronicles the most significant air disaster case of the 20th century which resulted in the largest financial recovery for a single disaster in aviation history; established a precedent for suing state sponsors of terrorism and marked a historic moment for the victims' families and the legal community.
 — *Kim Doleatto,*
 journalist, Sarasota Magazine

The Fight for Justice: Lee Kreindler and Lockerbie is a fitting monument to an extraordinary man who fought one of the great legal struggles of modern times and triumphed. It is a truly rewarding read.
 — *Michael H. Traison*
 partner, Cullen and Dykman LLP

ABOUT LEE KREINDLER

Lee was a great aviation law tactician and the most successful plaintiff's aviation attorney ever. But, for me, what drew me to him was his humanity, graciousness, and charm.

> — *Nicholas Gilman*
> *Gilman & Associates, Washington DC*
> *Aviation attorney*

Lee Kreindler was a wonderful man and a good friend. He helped me without being asked, and he always acted in my interest.

> — *Joseph Biden*
> *President of the United States,*
> *then U.S. Senator*

We would never have been here without your untinting, tireless efforts over almost 50 years to bring about a just and proper system [of air disaster compensation]. Personally, and on behalf of the entire U.S. government, you have our unrestrained thanks.

> — *Letter to Lee from Allan I. Mendelsohn*
> *Deputy Assistant Secretary for Transportation Affairs*
> *U.S. State Department*

Lee had an insatiable passion for the rule of law, for the pursuit of justice, for the pursuit of fair and just compensation for his clients, and for getting to the root cause for any aircraft accident. His "sue for safety" theme was scoffed and mocked at by the cynics in the early years, but even they became reverent disciples.

> — *George N. Thompson, Jr.*
> *Leading aviation defense lawyer*

He helped me when my husband was killed in an airplane accident. I was a homemaker with four children and very frightened. His compassion and advice contributed to our family being able to move on.

> — *Sue Kuchenbrod*
> *Client*

THE FIGHT FOR JUSTICE
LEE KREINDLER and LOCKERBIE

RUTH KREINDLER
and
CHRIS ANGERMANN

Published by Fight for Justice, LLC.
Sarasota, Florida
www.FightForJusticeLLC.com

THE FIGHT FOR JUSTICE
LEE KREINDLER and LOCKERBIE

Second Edition
Trade Paperback ISBN 979-8-9992226-3-3
Hardcover ISBN: 979-8-9992226-0-2
eBook ISBN: 979-8-9992226-2-6

Library of Congress Control Number: 2025944253

Copyright © 2025 by The Ruth B. Kreindler Revocable Trust U/A/D April 29, 2016

All rights reserved by the copyright holder. No part of this book may be used or reproduced in any form or by any electronic or mechanical means, including information storage and retrieval systems, without permission in writing from the authors.

Published by Fight for Justice, LLC.

Sarasota, FL

www.FightForJusticeLLC.com

This title was originally published by Bardolf and Company.

Cover design by *shawcreativegroup.com*

To my husband Lee Kreindler
who reached for the stars
and took us with him.

CONTENTS

PROLOGUE	9
1 NOTIFICATIONS	11
2 THE CLIENTS	21
3 ORIGINS	33
4 IN FITS AND STARTS	53
5 FIRST ATTEMPT TO SETTLE	57
6 DISCOVERY	63
7 BREAKTHROUGH	71
8 SHENANIGANS AT THE AIRPORT	87
9 DOCUMENTARY EVIDENCE	95
10 DEPOSITIONS IN GERMANY	101
11 THE ALERT DEPOSITIONS	111
12 DISINFORMATION CAMPAIGN	125
13 SECOND ATTEMPT TO SETTLE	137
14 INQUIRY AND TRAGEDY	147
15 STEPS TOWARD PROVING CAUSATION	157
16 FURTHER STEPS TOWARD PROVING CAUSATION	169
17 FRAU ERAC	179
18 HELP FROM THE CRIMINAL INVESTIGATION	189
19 ANOTHER ATTEMPT TO SETTLE	193

20	MONEY ISSUES	201
21	PROVING CAUSATION	209
22	MORE DISINFORMATION	213
23	THE TRIAL BEGINS	225
24	THE PLAINTIFFS CASE	239
25	THE DEFENSE PLAYS GAMES	251
26	THE DEFENSE CIRCUS	267
27	KURT MAIER	279
28	CLOSING ARGUMENTS	289
29	THE VERDICT	301
30	THE DAMAGES TRIALS	313
31	THE APPEAL	323
32	FINAL JUDGMENT	335
33	LIBYA	345
34	FRAZZLED	355
35	LIBYA AGAIN	363
36	AFTERMATH	379
EPILOGUE		383
ACKNOWLEDGMENTS		387
BIOGRAPHIES		389

PROLOGUE

On the evening of December 21, 1988, a Pan American airplane left the terminal gate at Heathrow Airport in London, England. The Boeing 747 slowly taxied on the tarmac toward the long departure queue. It was just after 6 p.m. and already dark outside. Because of the holiday season, the airport was busier than usual—red and green night lights of planes blinking everywhere—and Flight 103 took off 25 minutes late.

None of the 259 passengers and 11 crew aboard were worried about the delay.

They were from 21 countries and five continents, on their way to New York. Nearly two-thirds were Americans, including 35 students from Syracuse University who were going home for Christmas after a semester abroad. The atmosphere aboard the plane was lively and festive, permeated with holiday spirit. Many of the students knew each other and talked excitedly among themselves. The flight attendants were getting ready to serve drinks and snacks.

None of the passengers and crew knew that they had less than an hour to live.

The jumbo jet, named *Clipper Maid of the Seas*, climbed steadily, reaching a cruising altitude of 31,000 feet. As it left England and entered Scottish airspace, the captain, an experienced pilot, contacted Air Traffic Control and announced that he was getting ready to turn left to start the flight's transatlantic crossing. It was the last communication heard from the aircraft.

THE FIGHT FOR JUSTICE

Four minutes later, at 7:02, near the small town of Lockerbie, there was a loud bang, an explosion. It punched a hole in the fuselage, and in seconds, the high atmospheric winds tore the plane apart.

Passengers and crew plummeted to earth. Some, thrown from the aircraft strapped in their seats, tumbled through the air flailing and screaming. Others remained trapped inside sections of the fuselage crashing to the ground. The bodies and debris from the plane rained down over an area of many square miles.

None of them survived.

* * *

At New York's Kennedy Airport, the families of the passengers milled about the Pan Am terminal, waiting for Flight 103 to arrive. Several parents of the Syracuse University students had driven there, unaware of the disaster. When the announcement came that the plane had been lost, they were stunned.

One of the students' mothers collapsed, hitting her head on the floor. Screaming and wailing in anguish, she cried out, "My baby! My baby!"

As she trashed about, her arms and legs flailing, her husband threw himself on top of her, trying to calm her. "Stop it, please stop it!" he pleaded. "There is nothing we can do."

A television crew pushed through the shocked onlookers and filmed the scene. One of the reporters shoved a microphone toward the couple for a comment.

The husband waved him off, furious, "Go away, you idiot," he shouted. "Have you no decency?"

The reporter drew back, but the crew kept filming.

The mother's heart-rending sobbing continued for a long time.

1

NOTIFICATIONS

December 21, 1988

Lee Kreindler pulled his overcoat tight against the brisk winter cold and headed north on Park Avenue. He had been having lunch with a fellow attorney at the Union League Club on 37th Street in Manhattan. It was only three blocks from his law firm, and he returned to the office on foot.

At 64, Lee was the world's foremost aviation disaster attorney. He had litigated numerous air crashes. He had written a groundbreaking book on aviation disaster law and gave speeches on the subject at conferences all over the world. Some of his cases had led to changes in aircraft engineering and design that made air travel safer for everyone.

As he walked under the construction scaffolding of an office building, he listened to the familiar honking of New York's impatient drivers. He thought about the upcoming staff Christmas party. There were good reasons to celebrate. It had been a good year for his law firm, with two major cases being settled out of court.

At the ramp where Park Avenue rises to form a bridge over 42nd Street, he looked up at the familiar skyscraper looming behind Grand Central Station. For nearly 20 years, it had been the headquarters of Pan Am, America's largest international airline. Even after the company sold the building in 1981 and the Metropolitan Life Insurance

Company put its name "MetLife" up top, most New Yorkers still called it the Pan Am building.

Lee looked at his watch. It showed 2:30. He hurried to the office building at 100 Park Avenue and took the elevator to the 18th floor.

As he stepped into the lobby of his law firm, he sensed that something was up. The receptionist talking to a paralegal stopped in mid-sentence and gave him a startled look. The air felt charged with electricity.

Frank Fleming, one of the senior partners, appeared around the corner, as if he had been waiting for Lee for some time. "Pan Am just lost a 747 over Lockerbie, Scotland," he said with a stern expression. "A flight to New York and Detroit. An explosion. Or structural failure."

Lee felt a twinge in his chest. "What do we know so far?" he asked.

"Not much. CNN has no coverage other than the announcement. What do we do?"

"Let's see how things unfold," Lee said. "Keep me posted."

He headed to the office kitchenette to get a glass of water. The color television monitor, mounted on the wall, was turned to CNN. Above the newsflash "Plane Crashes in Scotland," there were nighttime images of houses ablaze and billowing smoke in an eerie orange glow.

Lee watched, experienced a jolt of horror and sadness followed by a sense of weariness in anticipation of dealing with the repercussions of the disaster. He knew, one way or another, he would be part of the legal battles that were sure to come.

He headed for his office, where his secretary, Pat Robinson, sat at her desk, opening mail. She had been with him for more than 30 years, ever since he and his father started the firm. Well-organized, warm-hearted, and outgoing, with a good sense of humor, she could be businesslike and empathetic, as the situation demanded.

"Nothing urgent, Mr. Lee," she said, smiling. "I guess things are going to get busy." She raised her eyebrows and nodded confidently to let him know she was ready, come what may.

As the afternoon wore on, Lee returned to the kitchenette to check on the television mounted on the wall. Lockerbie continued to be the lead story. The news feed from the Scottish town kept showing houses on fire where a section of the airplane had hit the ground. First responders at the scene—firefighters, police officers, and rescue workers—were milling about. A nearby street was lined with ambulances waiting, their emergency lights flashing.

The coverage also included a grief-stricken mother writhing on the floor at the Pan Am terminal. The scene played over and over behind news anchors reporting unemotionally on the disaster.

The first time he saw it, Lee looked away, wishing he could give the bereaved woman some privacy. His heart went out to her. He had met inconsolable families, angry survivors, and people stoically coping with the pain of losing their loved ones for more than three decades. After all that time, their distress still touched him deeply.

Late that afternoon, Lee received a phone call from Phil Bostwick, an aviation defense attorney in Washington, D.C. He and Lee had been on opposite sides of the litigation for a Turkish Airlines DC 10 which crashed near Paris in the early 1970s. A cargo door had blown off, destroying several cables needed to control the plane, and all 346 passengers and crew died in the crash. Lee had represented about 100 victims' families, and ultimately, McDonnell-Douglas and Turkish Airlines agreed to an out-of-court settlement. Like many of Lee's legal adversaries, Phil Bostwick found him to be trustworthy and became a good friend.

He got straight to the point. "Lee, I've given your name to a lawyer in Boston. His name is Walter Van Dorn, and his closest friend is the father of one of the Syracuse kids probably killed in the Pan Am accident today." He continued, "I've apprised Walter of how the Warsaw Convention affects airline disasters in international travel and told him you're the expert. If anyone can deal with it, it's you."

Soon after, Walter Van Dorn called from Boston. "The family is devastated," he said. "Margy Simon was the sweetest, loveliest girl. Her father is a basket case. I am going over to see them now. Can you give me an idea of what their rights are? If they ask me, what do I tell them?"

Lee said, "Nothing immediately. Just make sure the family is safe and has the necessary emotional support. I can't come myself, but I will send someone from my office to meet with them tomorrow afternoon."

After he ended the call, Lee asked two of the firm's attorneys to join him in his office. One was his son Jim, who had come five years earlier from the Brooklyn District Attorney's Office where he had gathered considerable trial experience. Half a foot taller than his father, he had the solid trunk of a college running back.

The other, Steve Pounian, had joined Kreindler & Kreindler in 1980 and had just made partner the year before. He was lean as a reed and had a gentle, engaging personality that put clients at ease.

They arrived together, and Jim asked, "Is this about Lockerbie?"

"Yes," Lee said. "This is going to be an extraordinarily difficult case, perhaps the most difficult we've ever handled. I'd like you both to work on it with me."

Surprised, Jim and Steve looked at each other. The firm had never put more than one attorney on an air disaster case, and now Lee wanted to have three!

"What do you want us to do?" Jim asked

"You and I can discuss that in Florida as things unfold," Lee said. "In the meantime, Steve, I know it's a lot to ask at this time of year, but would you call Walter Van Dorn and meet with the Simon family in Boston tomorrow?"

Steve did not hesitate. "I'll have Carole book me a flight," he said and hurried to his office to inform his secretary.

Lee looked at Jim who was lingering by the door. They had not teamed up on a case before. His partners would not think it was a good idea. But the time had come.

"I look forward to working with you, Jim," he said.

Jim allowed himself a smile. "Me too."

By the time Lee took the Metro North Train home to Chappaqua in Westchester County, it seemed everyone knew about the Lockerbie disaster. He heard several commuters who usually relaxed in silence, tired from their day's work, talk about it in muted conversations.

Lee kept to himself. He was looking forward to seeing his wife Ruth and sharing all that had happened with her. No doubt she had seen the television coverage and understood the implications. He imagined she would greet him with the knowing, quizzical expression she always had when he told her about a big new case that would occupy him to the point of obsession.

* * *

The following morning, the phones at Kreindler & Kreindler started to ring off the hook. Reporters, journalists, other attorneys, and potential clients all wanted information—more than Lee, Jim, and Steve could provide. The atmosphere at the firm remained on high alert throughout the day.

As the world media descended on Lockerbie, the extent of the disaster became more apparent, although there was still no explanation for what caused the crash. The Boeing 747 had broken apart in mid-air. Its remains, including the bodies of the passengers, were strewn over a large area surrounding the town. The mangled cockpit with the name *Clipper Maid of the Seas* visible above the blue stripe along the passenger windows had crashed in a field three miles away from the city center, establishing with certainty that it was Pan Am Flight 103 that had gone down. A large section of the fuselage had leveled five houses in the town, killing 11 people on the ground in a firestorm of destruction, and had gouged out a crater more than 150 yards long, filled with debris. Another part of the fuselage and two jet engines landed nearby but, fortunately, caused only property damage.

The Scottish authorities had assembled a large task force to comb the countryside and retrieve the bodies of the victims and their suitcases, clothes, half-wrapped Christmas presents, and other personal articles. They also confirmed that 35 students from Syracuse University were aboard the aircraft when it crashed.

By the early afternoon, Lee and Kreindler & Kreindler received their first retainer. The Cummings family in Connecticut had lost their father in the crash. Before the day was out, Steve Pounian called from Boston. He had met with the Simon family, and they had hired the firm as well.

When Lee met with his nine other partners in the conference room while Steve was still in transit returning from Massachusetts, there was none of the usual, jovial kidding. They sat around the table quietly, looking at him expectantly with serious expressions.

"It looks like we'll be retained by many clients. So, it's going to be a huge challenge, the most difficult we ever had," Lee said. "That's why I've asked Steve and Jim to work with me. I know we've never had three attorneys on a case before. We're a relatively small firm, and it will strain our human and financial resources to the limit."

He outlined some of the challenges of the case, notably the constraints of the Warsaw Convention of 1929, which limited airline liability in international plane crashes, capping damages at $10,000 per passenger death. In 1960 the Montreal Agreement had raised that figure to $75,000. The U.S. government had spearheaded the negotiations, wanting to preserve the Warsaw Convention. Foreign nations liked it because it prevented American passengers and families from recovering large damage amounts. The State Department liked it because it kept other countries' governments happy.

Lee did not care for it, however. Never one to mince words, he had called the agreement "stupid, irresponsible, and un-American" because it deprived bereaved families of fair compensation. In many situations, the payouts survivors received were the only means by which they could maintain their homes and pay for their children's education, and $75,000 did not go very far.

There were two ways to defeat the treaty's monetary strictures. One involved suing the manufacturer, in this case, Boeing. If they could prove that a mechanical defect had caused the crash, they could negotiate a larger settlement. The other would require finding Pan Am guilty of "willful misconduct," knowingly engaging in actions that contributed to the disaster.

"In either case, it will require months of discovery, going through documents, and conducting depositions and interviews in the United States and overseas," Lee explained. "It could be a year or more before we reach a settlement or go to trial."

He looked around the room at his partners, their subdued faces reflecting the gravity of the situation. Most of them were a generation younger than him, having come aboard when older partners retired. They had never dealt with a disaster of this magnitude.

"This is probably the biggest case our firm has ever taken on, and the risk is enormous," Lee said. "Expenses will mount with no increase in income and put everyone under great stress." He paused and concluded. "I won't be able to do it without your full cooperation and support."

THE FIGHT FOR JUSTICE

No one had any questions when he finished. The partners glanced at one another, communicating their agreement in silence with slight nods. Finally, Frank Fleming, speaking for everyone, said, "Okay. We're all on board. Let's do it!"

*　*　*

On Friday, Lee and Ruth flew to Sarasota, Florida, for a few days of vacation. Lee was looking forward to their stay at the Colony Tennis and Beach Resort on Longboat Key, where they owned an apartment. He liked to call it "our oasis." The Sarasota airport was tiny and quaint and felt almost abandoned compared to busy LaGuardia. A single-story building with a few terminals and an open area that had a single baggage claim carousel opposite two rental car counters. When the Kreindlers stepped outside into the balmy weather and sunshine, they immediately relaxed. After the bitter New York cold and hectic days at the firm, Florida felt like a peaceful paradise.

By the time Jim and their daughter Laurie and their children arrived the next morning, Lee had managed to get in a set of tennis. Later, he splashed in the resort pool with his two young grandchildren, Kate and Jason. After sending them off to get lunch, he floated in the warm water, letting his body unwind. He knew his respite would be brief at best.

And he was right. Pat Robinson telephoned and reported that the *New York Times* and other newspapers wanted to talk to him about Lockerbie. After lunch, NBC News in Tampa called, requesting a live interview. Lee agreed, and the following day—Sunday—a film crew traveled to Longboat Key by helicopter. The chopper landing on the white-powder sand beach attracted a large crowd of residents and vacationers. They followed the crew lugging cameras, lights, and sound equipment to the Kreindler condo and kept milling about, rubbernecking.

Notifications

Ruth was not happy with the all attention it brought to her family in full view of their neighbors. She had accompanied Lee on many of his high-profile cases and was used to the inevitable media circus, but in this instance, things threatened to spiral out of control much earlier than usual.

The news team set up their equipment in the small living room of the condo and peppered Lee with questions. He responded calmly in a firm tone of voice.

"What might have been the cause of the crash?" the reporter began.

Lee answered, "It could have been a bomb or structural failure."

"What if it turns out to be a bomb? Can you sue the terrorists?"

"Let's wait until we know more."

"How long before we will know?"

"I expect a week or so."

"What are the rights of the families? What can they hope to recover?"

"Only time will tell."

2

THE CLIENTS

December 1988 - March 1989

A week after the crash of Pan Am Flight 103, Scottish and American government investigators held a joint press conference in the city of Inverness. They announced that the explosion of a bomb in the luggage compartment of the Boeing 747 caused the disaster. The inquiry into an accidental airplane crash was now a murder investigation.

For days, more than 1,000 volunteers, police, military personnel, and other investigators had combed over 800 square miles surrounding Lockerbie for scattered debris and human remains. They had moved slowly across the fields in lines of eight or ten, holding hands to be sure not to miss the smallest remnant and clue.

Two of the metallic cargo containers they located showed unmistakable signs of an explosive device having detonated. The searchers also found a copper-colored Samsonite suitcase and the remains of a Toshiba radio-cassette recorder with the residue of the bomb that had been hidden inside. They'd stumbled upon that evidence early in the week but did not inform the international press until tests conclusively verified the initial assessment.

Watching the newscast with Jim in Florida, Lee noted grimly, "Bet you never thought you'd have to deal with homicide again after leaving the DA's office in Brooklyn."

The news that the downing of Pan Am 103 was an act of terrorism sent shock waves all over the globe. People everywhere were aghast that 259 innocent passengers and 11 Scottish residents on the ground had been murdered. Worldwide indignation led to angry demands that the culprits be found quickly and brought to justice.

For Lee, the proof of terrorist involvement complicated the legal situation. It closed off one avenue of litigation to overcome the Warsaw Conventions' limitations for damages—holding Boeing, the plane's manufacturer, responsible for possible defects. Now, he had to take on Pan Am Airlines and prove willful misconduct, a much more difficult undertaking.

Meanwhile, news outlets reported that there had been advanced warnings of the bomb attack.

In early November 1988, a month before the Lockerbie disaster, the German *Bundeskriminalamt* (BKA), the equivalent of the American FBI, raided the apartment of a terrorist group in a small town on the Rhine River north of the city of Frankfurt. They arrested 16 members of a cell of the Popular Front for the Liberation of Palestine, headed by the notorious Syrian terrorist Ahmed Jabril. They also discovered several bombs hidden in Toshiba radio cassette players, designed to blow up airplanes.

In response, the Federal Aviation Administration (FAA) sent out a security bulletin to all American airlines, advising that such bombs would be "extremely difficult to detect by normal X-rays."

Another warning came two weeks before the actual disaster according to an article in *The New York Times*. On December 5, the American embassy in Helsinki, Finland, received an anonymous telephone call from someone with a heavy Arab accent. He warned about a bomb threat against a Pan Am flight from Frankfurt, Germany. He did not specify which flight but insisted it would occur before Christmas.

Although there were some questions about whether the warning was authentic, the United States government took it seriously. Two days later, the FAA sent a bulletin to American embassies and airlines but did not inform the public of the threat. The U.S. embassy in Moscow posted the warning for its employees, and some diplomatic personnel changed their flights home to other airlines.

Many people, especially the families of the victims on Flight 103, questioned why Pan Am and the FAA chose to keep the Helsinki warning secret. They were upset and demanded answers.

Jeffrey Kriendler, a cousin of Lee's who spelled his last name differently, was vice president for communications at Pan Am. Speaking to the press, he said that when the airline received the FAA bulletin, "immediate action was taken, and the steps that were implemented at that time are still in place."

Watching his cousin on television, Lee wondered how the case would affect their relationship. The families were close and got together every year in Chappaqua for a big dinner. Now, he and Jeff were on opposite sides of what was bound to become a contentious legal battle. Would their long-standing family ties suffer? Would Jeff still accept Lee's and Ruth's invitation?

In the same press conference, aviation security experts weighed in: There were good reasons not to warn the public of the threats, they said. It would alert terrorist groups to how much the authorities knew. Ray Salazar, the director of aviation security at the FAA, commented, "If the security bulletins become public knowledge, people could circumvent the security measures. We have a process that works."

Another reason for secrecy was that public notice might lead to "copycat" threats, worsening the situation. Furthermore, the airlines would suffer economic losses when passengers canceled their flights even when the threats were not valid. President Ronald Regan, nearing the end of his second term in office, told reporters that issuing public statements about Lockerbie "would literally have closed down all the air traffic in the world."

None of these explanations satisfied the victims' families. They were already angry about the indifferent treatment by the U.S. government, which had a hands-off policy regarding air disasters. Lockerbie and its aftermath changed that. Now, the State Department contacts survivors right away and offers assistance, but at the time, it left the grieving families on their owns. The government siding with the airlines and their economic priorities added insult to injury.

The first indication Lee received that the announcement in Scotland and subsequent revelations in the news infuriated people came on New Year's Day. He was wearing his favorite, black-and white, plaid flat cap and watching his granddaughter, Kate, splash in the condo swimming pool. His grandson, Jason, who was five months old, sat on his lap. When the telephone by his side rang, Lee held onto Jason and picked up the receiver.

The voice at the other end sounded angry. "Mr. Kreindler, my name is George Williams. You have been highly recommended to me. My son, Geordie, was blown up on Pan Am 103. I want to kill all the bastards who did it. I won't rest until everyone responsible for the disaster is behind bars or dead. I will kill them myself if I have to—and that includes the terrorists and any Pan Am people who were to blame. Will you take my case?"

Lee tried to keep the tension he felt from affecting his grandson. He arranged to meet with George in New York the following week.

By then, the retired postman and former Marine had not mellowed. Although he looked worn out by grief, Lee could feel his barely contained fury. George was not in good health. He lived in a small home in Maryland with his wife Judy and dabbled in real estate. Geordie, their pride and joy, was finishing his final tour of duty in Germany as an Army First Lieutenant attached to a helicopter unit. He planned to join his father to start a small family real estate business. The high point of the week for George and Judy was when Geordie called them. Now he was gone, and Judy had plunged into a deep depression.

Lee empathized with George. "I will do everything I can to get you justice," he said.

He knew his promise was small comfort at best.

Another referral came from a Washington, D.C. attorney Lee knew in passing. Bert Rein called on behalf of his sister-in-law Denise and her children. "My brother, Marc, was on the Pan Am flight," he explained.

Lee had looked over a list of passengers on Flight 103 and recognized the name. Marc Rein had been the treasurer of the investment banking firm Solomon Brothers, a high-powered corporate position. Lee assured Bert, "I'll be pleased to meet with Denise as soon as she is ready, and I will do everything in my power to recover fair damages for your brother's family."

Three weeks later, Denise—Denny—and her father came to Lee's office in New York. She looked haggard, as if she hadn't slept in weeks, and kept rubbing her knuckles like worry beads. Her father, a white-haired man with patrician looks and bearing, never cracked a smile but occasionally reached out and covered her hands with his, trying to comfort her.

Lee spoke with them for about an hour, explaining the issues surrounding the Warsaw Convention and outlining what lay ahead. "In going after Pan Am, establishing simple negligence is not enough to win the case. We must prove willful misconduct. We must show that the airline or its agents knew they were doing something improper that could cause death and destruction, but they continued to do it anyway. It will not be easy, and it will take a long time."

Denny's father asked, "How good is our case, Lee?"

"I'm hoping it will be a strong case," Lee said.

Denny looked at him with big eyes. "Are you optimistic, Lee?"

"Yes, I am hopeful."

Denny and her father signed a retainer with the firm.

The parade of bereaved families went from morning till night. Many people came to the office with their attorney. Sometimes, only one family member showed up, sometimes more. Occasionally, it seemed the whole clan arrived. In one case, 12 people crowded into the conference room on the 18th floor.

Often, these meetings were exploratory. The families talked to several lawyers and visited Lee more than once before deciding who to retain. In the depths of shock and grieving, they wanted as much certainty as possible. Lee never overpromised but provided an outline of what lay ahead in the case and what services his law firm would provide.

He went over the fee structure with them. If a client retained Kreindler & Kreindler directly, the firm charged 20% in dependency cases and 25% in non-dependency cases of the amount recovered. The non-dependency fee for children who died was higher because New York State law severely limited recovery. If a client retained the firm through a lawyer who would continue to work on the case, acting as liaison with the family and obtaining documents for potential damages settlements, the net fee would be 15% or 20%, with the referring attorney getting 5%.

A few people were satisfied during the first visit that they wanted Lee and his team to represent them. When they said so, Lee would ask Jim or Steve Pounian to join them, the two alternating cases. Following introductions, they would take the clients to their offices on the floor above and introduce them to Virginia Parkhouse or Lisa Meacham, the two paralegals helping with the case. Then Jim and Steve interviewed the new clients for about two hours, getting the names of friends, co-workers, and business associates who could appear as character witnesses during the damage assessment portion of the trial. Later, they would schedule interviews to obtain reference letters and preliminary statements.

Lee fielded most of the initial calls that came to the firm himself. Pat Robinson scheduled meetings with the family members at the office or with their attorneys at restaurants for lunch.

Pat was efficient and well-organized but also kind and compassionate. Because of her warmth and sense of humor, clients quickly took to her. It was not unusual for them to be on a first-name basis by the time she shepherded them into Lee's office.

Lee knew how fortunate he was to have her. Many potential clients brought a host of pent-up emotions with them—fear, anger, anxiety, fury, sadness, anguish—and he wanted their initial experience to put them at ease. When they arrived, they did not encounter the stolid, often intimidating look of most established New York law firms—walls covered with dark, wooden paneling and oil paintings in heavy frames. Instead, they saw streamlined, modern-looking furniture and walls painted in appealing blues to suggest sunny skies. Ruth, who had a background in architecture and interior design, had designed the décor.

She was also responsible for the round glass table in the corner of Lee's office, whose base contained a hydraulic jack screw that could be raised and lowered remotely. When Lee adjusted it for his clients as he invited them to sit down, it often made for a good conversation piece.

Ruth had designed the table with the help of an expert engineering consultant after Lee won a lawsuit against Boeing in the 1961 Sabena Airlines 707 crash in Brussels, Belgium.

The crux of the case concerned the plane's horizontal wing stabilizer, which was regulated by a jack screw. Lee proved that the accident occurred when the thumb switch that controlled the turning of the screw had become stuck, locking the stabilizer in an extreme position. As a result, the Boeing 707 "porpoised" up and down for several minutes. The crew fought to gain control but to no avail. The plane crashed, killing everyone aboard, including the United States Olympic skating team members and its coaches.

Lee represented the families of the team and several other passengers and defeated the limitation of the Warsaw Convention by proving that Boeing was liable. While working on the case, he learned just about everything there was to know about jack screws, and Ruth decided to surprise him on his birthday following his victory.

The elegant-looking glass table with its lift mechanism always surprised clients and often acted as an icebreaker. As Lee told the story of how it was created, many anxious visitors relaxed. When he pushed a button that lowered the table, they were captivated and relaxed even more.

That did not happen, however, when Jeannine Boulanger and her husband Dave came to the office. Lee recalled the horrific scene on national television of Jeannine flailing on the floor of the Pan Am airport terminal when she realized she'd lost her daughter, Nicole, a promising young actress. Unbearable pain had overcome Jeannine then, but now she was on the other side of anguish and not in a friendly mood.

"We've seen everyone else. Why should we retain you," she challenged Lee as Pat ushered her into his office. Dave followed behind, looking a bit embarrassed.

"Why don't we sit down" Lee offered, but he never got to adjust the jack screw table.

"Why should you be my lawyer?" she challenged him again.

Over the years, Lee met with many angry clients who used him as a lightning rod for their angry feelings, and he knew that merely answering Jeannine's question would not defuse her rage. He said, "Mrs. Boulanger, I can't tell you that. Maybe I shouldn't be your lawyer. Maybe we won't get along. Maybe you would be more comfortable with someone else."

Jeannine sat down. So did her husband. "OK," she said, somewhat mollified, "But tell me why it should be you."

Lee took a seat across from her. "I'm serious. Maybe it shouldn't be me or my firm," he said. "What we have to offer you is fair and honest representation. That's all I can promise you. We have a superb staff. My two partners working on the case with me are excellent, experienced lawyers. We have a good track record. We have broken the limitation of damages of the Warsaw Convention more than anyone else, and I wrote the book on aviation accident law. But maybe we're not compatible."

Jeannine gave him a long, hard stare—she did not as much as glance at her husband—and said, "You're hired. I'm sick of talking to lawyers."

"Don't you want to know about our fee," Lee asked.

"No," she said. "I told you, I'm sick of talking to lawyers. Just charge us what you charge everyone else."

Lee wondered if taking on Jeannine as a client was a good idea. Would she cause trouble? Would she be impossible to satisfy? But he picked up the phone and asked Steve Pounian to come down to get a retainer signed and conduct the damages interview, trusting his gentle manner would dampen some of Jeannine's aggression.

It did and, in time, the Boulangers became one of Lee's fiercest supporters.

Not everyone arrived so openly hostile. Dona Bainbridge came in from White Plains, New York, with her lawyer. She moved gingerly because she was eight months pregnant. After she sat down at the round glass table, she wrapped her arms around her big stomach.

Her husband, Harry, had been a young lawyer in the legal department of PepsiCo's corporate headquarters in Somers, New York. He had been on Flight 103 with his boss, Robert Pagnucco, who was Assistant General Counsel of the company. Dona knew his wife Judy, who had already retained Kreindler & Kreindler.

PepsiCo gave its management employees excellent stock options. Just about every senior attorney in the legal department was a millionaire by age 50. But Harry had not been with the company long enough to reap that benefit. While PepsiCo was helping Dona financially, she was worried about money. She had left her job as an administrator for a non-profit organization in White Plains, New York, to have her baby. The small life insurance her husband had left her would not be enough to support them. She would have to go back to work.

Her lawyer brought out a letter and said, "We want to talk about this."

Glancing at the Pan Am logo at the top, Lee realized he had seen it already. It was from the airline's chairman, who had sent it to the families in mid-February, nearly two months after the disaster. Thomas P. Plaskett offered his condolences, mentioned developments in the investigation, dismissed the Helsinki warning as a hoax, and stated that families were entitled to "certain compensation as provided by international treaties."

"It felt like a slap in the face," Dona said.

"I can imagine," Lee said gently.

She frowned. "But what does the part about 'certain compensation' mean?" After Lee went over the Warsaw Convention issues with her, she asked, "How good is our case, Lee?"

"I'm hoping it will be a strong case," Lee answered. "We will have to prove willful misconduct to overcome the liability limitations."

"Is it possible to do that, Lee?" She clasped her hands tighter over her stomach, as if to protect her baby.

"Yes, it is possible, and we have been able to do it in other cases, at least to the point that the defendants recognized their liability exposure and settled voluntarily."

Dona signed a retainer agreement.

Every victim's family was different. Jack Schultz and his wife Jane were in their late 40s and lived on Manhattan's Upper East Side. As CEO of B. Altman, a large New York department store, and former president of Macy's, Jack was a recognized retail authority. Jane was a prominent public figure in her own right, overseeing charity events that involved New York's upper echelon of society. They were frequently invited to the White House and attended important retailing conferences worldwide.

Preparing for the meeting, Lee expected a power couple used to being in charge. But that day, they seemed tentative and uncertain, like worried parents at a student-teacher conference.

Lee was surprised until they told him their heartbreaking story.

Two years earlier, they decided to move with their two teenage sons to Stamford, Connecticut, and bought a beautiful house there. The previous owners had left some items behind, and on the Schultzes' first visit to their new home, their youngest son, Andrew, noticed an object he did not recognize. It was an old grenade, a relic of World War II. As he examined it more closely, it exploded in his hands. He suffered terrible injuries all over his body and lingered in a hospital for weeks before he died. His older brother Tom, witnessing his parents' anguish, supported them as best he could before he had to leave for college.

As a sophomore at Ohio Wesleyan, Tom signed up for the overseas study trip sponsored by Syracuse University. He had spent a semester in Germany and was on his way home on Pan Am Flight 103. In less than two years, the Schultzes had lost both their children.

When Jack finished telling the story, he stared straight ahead, like gazing down a long, empty corridor. Jane looked down at the hands in her lap, overcome with emotion. Feeling her desolation and sorrow, Lee got up and asked Pat to bring some tea to give them time to recover.

But the Schultzes were not done. Their ordeal continued when they went to pick up Tom's body. It had been shipped to a cargo hangar at Kennedy Airport. Although they advised Pan Am that they were coming with a hearse, no airline representative met them. Instead, a ground crewman ushered them into a small office where they sat waiting on uncomfortable metal folding chairs for what seemed like an eternity. Finally, he returned and asked them to fill out a stack of forms. After that, a forklift operator brought a pine box from a storage compartment and dropped it unceremoniously on the tarmac. He drove off without a word, leaving them to deal with Tom's remains alone.

"They killed my son and then made us struggle to get his body," Jane said, lips thin and white with anger.

Jack growled, "I was ready to kill every one of them."

Lee could only shake his head in disbelief.

Out of the blue, Jack asked, "What is the American International Insurance Company? I had a call from this guy, Ted Dickenson, who claimed he represented them. He said his company was Boeing's carrier, and they were located on LaSalle Street in Chicago. What is that all about?"

Lee had heard similar questions from other clients. "It's a solicitation effort by a disreputable firm in Washington, DC.," he explained. "They use that approach after every airplane accident. They claim they are Boeing's insurers and would like your lawyer's name. If you say you don't have one, you get a call the next day from Ted Dickenson, who tries to hustle you to sign up with him."

Jack spat out, "They are vultures!"

The Schultzes agreed to retain Kreindler & Kreindler. As Jack shook hands with Lee, he said, stern-faced, "Incidentally, this was no accident, Lee. Don't call it an accident."

Jane nodded, seething.

The Clients

When Jim came downstairs to meet the Schultzes and escort them to his office for the initial damages interview, Lee took him aside and told him, "We have to be very careful not to refer to Lockerbie as an accident. Jack really took offense at that. So did Jane. Probably all the families would. From now on, the word is 'disaster.' Please tell Steve."

As the Schultzes went upstairs, Lee sat alone in his office for a moment, digesting all he had heard.

Clients were never "just clients" to him. He felt their pain and concerns physically, in his gut. On the way home to Chappaqua, images of their drawn faces and fragments of their indignant, worried questions kept whirling around in his mind, too. He entered his house like someone carrying a heavy weight. Ruth could always tell when he had a trying day. In the evening, he would unburden himself with her.

At some point, she told him, "Honey, you've got to get this out of your stomach and into your brain. If you can't sleep thinking about these things at night, you won't be able to help anyone. You have to concentrate on what's ahead."

It was good advice but not easy to follow.

* * *

Throughout February and early March of 1989, Lee continued to get retainers from Lockerbie clients. Kreindler & Kreindler ended up representing 98 passengers' families, about 45% of the total. People came from all over—New York, New Jersey, Connecticut, Massachusetts, Pennsylvania, Virginia, Texas, Maryland, England, Scotland, France, Germany, South Africa, and Argentina. They were business owners, high-powered corporate executives, professionals, everyday workers, retirees, and college students. With only a few exceptions, the legal team met them and came to know them well.

Lee maintained personal contact with each client. He made visits and frequent telephone calls, and many of the families became friends.

They also developed warm, close relationships with Ruth. And, of course, many became good friends with Pat Robinson.

Collectively, the Lockerbie families forged three groups, two in the United States and one in the United Kingdom. The Victims of Pan Am Flight 103 was the most vocal and became a formidable political force. Its members forced a meeting with President George H. W. Bush over the objections of his chief of staff, John Sununu, by demonstrating in front of the White House and daring him to have them arrested in full view of the international news media. As a result of their lobbying efforts, President Bush appointed a commission that explored terrorism in general and the Pan Am bombing in particular. Later, President Clinton met with members of the group, held ceremonies at the White House with them, and personally participated in the groundbreaking of the Lockerbie cairn project at Arlington Cemetery.

As far as Lee was concerned, they were the most unusual group of clients he ever had—engaged, motivated, and driven, as though propelled by some unaccountable force. They sought answers. And they wanted justice.

Many were bright and well-educated and wanted to know everything about the case. Some called daily for updates on the latest developments. Lee began to worry that he would never get off the telephone. So, at the beginning of February 1989, he decided to send out a clients' letter, a report called "Summary of Activities and Approach."

A month later, he dispatched another. After that, he mailed one every six weeks or so, some over 40 pages long. Lee wrote every letter himself and agonized over making it perfect. He showed the drafts to Ruth, Steve, and Jim, and they made suggestions and corrections.

Lee knew he took a risk because some letters contained privileged information. Yet, his clients never betrayed his trust, never leaked any of the content to reporters or other parties. They had faith in him.

3

ORIGINS

In many ways, Lee was the perfect attorney for the Lockerbie litigation. Born on March 11, 1924, he was part of the Greatest Generation that fought in World War II and came home with an unyielding optimism about the future. Like many fellow soldiers, he wanted to make a difference and believed he could make the world a better place.

He had grown up in the Crown Heights neighborhood of Brooklyn near the botanical gardens. His father, Harry Kreindler, a respected litigation attorney, had a small office on Flatbush Avenue. He often brought cases home with him, sharing the ins and outs at the dinner table. His passion for the law and helping his clients was infectious and inspired his son from an early age. Lee wanted to follow in his father's footsteps, although he also considered becoming a writer or a politician.

School came easy for Lee. He was a straight-A student at James Madison High School and attended Dartmouth College in New Hampshire at a time when students from Jewish backgrounds were a small minority there. By then, his father had moved his law practice to Manhattan and bought an apartment on 75 Central Park West, a stone's throw away from the Tavern on the Green.

Lee was in his first year at Dartmouth when the Japanese attacked Pearl Harbor, precipitating America's entry into World War II. Two years later, he left school and enlisted and served in the Pacific War

Theater in the Philippines. He did not see combat, writing articles for the Far East news edition of *Stars and Stripes*, the U.S. military newspaper instead.

Some of the staff were experienced newspapermen, and they taught Lee to write in a conversational way, which benefited him for the rest of his life and career. When he became a lawyer, his briefs and letters to clients were always thorough, clear, and easy to read.

After Japan surrendered, Lee came home and finished his B.A. at Dartmouth College. From there, he went to Harvard Law School. With a burning interest in politics, he started a club for like-minded Democrat students. The speakers who addressed the group included John and Bobby Kennedy. At the time, John F. Kennedy was a U.S. Representative for a working-class district in Boston. He already exuded the warmth, charm, and confidence that would make him a popular senator and president. His ambition and readiness to serve others appealed to Lee. By the time Kennedy challenged Americans in his 1961 inauguration speech, "Ask not what your country can do or you but what you can do for your country," Lee had lived those words for more than a decade.

After graduating from Harvard Law School in the spring of 1949, Lee passed the New York bar exam with flying colors and joined his father to form the law firm of Kreindler & Kreindler. He admired his father tremendously and wanted to learn from him.

The Kreindler & Kreindler office was located at 51 Chambers Street in Manhattan on the 12th floor of the Emigrant Industrial Savings Bank Building across from City Hall. As senior partner, Harry had the only room with a window, while Lee occupied a cubby hole surrounded by law books and files. Their young secretary-receptionist, Pat Robinson, sat at a desk in between. She called Harry "Mr. Kreindler" and her younger boss "Mr. Lee," a habit she continued for the next 50 years she worked for him. A smaller desk for Tom Feinman, the part-time private investigator, was off to one side. Whenever Tom came to the office, he brought along his big dog. Its name, Tiny, never failed to amuse clients who happened to visit.

New York City has always been a bustling place, and the 1950s were no different. Lee loved the energy of the busy traffic and people crowding the streets and avenues. Young and ready to make his mark in the world, he drove a sports car, a graduation present from his parents, and pursued New York politics in his spare time. Gregarious, energetic, and charismatic, he soon came to the attention of New York's Democratic party bosses as an up-and-coming young talent. Tammany Hall, headed by Carmine DeSapio, asked Lee to run for the U.S. Congress to represent the 17th District in the Democratic primary. Also known as the Silk Stocking District, it stretched from mid-town Manhattan to the Upper West Side, including the apartment where he and his parents lived. Lee reluctantly agreed, aware of the rumors that Tammany Hall had ties to organized crime. He did not want to become anyone's stooge.

Once Lee threw his hat in the ring, however, he worked tirelessly to get the nomination. Many friends and other idealistic young people worked on his campaign, and their enthusiasm and energy paid off. Shortly before the primary, Walter Winchell, the influential columnist, wrote an article in *The Wall Street Journal*, all but anointing Lee for the Congressional seat. But one evening, when the party bosses demanded his support for their pet projects, Lee made it clear that he was his own man. The next day, he received a phone call informing him he was no longer on the primary slate. They had replaced him with another, more pliable candidate. Lee felt angry, embarrassed, and disappointed, but not disheartened. He was gratified that he had remained true to himself.

With his political career on hold, he worked hard to become an attorney like his father. Over the next year, Lee supported Harry by doing research and preparing legal documents for various automobile accidents and other personal injury cases. He accompanied him to court and learned how to conduct depositions, make opening statements, examine and cross-examine witnesses, and deliver closing statements that appealed to jurors' emotions. Although Harry was a highly experienced and accomplished litigator, he preferred to settle cases out of court. Lee decided to emulate him. During his long, successful career, he settled more cases than he tried.

Pursuing the legal profession with all his energy, Lee soon forgot about his failed foray into politics. By early 1952, he had other things on his mind. He met the love of his life and embarked on what proved to be a career-defining legal case.

In March, Lee went to a debutante ball, a once-a-year coming-out party for the sons and daughters of prominent New York families. It took place in the ballroom of a hotel in Manhattan, and everybody who was anybody on the social scene attended. At some point, Lee noticed a pretty young woman dancing with her escort. She was graceful and vibrant, and he was smitten. But he was reluctant to ask her to dance. He knew he wasn't the nimblest man and didn't want to start things off "on the wrong foot," as he told friends later. His strengths were his conversational abilities and sense of humor.

So, he asked one of the chaperones, pointing covertly toward the dance floor, "Can you tell me that young woman's name?"

She raised her eyebrows and gave him a meaningful smile. Then, she whispered conspiratorially, "That's Ruth Bilgrei."

Mustering his courage, Lee approached the young woman and said, "Aren't you Ruth Bilgrei?"

She replied, "Yes."

"My name is Lee Kreindler. Don't I know you from someplace?"

She took a long, evaluating look and said, "No," and turned away.

But Lee was not easily deterred. He called up Ruth the next day and asked her out on a date to see a Broadway play. When she said yes, he felt like walking on air.

Although it was a long way to 930 Grand Concourse in the Bronx where she lived, he drove his sports car, hoping to impress her. When he knocked on the door of her home and Ruth opened, he greeted her with a bouquet of flowers and a winning smile.

But her expectant look turned to surprise. Puzzled, Ruth said, "You aren't Andy Rosenbaum."

It took a moment to sort out the case of mistaken identities. When Ruth said yes over the telephone, she thought she would go on a date with a young dentist she had met at the dance. Lee, in his eagerness and delight that she had accepted, never said his name.

Rather than apologize, Lee threw up his hands in a "what-the-heck" gesture and burst out laughing. "So, what do we do now?" he asked when he recovered.

Ruth smiled with a twinkle in her eyes and said, "Well, now that you're here, you might as well come in and meet my parents."

She led Lee into the living room, where her father, Samuel, whom everyone called Sam, and her mother, Hannah, eyed him with appraising looks. After the introductions, Sam sat in a comfortable armchair and gestured Lee to the sofa across from him. Ruth and Hannah went into the kitchen to find a vase for the flowers.

When Lee admired the ivory chess set sitting on a side table, Sam, a championship-caliber player, perked up. "Do you play?" he asked.

Lee shrugged regretfully, "I know the rules, but I'm more of a golf and tennis man."

It was not the most auspicious beginning, but by the time Ruth and Hannah rejoined them, the men were talking about Sam's automobile parts business and Lee's experiences as a young lawyer.

Ruth appreciated how Lee held his own in the face of her father's interrogation.

At some point, Lee checked his watch and said, "We better get going, or we'll miss the opening curtain," finding a graceful way to end the visit.

In the car, Lee thought he'd acquitted himself rather well. He later found out that Ruth's father pegged him as a loser because when he sat down and crossed his legs, there was a hole in the sole of his shoe. Fortunately, Ruth's mother thought Lee had potential, or that first date might have been their last.

It was a pleasant drive down Broadway to the Ziegfield Theater to see *Caesar and Cleopatra* by George Bernard Shaw, starring Vivien Leigh and Laurence Olivier. But Lee and Ruth didn't like the acting or the play and left after the first act. Fortunately, the ice cream they enjoyed at Rumpelmayer's café in the Hotel St. Moritz dispelled any unpleasant aftertaste. Both parties deemed the outing a success.

They continued to see each other throughout the spring and summer. Ruth studied architecture at New York University, so they often met in Washington Square Park for lunch. They also took walks, went to the theater and the movies, and double dated. Lee thought Ruth was the most beautiful woman in the world. Ruth found him dashing and exciting. She liked that he never put on airs and talked to everyone the same way, whether it was a waiter, an elevator man, a professor, or a fellow attorney.

They were young and head-over-heels in love.

Soon, Lee invited Ruth to meet his parents and sister Rosamond, whom everyone called "Babe." They had dinner at the spacious apartment overlooking Central Park.

Lee's mother, Doris, was a painter. Her canvasses, which adorned the living room and hallway walls, were evocative, impressionist nature scenes in mottled colors. Admiring them, Ruth said, "They're like Debussy's music made visible," earning her an appreciative smile from Doris.

Dinner was a boisterous affair, with lively conversation accompanying the different courses. To Ruth's surprise, everyone in the Kreindler family called Lee "Jim." When she asked why, Babe explained, "When Lee was born, he had a smile on his face, so my parents called him Sunny Jim and the name stuck."

Ruth felt at home among the Kreindlers, and the evening was a great success. Everyone adored her. She and Babe became lifelong friends. In time, her father came around and enjoyed Lee's company, too.

In late May, Lee took Ruth to dinner at L'Aiglon, a fancy French restaurant on 55th Street just east of Fifth Avenue. It was known for its romantic décor—red chairs, banquettes and drapery, and luminescent wall sconces and chandeliers—and its exquisite food. He waited until after desert to get down on one knee at her side, proffering a diamond ring and asking her to marry him. When Ruth said yes, and they kissed, the waiters and other patrons applauded.

The wedding ceremony occurred on Monday, September 1, in Manhattan. Ruth wore an antique, ivory silk gown and a head garland of orange blossoms, and carried a bouquet of orchids. Lee had on an elegant tuxedo with a white bow tie. At the reception in the nearby Plaza Hotel by Central Park, they finally had their ballroom dance—Lee had practiced—and everyone agreed they were a dashing couple. The wedding made the society pages of the *New York Times* the next day.

They spent their honeymoon at the The Greenbrier, a golf resort in West Virginia. To get ready, Lee had Ruth take golf lessons in Bryant Park behind the New York Public Library. She did her best but never took to the game. On their first outing, when someone yelled "Fore," Ruth was so frightened she leaped into Lee's arms.

She did buy Lee a blue cashmere sweater at the pro shop, which he wore for years until it became threadbare.

Upon returning to New York City, they lived at the Ansonia Hotel on the Upper West Side until they could move into an apartment at 25 Central Park West. Lee hadn't given up his political ambitions entirely and wanted to reside in the 17th District. Their place on the sixth floor was small but cozy. The kitchen was so tiny if you opened the door to the oven, you could not step inside the living room. But the view of Central Park made up for any inconvenience.

The afterglow of their honeymoon lingered as the Yankees won the World Series against the Brooklyn Dodgers in seven games. The rivalry led to mutual teasing as they cheered on their respective teams. Although she'd never attended a game at Yankee Stadium in the Bronx, Ruth was a Yankee fan by default. With fond memories of his father taking him to Ebbets Field, Lee rooted for the Dodgers. Fortunately, neither were die-hard baseball fans, so the outcome didn't put a damper on their relationship.

Instead, Lee started the practice of what Ruth later called their "pillow talk," sharing at night with her what had happened at the law firm and in court during the day. They continued that tradition for the rest of their life together.

In November, Dwight D. Eisenhower was elected president, beating Lee's preferred candidate, Democrat Adlai Stevenson, in a landslide.

Soon after, a woman walked into the law firm, supporting herself with a cane, and announced in a loud voice, "I am Sylvia Rothenberg, and I survived an airplane crash in Elizabeth."

Her strident tone brought Lee out of his cubby hole. The disaster had been big news earlier in the year. On February 11, a National Airlines flight to Miami crashed in the New Jersey town shortly after take-off. On the way down, the plane sheared off the corner of a four-story apartment building, killing several residents. Then, it ricocheted off another building, strewing wreckage over several city blocks. After the fuselage broke in two, the front section crashed into the playground of an orphanage and burst into flames, killing 26 passengers and three crew members aboard. The tail part settled on a treetop before plummeting to the ground. Miraculously, 34 passengers and one stewardess survived.

Sylvia Rothenberg looked to be in her 40s. She wore a dark blue dress and a matching women's Gatsby hat. From one gloved hand, she dangled a black leather clutch purse. In the other, she held her cane. Her face was drawn and haggard.

"I've been to several law firms already, including Stroock, Stroock and Lavan; Proskauer Rose; and Skadden, Arps, Slate, Meagher & Flom. None of them want to take my case. They're only interested in automobile accidents," she said dismissively.

Lee realized she had started with the most famous Jewish law firms and worked her way down the list to Kreindler & Kreindler. But he kept that knowledge to himself.

Harry, arriving from a meeting, overheard Sylvia's last statement and said, "Why don't you come into my office."

When he ushered her inside, Lee moved to help Sylvia sit, but she waved him off. She settled into the chair before the desk with difficulty and stoic determination. Lee went to the window and leaned against the nearby bookcase.

"How can I help you?" Harry asked.

"I want you to sue National Airlines," Sylvia said, her dark eyes fierce and resolute. "I was in a coma for six days and have had twelve operations over the last six months. I was going to join my husband on vacation in Miami. When Samuel heard about the crash, he immediately flew up and rushed to my bedside. He got so upset he had a heart attack and died a week later." Her lips became a thin line as she looked away.

"Why don't you tell me what happened to you," Harry said kindly.

Sylvia took a deep breath. "The plane took off and was still climbing when there was a dreadful noise, like an explosion. As we began to tilt downward, there was another bang. We were getting tossed about. People around me were screaming and praying. We were going down! So, I hooked my hands to my seatbelt and yelled, 'Let 'er rip!' There was more noise, and I was flying in the air. Next thing I was in a tree. I remember thinking, 'What are all these leaves doing here?' And then everything went black."

Lee and Harry glanced at each other in amazement. Sylvia was a very lucky woman who had displayed remarkable courage in the face of death.

"I woke up in the hospital," Sylvia resumed. "The doctors told me I'd been out for six days! I had twenty-two bone fractures and spent six months in St. Elizabeth's Hospital recuperating. Since I got home to Queens, I've been in and out of the hospital for more surgeries."

She looked up, meeting Harry's eyes, challenging him. "Will you help me?"

Harry pursed his lips as if giving her request some thought. In those days, getting on an airplane was considered an ultrahazardous activity, and passengers assumed all the risk. Crashes were treated as acts of God. There was no precedent for air disaster litigation. If an airline paid any compensation to the victims' families, it was a pittance, barely enough to cover burial costs.

Sighing, Harry said regretfully, "I'm sorry, but I don't think there is anything we can do for you, as I'm sure the other firms explained."

Lee saw Sylvia's face fall, revealing an exhausted, deeply hurt, despairing woman beneath the mask of determination. On impulse, he said, "Wait a minute, Dad. Why don't we try to figure out why the plane crashed? There might be an angle we can explore that hasn't been tried yet."

Harry's surprised look turned to amusement—the seasoned veteran indulging a young whippersnapper. "All right, since you have nothing else on your plate right now, knock yourself out," he said. "If you succeed, I will try for damages."

Feeling growing excitement, Lee smiled and said to Sylvia, "We will take your case."

Sylvia signed the retainer papers which Pat typed up without glancing at the terms. She had made her assessment of Lee and decided he was a man of his word. That was all she needed to know.

Later that evening, Lee told Ruth about his first client and case.

"Did she really say 'Let 'er rip!'?" Ruth asked, wide-eyed.

Lee laughed. "Yes."

Ruth thought for a moment. "So, how are you going to do this?" she asked

He answered happily, "I have no idea."

But the next day, he got going in earnest and approached the case with the creativity and attention to detail for which he became famous. In those days, there was no discovery process in which the plaintiff could get documents and other information from the defendants. You had to have all your ducks in a row before you filed a complaint and went to trial a few weeks later. Lee had to start from scratch.

When he learned that the Civil Aeronautics Board (CAB) investigated every airline accident in the United States, he sent to Washington for a copy of their report. It provided a cause for the crash but raised more questions than it answered. Flight 402, a four-engine, propeller-driven Douglas DC-6, had arrived at Idlewild Airport in New York from Miami, Florida. Following a routine inspection and refueling, the plane made a 15-minute ferry flight to Newark Airport. After another inspection, it took on passengers and their baggage. Now, as Flight 101, the aircraft departed 17 minutes after midnight for the return flight to Miami.

Observers at the airport control tower reported that the take-off and climb-out seemed normal. But suddenly, the aircraft lost altitude and veered to the right. When the controller called the cockpit, the captain replied, "I lost an engine and am returning to the field." The plane was immediately cleared to land but never made it. Instead, it continued to drop further and disappeared. At 00:20, tower personnel observed a fire in the area of Elizabeth, New Jersey, where the plane had crashed.

The CAB investigation determined that the probable cause of the accident was a "mechanical difficulty" during the climb after take-off and a failure in the pitch-control system, leading to "the reversal of the No. 3 propeller with relatively high power and the subsequent feathering of the No. 4 propeller, resulting in a descent at an altitude too low to effect recovery."

Various conjectures blamed exposed wiring causing the disaster, but there was no concrete evidence to prove it. Nor did the report suggest that any person was at fault.

Pouring over the document, Lee noted that "mechanical difficulty" was a vague term. He understood that the plane had controllable pitch propellers, which let the angle of the blades change in flight. But he had no idea what the technical terms "reversal" and "feathering" meant.

Calling around, he discovered that "feathering" referred to the propeller blades being tilted 90 degrees, or approximately parallel to the on-coming airflow. The procedure reduced drag during taxiing on the ground. "Reverse pitch" meant adjusting to a negative blade position, which reversed thrust and slowed the aircraft. That was especially helpful during landing on a wet runway where the wheel brakes were less effective. But it was catastrophic during take-off. When the propellers locked in reverse or feathered during Flight 101, they prevented the plane from gaining altitude, sending it plunging to the ground.

However, that did not explain *why* it happened. Lee decided that he needed first-hand knowledge of how propeller engines worked.

Searching the *Yellow Pages*, he found a propeller shop in Mineola, Long Island, about 10 miles southeast of LaGuardia Airport. He drove to the factory building and talked to the owner, a plump, middle-aged man wearing grime-covered overalls. Lee shook his grease-stained hands without batting an eye. When he explained that he wanted to come work at the shop to learn about propellers, the man looked at him dubiously, scratched his head, and said, "I suppose it's all right."

Ruth thought she had married a lawyer, but for the next 10 days, she found herself packing a lunchbox for a mechanic. Lee put on a pair of overalls and drove in his sport scar across the 59th Street Bridge to Queens and Mineola. He put in a solid day's work at the shop, earning the other employees' respect.

Afterward, he took his co-workers and the owner out for beers and asked a slew of questions. In the process, he learned about propeller manufacture, repair, stress, fatigue, thrust bending, aerodynamic twisting, and vibratory disturbances; how the blades are attached to the rotating part of the propeller's motor; and how, in flight, they're adjusted automatically or manually by the pilots for ideal thrust.

When Lee got home, he shared with Ruth what he "learned" that day. After dinner, he laid out drawings of propellers on the floor of the apartment to get a clearer idea. Ruth helped him mark them up with colored pencils to illustrate his findings.

By the end of the first week, Lee had four theories of what might have caused the failure. At the end of his 10-day stint, he had six. Unfortunately, the first deposition with an aeronautical engineer invalidated all of them.

Over the next half year, Lee deposed the surviving passengers and stewardess, as well as airline pilots, ground crew, maintenance men, engineers, and other experts. He kept Sylvia Rothenberg informed throughout his research and appreciated that she continued to believe in him. His pursuit of a credible explanation for what had happened became an obsession. Harry was amazed at his drive and persistence. He told his son several times that he was on a wild goose chase, but Lee refused to give up.

Finally, Lee met with an airplane engineer in Miami, Florida, and found out that the oil pressure in the delivery system controlled the automatic tilt changes of the propeller blades in mid-flight. If that system was compromised by too much or too little oil, it could lock the blades in place so the manual override would not work. Lee now had a workable theory of why the plane had crashed.

Follow-up depositions with ground maintenance crews revealed that they never looked at the oil level during the routine inspections before clearing an aircraft for flight. Doing so was not part of the checklist provided by the airline, a critical oversight.

Armed with that knowledge, Lee filed a lawsuit against National Airlines in Manhattan Federal Court, claiming negligence and seeking punitive damages. He had lined up an impressive group of witnesses—experts and maintenance men—to prove the company's culpability. Even his father was guardedly optimistic about the possibility of succeeding.

By the time Lee shared his evidence with the defense attorneys, as required before the start of the trial, they had met the young, personable attorney several times. They knew about his detailed research and numerous depositions and were impressed with his thorough knowledge of how propellers worked. When Lee laid out his discoveries in clear, easy-to-understand language, the airline's lawyers could imagine his impact on a jury.

So, in late September, three weeks before the trial was to start, National Airlines caved and agreed to settle. Harry helped with the negotiations. In the end, the airline agreed to a payout of $169,398.63.

The announcement on September 30—Harry let Lee take the well-deserved credit—made all the newspapers in the Tri-State area. It was the largest settlement ever in a personal injury airplane accident case. Sylvia Rothenberg received the check while lying in a Queens hospital bed, recovering from yet another operation. A picture accompanying the article in the newspaper showed her smiling at her nurse.

For Lee, the thrill of winning a near-impossible case did not outweigh the satisfaction of giving Sylvia some compensation and joy for her ordeal and personal loss. The deep sense of accomplishment told him he had made the right decision to pursue a legal career.

The case created a big stir in the insurance industry and came to the attention of Melvin Belli, a prominent personal injury lawyer. Known as "The King of Torts" and to insurance companies as "Melvin Bellicose," he held several meetings a year for other attorneys presenting new and radical litigation developments and trial techniques. When Lee appeared on his program to discuss the Elizabeth case, he impressed everyone. From that day on, he was well on his way to becoming the go-to person in aviation disaster cases.

As a result, Lee never solicited clients and never advertised to drum up business. People came to him—other lawyers and their clients—for representation. It helped that the 1950s and '60s saw an expansion of air travel, fueled by the development of jet engines for national and international flights. Although airplanes became increasingly safe, accidents occurred, and Lee's expertise became widely known as his reputation grew.

Kreindler & Kreindler expanded. The firm took on partners and moved to a high-rise building on Park Avenue. By the time Harry retired, it occupied two floors.

Still, litigating airline accidents was always an iffy proposition. Ruth often compared it to being a riverboat gambler who puts up the money for his clothes, berth, and food but gets paid only if he wins the jackpot. Lee and the firm took on all the financial risks without any guarantee of compensation. And unlike a gambler, he had no aces up his sleeve. He did not cheat but worked with the cards dealt to him.

Eventually, Lee hired five former military pilots who had served in the Army, Navy, Air Force, and the Marines and become lawyers. That distinguished Kreindler & Kreindler from all other aviation litigation firms.

Keeping up with technological advances, Lee was the first attorney at his firm to use a computer at a time when he was the oldest partner! It was Ruth who first introduced him to the new technology. She had read about computers and gotten curious. While Lee was busy attending a trial in Seattle, she had one of the expert witnesses on retainer take her to a Radio Shack, buy her a computer, and teach her how to use it. After she sent letters to Lee about "computation," he decided to give it a try, too. Then he introduced computers to the office, over the initial objections of the other lawyers and secretaries who feared they would lose their jobs.

Lee understood that he could no longer figure out the intricacies of airplane design, construction, and propulsion on his own. So, he hired engineers and aeronautical experts to help him win cases, including Carl Oppendahl, the son of the man who had participated in developing jet engines. Of course, defense attorneys soon hired their own experts to contradict the plaintiff's position.

But Lee did extensive research and usually came better prepared. His trial notebooks, covered with colored Post-its, were legendary. When he ran out of stickers and everyone at the firm was busy, if Ruth was visiting, he sent her to the stationary store around the corner for more. The proprietor would greet her with, "I know what you're here for," and hand her several packets of sticky notes.

Because of his thorough preparation and ability to integrate massive amounts of information, Lee was known as a man who knew what he was talking about. As a result, he settled many cases out of court. In one, he reached an agreement with the opposing attorney during an elevator ride. When asked later why he chose to settle, the attorney said, "If it had been anybody else, I wouldn't have. But I knew Lee to be a man of his word."

It helped that Lee was a great negotiator, sensitive to the needs of all parties involved. As Ruth told others on several occasions, "Although I never won an argument with him, I never felt as if I lost."

* * *

When he and Ruth had their two children, Jim and Laurie, they moved from Manhattan to Chappaqua in Northern Westchester County. The town was a 30-mile train ride from Grand Central Station, which was only three blocks from the firm's office. The trip took little more than an hour.

With her background in architecture, Ruth designed the modern house they built and supervised its year-long construction. Getting up early in the morning, with Laurie in the baby carriage, she walked to the site and talked to crew leaders to check on the progress. She designed the interior, too, to meet Lee's needs for efficiency. He could get out of bed in the morning, shower, get dressed, have breakfast, and be on his way to the front door without ever having to backtrack. In time, they put in a tennis court and swimming pool.

Although Lee liked to think of their house as a refuge, he brought his cases home with him. Like his father, he discussed them with Ruth and the children at the dinner table. When he got carried away, Ruth would gently tap his hand and whisper, "Darling, you can talk to me all night, but let's give the children a chance, too, to tell us about their day."

Lee tried to restrain himself and listened for a minute or two before getting carried away again about various aspects of his cases. He even talked about them in his sleep.

Over time, he and Ruth became involved in the Chappaqua community. They were the driving force behind building a second town swimming pool—Ruth found suitable land, held fundraisers at their home, and spoke to local organizations including the League of Women Voters, asking for financial support. When the facility was finished, even the most vocal early detractors were happy to spend time there.

In time, the Kreindlers became an integral part of Chappaqua. They held tennis, pool, and dinner parties at their house, socialized with their neighbors, and attended the local synagogue.

Lee was living the life he wanted to, fulfilling the American Dream.

4

IN FITS AND STARTS

February—March 1989

As he started working to make the case that Pan Am bore responsibility in the Lockerbie disaster, Lee first focused on the FAA warning bulletins. They raised several questions: What did Pan Am do about them? Did it take extra precautions, as Jeff Kriendler, their spokesman, claimed? And if so, were these measures thorough enough to justify Pan Am's claim that the tragedy was an act of terrorism and there was nothing it could have done to prevent it?

To get a head start on finding answers, Lee retained a German law firm and its investigator in Frankfurt. They were to monitor media coverage and closely examine airport security measures there to discover how the suitcase with the bomb might have gotten on board Flight 103.

Lee did the same in London through Kreindler & Kreindler's correspondence firm to get a handle on what had occurred at Heathrow Airport. The English law firm also recommended hiring a Scottish attorney to advise on legal procedures and act as liaison with the criminal investigation taking place in Lockerbie.

Because terrorists had murdered 270 people, the scope and intensity of the inquiry were extraordinary—the most extensive in history, conducted jointly in cooperation between the governments of Scotland

and the United States, with Germany assisting in some aspects. The officials in charge considered it paramount to apprehend the perpetrators and bring them to justice. They sealed off the criminal investigation from the public and made no effort to contact the victims' families or their attorneys to share information about the crime.

Still, it wouldn't hurt to have "eyes and ears on the ground" in Scotland. So, Lee engaged Michael Hughes, a Glasgow attorney. He was serving as secretary of the Lockerbie Disaster Group, a consortium of a dozen or so Scottish solicitors representing the families of the victims on the ground and a few families of U.K. passengers who died in the plane crash.

Lee flew to Glasgow and met with Michael in the pub room of the Babbity Bowster Hotel near the River Clyde where he was staying. The Scottish attorney was an energetic man in his early 40s with chestnut brown hair, penetrating blue eyes, and a slightly crooked smile. Lee found him likable and well-versed in Scottish law and the case's particulars. As a family man who adored his wife and five children, Michael had a strong sense of justice and was outraged at what the terrorists had done.

Lee took to him immediately, and they quickly developed a close professional working relationship. They talked by phone every day and exchanged faxes frequently. When differences developed within the Lockerbie Disaster Group, Michael left and gave his full attention to advising Lee and the American litigation. It was a matter of great pride to him to be the Scottish legal representative of the Lockerbie Plaintiffs Committee, and he took his responsibility very seriously.

When the first batch of documents arrived from the law firm in Frankfurt, most of them were in German. No one at Kreindler & Kreindler spoke or could read that language. Expecting more papers to come from there, Lee looked to hire a translator.

Coincidentally, that afternoon, Phyllis Rosenthal and her husband Charles came to the office. Phyllis, who had lost her daughter Andrea in the disaster, was in a murderous state of mind. "I'm so mad I'm going to Washington to shoot President Bush," she raged. "How dare he say the public should not be notified of bomb warnings unless the information is credible and about a specific flight, and that it was probably not the case with Pan Am?"

After Lee took them into his office, the reason for Phyllis' fury became clear. When Andrea wanted to buy a ticket on a charter flight home, Phyllis told her, "No, honey, that's not safe. Go on Pan Am." Lee realized that she blamed herself for Andrea's death but could not face the pain and guilt.

Phyllis remained so distraught that Pat Robinson took her to the ladies' room to help calm her.

While they were gone, Charles said to Lee, "I'm really worried about her. She's very smart—she speaks six languages fluently, including Hebrew and German—but her intellect doesn't help her. I'm afraid she'll kill herself."

When Phyllis returned, Lee said, "I've been talking with your husband, and I have an idea. I understand you speak German."

Phyllis nodded, surprised. "Why?"

"I'd like you to come to work for us as a translator," Lee offered. "We have a number of German documents in the case and need to know what they say."

Looking at him askance, Phyllis asked, "What's the deal? Are you trying to buy me off?"

Lee put up his hands. "No, not at all. You can help us a lot," he insisted. "You could take a look at the documents and tell us what's important in them."

Phyllis glanced at her husband, who had not said a word. "I'll do it," she agreed. "But I don't want to be paid."

Smiling, Lee said, "If you do this, I will assign you to our head paralegal, and you won't see much of me. But you'll have to be treated like everyone else. What you do with the money you earn here is your business."

Phyllis examined her fingernails for a moment. Then she said, "Okay."

Charles looked pleased and relieved.

When Lee mentioned recruiting a new employee to the partners, most were against it. "You can't hire her as a paralegal!" they protested. "No other law firm would do that."

"So what?" Lee replied. "She can help us with the case."

Having something to do in the litigation allowed Phyllis to get her life back on track. Years later, when her other daughter was getting married in Texas, in the newspaper announcement, Phyllis, who had continued to work at the firm, proudly listed as one of her accomplishments that she was a paralegal with Kreindler & Kreindler.

5

FIRST ATTEMPT TO SETTLE

February—March 1989

In mid-February, Lee filed a wrongful death action suit in New York against Pan American Airlines and its security subsidiary, Alert Management. It accused the airline of failing to warn passengers of a bomb threat for which it received notification. The action further claimed that Pan Am was derelict in the supervision and training of security personnel and contractors and did not monitor, maintain, and otherwise secure the aircraft to prevent its destruction.

Some of the accusations were speculative, based on informed assumptions. Lee had no conclusive proof of negligence or willful misconduct yet. He hoped the investigators in Frankfurt and London would find sufficient evidence and that the documents Pan Am turned over during discovery would confirm the accusation.

When other law firms with Lockerbie clients brought suits against the airline in Connecticut, Ohio, and Florida, the cases were consolidated for pretrial discovery and litigation under one jurisdiction. Chief Judge Thomas C. Platt in the U.S. District Court for the Eastern District of New York in Brooklyn became responsible for all Pan Am and Alert proceedings.

A year younger than Lee, Platt had been appointed to the Federal bench by President Nixon in 1974. White-haired, with a thin nose and penetrating eyes, he was a soft-spoken man with a sense of humor.

But he had a reputation of toughness and tolerating no nonsense in his courtroom.

In 1981, Judge Platt had presided at the hearing to settle the contract negotiations between the Air Traffic Controllers Organization and the Reagan administration. When the union threatened to walk out despite the ban on strikes by federal employees, Judge Platt warned its representatives, "People will tell you I'm not exactly known as a soft judge." After the union violated his order to return to work, he imposed hourly fines, which grew to more than $4 million before President Reagan fired the air controllers who disobeyed. That led to the union's decertification and dissolution as a bargaining agent.

Lee was not worried about Judge Platt's reputation, though. He had argued several cases before him and always found him to be fair.

As the first order of business, Judge Platt appointed a Plaintiffs Committee to act as the umbrella group for all the legal actions. It consisted of aviation law attorneys Mitch Baumeister, Frank Granito Jr, and his son Frank Granito III, all three from New York law firms; Nick Gilman from Washington; Stanley Chesley from Cincinnati; Richard Brown from Los Angeles; and Lee Kreindler, his son Jim, and Steve Pounian. The New York firms had the most clients.

Mitch Baumeister had worked for Lee in the 1970s, first as an associate and then as a partner, before starting his own firm, Baumeister & Samuels, in 1984. They were a study in contrast. Lee was genial and easy-going. He did not look or talk like a lawyer. Mitch had narrow features and wire-rim glasses that gave him the appearance of a research-oriented corporate attorney. But he was a fiercely competitive litigator. The only Committee member with a private pilot's license, he liked to fly propeller planes in his spare time.

Frank Granito Jr also came from a firm he helped establish, Speiser, Crouse, Nolan & Granito. Seven years younger than Lee, he had served as a fighter pilot with the Pacific Fleet during the 1950s

First Attempt to Settle

and early 1960s before becoming an aviation attorney. He liked good food, had a good sense of humor, and got along well with others.

Frank Granito III, whom everyone called Frankie, was the youngest member of the group. Shorter and stockier than Frank Jr, he had graduated from law school two years earlier. This was his first case working with his dad, and like Lee's son, Jim, he wanted to make him proud.

Jim was the only one in the group who sported a mustache, and his curly brown hair contrasted with Lee's mostly bald head. As a younger attorney still proving himself, Jim often came across as more serious-minded than Lee. But they shared an outgoing, quick-witted personality and purposeful, high-energy approach to pursuing cases.

Steve Pounian was lanky and more reserved. However, behind his casual, unhurried manner and ability to put clients at ease was a razor-sharp legal mind. Lee often said that Steve was his favorite kind of lawyer. As Kreindler & Kreindler had the most clients, Steve took on the role of liaison counsel to act as an intermediary between the various firms and the court.

Because of Lee's vast experience and reputation, it was a foregone conclusion that the others would elect him Chairman and Lead Counsel at the first Committee meeting. Lee accepted, knowing it would be a heavy burden to head up the investigation, prepare for the liability trial, and support the victims' families along the way. But he knew he was the most experienced and best suited and felt ready as if he'd been preparing for this case his whole life.

* * *

Shortly after his appointment, and with the blessing of his fellow Committee members, Lee called John Brennan, Chairman of United States Aviation Underwriters (USAU); Pan Am's insurer. The company was a subsidiary of USAIG and would have to pay whatever compensation might be recovered in the legal proceedings.

Lee had a long professional relationship with Brennan, and speaking directly with him about cases was not unusual. In the past, he had found him to be contentious and calculating but ultimately fair and reasonable. As always, Lee sought to settle the case rather than go to trial.

He knew from experience that three factors were at play in settlement negotiations, depending on the strengths and weaknesses of a case:

1. The inherent value of each claim from the standpoint of provable damages.
2. The question of liability, which involved the probability of winning and the risk of losing, if it came to a trial.
3. The attitude of the plaintiffs because they were the ones who accepted or rejected a given offer.

Obviously, the greater the risk of losing a case, the more likely a party would settle. That usually went for both plaintiff and defense. Generally speaking, a settlement was desirable for both sides—the cheapest, quickest, and most assured way to resolve the dispute.

In this situation, Lee felt stronger about the first and third than the second point. So, he arrived at USAU's headquarters near Battery Park not expecting an immediate agreement but an exploratory conversation regarding some of the issues that might lay the groundwork for a future settlement.

However, when the secretary ushered him into the elegant, wood-paneled chairman's office, John Brennan, who was only a few years younger than Lee, acted without an ounce of courtesy. There was no offer of coffee or tea, no small talk about their families, no effort to exchange pleasantries before getting down to brass tacks.

Brennan remained seated behind his desk, looking like a bull terrier guarding his territory. Barely glancing up from the papers

First Attempt to Settle

before him, he nodded hello and said, "I don't know why you called for this meeting, Lee. There isn't any point in having it."

His aggressive tone took Lee aback. But he decided not to respond immediately.

Straightening, Brennan poked his chin out and continued, "I won't cough up a dime more than $100,000 per death until the Supreme Court for the World tells me to pay more."

Lee looked puzzled. The offer of $25,000 above the Warsaw Convention maximum was almost insulting. "Well, it may come to that," he ventured. "You never know."

Brennan gripped the arms of his leather chair. "The terrorism was directed not at Pan Am but the United States government," he snapped. "You know as well as I there is no way an airline, in this day and age, can effectively protect itself against a terrorist attack."

Seeking to defuse the tension, Lee scratched his head and smiled. "I guess you and I see this case somewhat differently," he said. "There are security issues within Pan Am's purview, after all."

After locking eyes briefly with him, Brennan returned to the pages on his desk and said dismissively, "I've got a busy day. If any facts come to my attention to change my mind, I'll call you."

Surprised by his utter lack of courteousness, Lee gave him an evaluating glance. Then he said, "Don't bother getting up. I'll see myself out."

In the taxi on the way back to his office, he felt bewildered. The meeting had felt like running into a brick wall. On top of that, Brennan had been uncharacteristically rude. Whatever the reason, it promised a long, difficult, and complicated case ahead.

6

DISCOVERY

March 1989

The documents from Pan Am arrived at 100 Park Avenue in a big truck. The driver and his helper carted 16 large boxes jam-packed with papers to the Kreindler & Kreindler office. Legal aides and secretaries lugged them to the conference room on the 19th floor which became a kind of command center for the team.

A cursory examination showed that the documents—ledger, legal, or letter size, or just small pieces of paper—were in no particular order. If there were any incriminating records, they were well hidden among the massive quantity of material. The defense was obviously making every effort to overwhelm the plaintiffs. This practice was not unusual, but Lee suspected John Brennan had made sure of it.

The Lockerbie Plaintiffs Committee had served the defense with a wide-ranging document request of all memos, letters, faxes, e-mails, and telexes sent or received by Pan Am and Alert Management in New York, Frankfurt, and London for five years. Because they ran in the tens of thousands of pages, it would take several months to analyze them. When so informed, Judge Platt set a deadline of July 31 to complete the process. Then, depositions with people involved in the case could get started.

There were some ways to classify the trove of documents. Papers from Pan Am's headquarters in New York were stamped PN; from the airline's Frankfurt station, PF; and from London station, PL. Other classifications covered Pan Am's correspondence regarding its security subsidiary, Alert Management, and FAA regulations, violations, causation, and more. Often, the same message showed up in two or more places.

Lee and his two partners put an associate, Noah Kushlefsky, in charge of the initial screening process. Noah had joined the firm just a year before Lockerbie after getting his law degree from George Washington University. His gregarious personality and strong organizational skills soon earned him Lee's confidence.

They hired eight high school students, sons and daughters of the firm's partners and their friends, to comb through the documents. Every afternoon during school and all day long during their spring break, the youngsters sorted the papers into categories. "Pan Am 103 Staffing" was one, "Screening at the Airports" another, "Screener Training" another, "X-ray Procedures" yet another. Other classifications covered Pan-Am's correspondence regarding its security subsidiary, Alert Management, and FAA regulations, violations, causation, and more.

Lee popped his head into the conference room at least once a day to encourage the youngsters. He was delighted to see how seriously they took their assignment.

With stacks of paper everywhere, the conference room soon looked like a hoarder's paradise. Many of the pages were poor copies and illegible. That required contacting the Pan Am legal defense team and demanding they provide readable documents, which wasted time.

Associates at the firm performed the next sweep-though by subject matter. They pulled out the pages that appeared to be important and distributed them to Steve, Jim, Lee, and the other Plaintiffs Committee lawyers for further evaluation. After that, clerks copied the relevant documents so that each member of the trial preparation team had a complete set to use in depositions.

Discovery

The process was cumbersome at best and felt like an exercise in frustration that failed to yield any useful results.

* * *

In the meantime, the investigators in Germany reported that they had found nothing unusual in Pan Am's and Alert's security practices and presented Kreindler & Kreindler with a bill for $60,000. The London detectives found nothing helpful either. Michael Hughes made some potentially valuable contacts in Scotland, including meeting the main administrator of the criminal inquiry, but nothing came of them.

The case was at a standstill. Bills were mounting, and the plaintiffs' attorneys had nothing to show for their efforts but useless piles of paper.

Lee often called this stage of trial preparation the horse latitudes. The term refers to the area of the world's oceans north and south of the equator that usually has calm weather and little rain. In the days of sailing voyages, ships could sit there for weeks waiting for a gust of wind. Sometimes, the crew threw the horses overboard to conserve drinking water. As a result, horse latitudes came to mean "stuck without any progress."

It would have been easy to give way to despair when nothing was happening, and the case hung by the thread of hope that something would come up to move things forward. No doubt, Lee had moments when he wished he'd never gotten involved in Lockerbie. But they were fleeting, and he only shared them with Ruth. When asked about it, he always put on a good face and said, "It's just too big, too important, too mind-boggling for us to stay out of it."

In the office, he kept encouraging everyone to "keep digging."

It helped that Lee was naturally an optimist who believed with all his heart that the law could make the world a better place. He often wrote and spoke of lawyers' role in bringing about world peace.

That belief had deepened during a trip to Israel with Ruth, where Gideon Hausner, the country's former attorney general, invited them to stay at his home in Jerusalem. Hausner had been the prosecutor at the Adolf Eichmann trial, which was televised worldwide and drew public attention to the Holocaust which was little known at the time. It set the precedent that the defense "I was only following orders" is invalid if the orders are criminal and illegal.

Hausner was nearly a decade older than Lee. He had the same balding head with black, close-cropped hair on the sides. His face was chiseled, his nose aquiline, and his forehead furrowed, with bushy eyebrows above lively eyes. Yet, he seemed rather shy for someone who had occupied the spotlight on the world stage.

He and his wife Judith lived in a small apartment with a guest bedroom, and they treated their guests like family. Lee and Ruth cherished their time with them, discussing the law and its greater purpose. Hausner told Lee that he had thought a great deal about how to make the Eichmann trial an indictment not just of the defendant but of all Nazis and the horrific crimes they had committed against humanity and the Jewish people.

In an extraordinary decision, Hausner had survivors of the concentration camps and ghettos testify about their horrific experiences, even when they had no direct proof of Eichmann's culpability. For many witnesses, it was the first time they spoke about the horrors they had endured. Until then, they had kept them bottled up inside. While bringing an evildoer to justice, the trial made it possible to speak about the unspeakable, lift the curtain of self-imposed silence, and encourage healing conversations among Holocaust survivors.

Lee never forgot the lesson that a trial could serve a larger public purpose. He vowed to use airline disaster trials to make flying safer for everyone worldwide, and pursued a "sue for safety" approach in many of his air disaster cases.

Discovery

In July 1971, Lee organized the fifth "World Peace through Law" conference to encourage dialogue and understanding among judges and attorneys of different countries. The International Court of Justice in The Hague could only hear disputes between member nations. Lee thought expanding its jurisdiction to legal disputes between private citizens would benefit everyone. He invited supreme court justices and other important legal practitioners from around the world to engage in a mock trial to better appreciate each other's legal systems.

The conference took place in the Yugoslav capital Belgrade, and attracted over 4,000 lawyers and observers from 114 countries. It was an epic undertaking and required much preparation, including arranging simultaneous translations of the proceedings in many different languages.

Lee wrote the script for the mock trial himself to make it a truly international event that involved countries from all over the world. He devised a complex and clever scenario: Japan builds a retrorocket for an Italian satellite which is launched from a NASA spaceport. The rocket crashes into the Kremlin in Moscow, injuring a Venezuelan man and killing an Ethiopian tourist and his son. The Soviet Union, Venezuela, and the deceased's widow bring suits against the governments of Japan, Italy, and the United States.

The six parties had 20 minutes each to argue that another nation's law should apply because it would be more favorable to their cause. The attorneys were the heads of the legal systems of the six countries involved, except for the United States. Because U.S. Supreme Court Chief Justice Warren Burger acted as the presiding judge of the mock court's panel, Leon Jaworski, who had served as the second special prosecutor in the Watergate scandal, argued for the American side.

When everyone finished their presentations, Lee addressed the court, "Your honors, I have wanted my entire career to say this: 'You now have 10 minutes to recess and return your decision.'"

Uproarious laughter from all the attendees echoed throughout the meeting hall.

The conference was a big success and led to fruitful exchanges among the participants, increasing understanding of the positive role law and justice could play worldwide. Many of them became Lee's friends and encouraged him to continue to advance the rule of law in other parts of the world. One of the mock trial judges, Azu Crabbe, later became Ghana's Chief Justice. He and Lee got along well, and when Lee organized another conference, he chose Bolgatanga, Ghana.

Soon after, he joined the International Academy of Trial Lawyers, a group of the top 500 trial lawyers worldwide, and served as the youngest dean and president of the organization. His position allowed him to choose the location of the annual conference, and he picked the Ivory Coast in West Africa for the first meeting of his tenure.

When traveling without their children, Lee and Ruth took separate planes to ensure that, in case of an air tragedy, one of them survived to take care of their family. On this trip, Ruth arrived first in Abidjan, the country's largest city. Riding in the taxi from the airport behind one of the delegations, flags on their limousines fluttering in the wind, she felt like a head of state. Because Lee's plane was late, she gave the opening remarks in her best French. Although nervous, she acquitted herself well but was happy when Lee came and took over midway through her speech.

All influential West African jurists attended. Ruth found some of the local leaders dressed in their colorful tribal clothes a beautiful sight.

As luck would have it, the hotel where Lee and Ruth were to stay was owned by a cigarette factory and had burned down. Fortunately, one of the tribal chiefs at the conference invited them to join him at another hotel. He had booked an entire floor for his family and entourage. Lee was happy to accept.

The Friday evening they moved in, the locals came out for their usual weekend celebration. Ruth felt like they were walking through a casino.

No one got much sleep that night. But the conference was a success.

Lee was nominated for the 1978 Nobel Peace Prize for all his efforts to make the law a force for good worldwide, although he didn't win. That year, the honor went to Menachem Begin and Anwar Sadat for making peace between Israel and Egypt.

Lee was not disappointed. He felt that he had been a long shot anyway. He continued to pursue his career with determination, believing that it was his job to make life better for his clients.

7

BREAKTHROUGH

March—May 1989

Toward the end of March, Lee heard from one of the German lawyers in Frankfurt. The attorney faxed him a copy of an article that had appeared in *Stern* magazine. The illustrated weekly, which means Star in English, was a popular current affairs publication, somewhat like *LIFE*, with photographs and some investigative reporting.

The piece, written jointly by Frank Muller Moy in London and Tom Kettner in Frankfurt, reported that on the afternoon and early evening of December 21, 1988, the day of the Lockerbie disaster, a big party took place at Pan Am's Frankfurt airport headquarters. The occasion was the retirement of the airline's station manager, Herbert Leuniger. People who should have been performing security duties were enjoying the festivities instead.

When Lee and his team read the English translation—provided by Phyllis Rosenthal—they got very excited. The information offered the first glimmer of hope that they would find evidence of serious misconduct by Pan Am and its subsidiary Alert Management.

Enlisting the help of one of the firm's clients in England, Lee tracked down Frank Muller Moy. It took over a month, but when he finally contacted him by phone and introduced himself, the reporter was eager to talk. So, Lee and Steve Pounian flew to London to meet with him. They stayed at Brown's Hotel in the heart of the Mayfair district within walking distance of Charring Cross and Hyde Park.

Their encounter occurred the following day in the hotel's Tea Room, whose original wood paneling and old paintings go back to 1837 when the hotel first opened. In contrast to the cold and clammy English weather outside, it was warm and cozy. Steve and Lee sat on the L-shaped sofa in the corner while Muller Moy occupied one of the plush red chairs across the table from them. He was in his late thirties with chestnut brown hair and the discerning, weary eyes of a reporter who never gets enough sleep.

Lee and Steve asked him many questions, but their initial excitement about finding chinks in Pan Am's security armor quickly dissipated. Yes, there had been a party, but the Alert screeners whose job was to do the security functions had not been invited and did not attend.

Putting his hands together steeple-like, Lee said, "It really is very important for us to get solid information on Pan Am and Alert, Frank."

"I understand, and I'd like to help," Muller Moy replied. "The world cries out in sympathy for all the Lockerbie families." He reached into the leather satchel he'd brought with him and pulled out several pieces of paper. "Look, I shouldn't show you this, and you must keep it confidential until it appears, but we have another story coming out next week."

It was a fax copy of the article's galley sheets. The story in German was written primarily by his co-author, Thomas Kettner. Muller Moy translated it into English and showed Lee and Steve the accompanying pictures. The piece focused on Oliver Koch, the 21-year-old chief of training at Alert in Frankfurt. He had made public accusations against his boss, Ulrich Weber, the general manager of Alert for all of Germany, and complained about the lack of adequate security at the airport. As a result, Koch was fired and his life threatened. But before he went into hiding, he told his story on Munich television.

Somehow, Kettner had tracked him down, befriended the young man, and gotten him to agree to an interview.

In the story, Koch described shocking conditions at Alert Management in Frankfurt. He said Weber was a promiscuous bisexual who hired and fired security screeners based on personal favors rather than experience or competence. The X-ray machine operators who scanned the luggage had received no adequate training. The Helsinki warning that a Pan Am flight from Frankfurt to the United States would be bombed had been sent to Alert but was never passed on to the screeners. Koch found it a pile of papers on his boss's desk the morning after the disaster. When Weber heard that the FAA was coming to interview him, he backdated the document to December 9.

As Muller Moy translated the article, Lee and Steve Pounian listened with disbelief, but the reporter's sober account and quiet confidence soon dispelled their skepticism.

Lee realized that if they could locate Koch and depose him, they would have the beginning of a case of willful misconduct. He asked Muller Moy, "Can you find Koch for us? We want to get him to testify."

The reporter shrugged apologetically. "Only Kettner knows Koch's whereabouts, and he promised not to reveal that information."

Lee thought for a moment and asked, "Can you get Kettner on the telephone for me?"

Muller Moy nodded OK.

While he left to make some calls, Lee booked a seat on the 7 p.m. Concorde to New York to attend a pretrial conference scheduled the next day with Judge Platt. He hoped taking a late flight would give him enough time to reach Kettner and find Koch.

When Muller Moy returned to the Tea Room, he had good and bad news. He had found Kettner in Hamburg at *Stern's* main office and spoken with him. "But Kettner says it is impossible for you to talk to Koch," he explained. "The young man is scared out of his wits. He's in hiding. He has a new job and is using a pseudonym. "

Lee refused to give up. "Please call him again. I want to talk to him personally. Does he speak English?"

Within minutes, he and Kettner were on the line together. The German reporter was adamant. "I'm sorry. I already told Frank that I can't do anything."

"Mr. Kettner," Lee said, "I am chief counsel for all the Lockerbie families. We are trying to find out how Lockerbie happened, and ultimately, we will try to recover some money for these poor families. I need your help. I want to meet with Koch and persuade him to come to New York to testify. We will pay all his expenses and yours too, if he would feel more comfortable having you accompany him."

There was a long silence at the other end.

"Tom," Lee continued. "Let's get on a first-name basis. Please call me Lee. I want to work with you on this. There might be a great exclusive story in *Stern* for you if we pull it off. We must talk to Koch. He has to understand that the Lockerbie families need him. The best protection for him is to go on the record in our case. Once he has testified, Pan Am will be afraid to go near him."

After some back and forth, Kettner said, "Okay. I will try to find Oliver and talk to him." He added, "There's another Alert employee, Werner Schutz, who also appeared on Munich TV. He echoed Koch's criticism of the Alert operation, although he was not directly involved with Flight 103. But he knows of Oliver's whereabouts and will be able to tell him to give me a call."

"Thank you, Tom," Lee said. "And we would like to talk to Schutz, too. If it makes getting Oliver on an airplane to New York easier, we'll pay his expenses as well." He concluded, "I will wait for your call here at Brown's Hotel until 5 p.m. Then, I have to leave for New York. My colleague, Steve Pounian, will stay in London. If necessary, he'll be

Breakthrough

available to fly to Munich to talk to Oliver and Werner. In any event, I will speak with you tomorrow from New York."

When Lee got off the phone, Steve looked at him in astonishment, his dark eyes wide as saucers. Lee grinned, realizing that his colleague thought he'd lost his mind. How could they possibly pull this off?

They said their goodbyes to Muller Moy, thanking him for everything and promising to stay in touch. Then, they went to Lee's room to strategize.

Lee knew Judge Platt's order prohibited taking depositions before July, and it was early May. The federal rules and rules of fairness required adequate notice of depositions, to give adversaries a reasonable amount of time to prepare. But Lee also knew that if he gave Pan Am and Alert any inkling of what was going on, they would move heaven and earth to prevent Koch from testifying. His life had already been threatened. They might rehire him or otherwise buy him off.

"We have to get Koch on a non-stop flight to New York," Lee told Steve. "When we know he's on the airplane, we'll give notice."

By the time he returned to New York, Tom Kettner had found Oliver Koch. Once again, there was good and bad news. Koch and Schutz were willing to fly to New York if Kettner came with them. But Kettner, an enthusiastic tennis fan, had tickets for the French Open in Paris. "There is no way I can make it to New York," he said during the phone call.

Lee pleaded, "Tom, please, the Lockerbie case may depend on your coming. I have a tennis court at my house. Not only will I play with you, but I'll buy you dinner."

"Lee, I don't know you, but you must be out of your mind," Kettner said. "You want me to give up the French Open and a marvelous weekend with a beautiful woman to babysit two Alert screeners for three days in New York? Besides, I'll have to ask my editor if he will allow it."

That was all the opening Lee needed. "Wonderful. Talk to your editor and work it out. We need you."

The next four days were a nail-biting roller coaster ride. Every time things took a turn for the better, some setback would occur to plunge everyone into a state of frustration and despair. First, Kettner got *Stern* to agree to the trip. Then, Koch's mother got sick, and he said he couldn't go. Then, Schutz, who wanted to make the trip, persuaded Koch it was his duty to go. But Koch's girlfriend said he couldn't go to New York without her. Throughout the negotiations, Kettner had to communicate with Schutz and Koch in roundabout ways because Koch had a small apartment somewhere in Munich and no telephone. He was still scared and would not give Kettner his employer's name or telephone number. At some point, overwhelmed by his mother's deteriorating health and his girlfriend's demands, he refused to talk to Kettner.

From a distance, Lee could only listen on the telephone to the reporter's blow-by-blow account. Sometimes, it sounded like a Three Stooges routine—none of it funny at the time. But he kept his composure throughout, sharing his frustrations only with Ruth at home.

Finally, Kettner called that Schulz had persuaded Koch to come. "Send me the tickets by DHL!" he said triumphantly.

Lee had Pat book seats on a Lufthansa flight and deliver the tickets.

The next day, Kettner called Lee to say Koch had changed his mind again. "His girlfriend insists he shouldn't come, and his mother has taken a turn for the worse and might die," he explained.

Pacing in his office, Lee urged, "Tom, you can do this. Go to Munich. Get Schutz to help you. Talk to the girlfriend. If necessary, bring her with you, too."

"Lee Kreindler, you are a crazy man," Kettner marveled. "I will call you from Munich. You'd better buy me some nice dinners!"

Lee spent the next 24 hours fretting and worrying.

On Sunday at 6 p.m. New York time, Kettner called. "I want you to kiss me," he said. "I am at the Hotel Altmeier in Room 606, in Munich. I didn't take any chances. In the next room are Koch and Schutz; they are now roommates! I thought that was the safest way. And I am watching their door. Call here tomorrow at 9 a.m., our time. Our flight to New York leaves at 10. If I have checked out of the hotel, you know we are on our way. If there is a problem, I will still be here."

"That is great news!" Lee said. "I can't thank you enough."

"There is a hitch," Kettner admitted. "I left Frankfurt without the plane tickets! I don't have the tickets to New York!" Before Lee could reply, he added, "Oh, another problem is that Koch could only get three days off from work. He has to be back here on Friday."

Lee got off the phone and threw his hands in the air in frustration. Then he got to work. With Pat Robinson's help and a few transatlantic phone calls, Kettner got the tickets.

At 3 p.m. New York time, Lee called the hotel in Munich. Kettner had checked out. They were on their way!

Anticipating a good outcome, Lee and the team had already prepared the notices of depositions of Koch and Schutz, leaving the date and time blank. To give the defense some idea of the scope of the testimonies and avoid the argument that it could not adequately prepare, they attached copies of the *Stern* magazine article that was about to appear, together with an English translation.

Lee was at the Kreindler & Kreindler office at 8:30 the next morning to meet with his team, finalize the deposition notices, and have them served on the defendants. It would be a difficult challenge because he and his colleagues only had three days to make it all happen. They hadn't even met Koch and Schutz yet but had to give notice, and the most lead time they could provide was two days! They set the depositions for Wednesday at 9 a.m. at the firm's office on Park Avenue and informed the defense.

An hour later, Lee called Steve Fearon, whose firm represented Alert Management. Fearon was a generation younger and also practiced aviation law. Lee respected him as a lawyer. He had always found him to be fair and reasonable and thought a phone conversation might blunt the shock of the unexpected notice and pave the way for an amicable resolution.

Fearon listened. Then he exploded, "You've got to be kidding, Lee! Two days isn't enough notice for anyone, and it violates the scheduling order. Furthermore, you, yourself, haven't finished going through all the documents we're producing, so even you aren't ready."

"These are unusual circumstances, so please reconsider, Steve," Lee said. "Why don't you talk to Jim Shaughnessy and get back to me." Shaughnessy of Windels, Marx, Davis & Ives was the lead attorney representing Pan Am.

Lee hung up, not feeling very confident about the defense's reaction, but he had learned to deal with such obstacles one at a time. So, he focused on preparing for Kettner, Koch, and Schutz arriving on the Lufthansa flight from Munich. They were scheduled to touch down at about 1 p.m. Pat Robinson had arranged to pick them up and bring them directly to the Kreindler & Kreindler office.

At 2 p.m., the defense served Lee and the Plaintiffs Committee with motion papers to strike the deposition notices. Duplicates went to Magistrate Allyne Ross, whom Judge Platt had assigned to all discovery disputes.

While waiting for Koch and the others to arrive at the office, Lee, Jim, and Steve put together responsive papers as best they could. They tried to reach the attorneys for Pan Am and Alert to agree on when to appear before Magistrate Ross and argue the defendants' motion. As Lee expected, the defense lawyers were all "out" someplace. They knew the clock was on their side and time was slipping away. Had he been in their shoes, he would have done the same thing.

When Koch, Schutz, and Kettner arrived, Lee's office was still a whirlwind of activity, as his team tried to get papers together for Magistrate Ross and locate the defendants' lawyers.

Oliver Koch was a rail-thin young man with high cheekbones, blue eyes, and a shock of blond hair falling on his forehead. He wore a striped, long-sleeve shirt and denim jeans popular with European youth. He shook Lee's hand, introduced himself, and said in halting but clear English, "I'm excited to be here in New York."

Werner Schutz was half a head shorter than his lanky companion, a chubby Bavarian with the beginnings of a beer gut hanging over the belt of his jeans. He seemed just as eager, leaning toward Lee, but only said his name.

Tom Kettner kept to the back. He was tired from the long trip and his role as babysitter, but his dark eyes darted about as if he was taking it all in and making mental notes for future articles. He looked different from how Lee had pictured him listening to his voice over the telephone, more athletic and down-to-earth. When Lee explained that he needed to talk to Oliver and Schutz for an hour or so, and then they would have the night off to rest, Kettner seemed visibly relieved.

While Steve and Jim were busy putting the final touches on the responsive papers for Magistrate Ross, Lee took Oliver Koch to his office. Sitting at the jack-screw table, he did his best to make the young man feel at ease while evaluating him as a witness. He was pleasantly surprised by Oliver's clear and thorough responses.

Lee confirmed that Koch had been Alert Management's director of training and that he was responsible for giving the screeners instructions and warnings.

At 4 a.m., following the Lockerbie bombing, Koch had gone to his office at Frankfurt Airport. His boss, Ulrich Weber, had directed him to clean up the place in anticipation of visits from the police or the FAA. Weber had a desk in Koch's office where he kept his computer. Next to it was a large pile of papers. Halfway sorting through it, Koch saw the Helsinki warning. "I cried out, 'Oh my God.' I couldn't believe it," he told Lee. "This was the warning of the Lockerbie bombing!"

The required procedure was to disseminate warnings and instructions immediately. First, a paper was date-stamped to show when it was received. That was usually done by Weber's secretary, Stella Schneider, at his direction. Then, it would be given to Koch for distribution to the screeners.

"I never saw this warning and never gave it to the screeners! And there was no date stamp on it," Koch said. "I realized I would be blamed for not giving out the warning. So, I made a copy to show there was no date stamp." He handed Lee a paper, "This is the copy I made, without the date stamp. When Weber came in, I took it to him and said, 'Herr Weber, this was the warning of Lockerbie. It was on your desk. It was not date stamped!'"

As Lee looked at the document typed in German in astonishment, Koch handed him another paper. "And here is the warning with the date stamped December 9," he explained. "Two days after I gave Weber the undated warning, we heard that the FAA was coming. Weber asked me to give him the document again, and he backdated the stamp machine and marked it so the FAA would think we'd given it out."

Lee shook his head and sighed. The incompetence that led to 270 people losing their lives was terrible enough. But the duplicity of the cover-up was inexcusable.

Breakthrough

Koch's description of the condition of Alert Management was just as appalling. The company employed untrained screeners, guards who did not know what they were doing, and X-ray operators who did not know what they were looking for. None followed procedures or took the minimum X-raying time required per bag. It all added up to a contemptuous attitude toward security by everyone at Pan Am and Alert. In addition, there were tales of promiscuity and playing favorites by Ulrich Weber.

As he listened, Lee marveled what a monumental breakthrough in the case Koch's testimony represented. He had to take his deposition!

After talking to Koch for more than an hour, Lee invited Werner Schutz into his office. Since the German spoke no English, Lee asked Phyllis Rosenthal to join and translate. Schutz had similar damning things to say about Alert—confirming a lazy, lax corporate culture regarding security and some of Weber's most outrageous shenanigans. But because he had worked only at the Munich-Riem Airport, he had no direct connection to Pan Am 103, and Lee spent only 15 minutes with him.

He then excused Koch, Schutz, and Kettner for the night and sent them to their hotel to rest. As it turned out, Kettner did just that, but Koch and Schutz wanted to explore Manhattan. Lee had Pat Robinson make sure one of the Kreindler & Kreindler staff members went along as a minder. He reported the next day that they'd gone out looking around and bar-hopping till three in the morning.

Meanwhile, Lee, Steve, and Jim finalized the responsive papers for Magistrate Allyne Ross, served them on the defendants, and filed them in court. Lee had dealt with her on several occasions, and Jim knew her from his time in the Brooklyn's DA office as well. Her blue eyes, striking blond hair, and ready smile turned the heads of many a young attorney, whether she was wearing her judge's robe or street clothes. But no one who dealt with Ross professionally underestimated her. She had a keen legal mind and little time for attorneys who showboated or tried to muddy the waters.

On Tuesday morning, the litigation team advised the defendants they would attempt a conference call with Magistrate Ross to argue the motion. She responded quickly, scheduling the telephone meeting for 2 p.m. that afternoon.

After listening to the arguments by both sides, she gave her judgment, "Mr. Kreindler, the rules require fair notice, and this is not fair notice. There is no way the defendants can properly prepare for these depositions. Furthermore, the court has ordered that depositions not start until July. The defendants' motion to strike the deposition notices is granted."

"I understand your decision, Your Honor, although I disagree with it," Lee said. "You must know that I represent all the Lockerbie passengers' families, and, to protect their rights, it is critical that we obtain the facts which until now have been barred to us. I believe the circumstances are extraordinary. As you know, we have a serious time problem. So we have no choice but to appeal to Judge Platt."

Magistrate Ross said she would facilitate the appeal. "I can take the papers to Judge Platt myself. He is right here in the building, which will save you some time."

"Thank you, Your Honor. I appreciate that," Lee said.

When he got off the phone, he called Judge Platt's chambers and alerted the clerk. "We would like a conference as soon as possible to resolve our appeal. We have a witness here who has to go back to Germany on Thursday, and it is already Tuesday."

At 5 p.m., he received a telephone call from Judge Platt's law clerk. "Please be here tomorrow morning at 9:30 a.m. and advise your opponents to be here also."

Because the notice to the defense specified that the depositions would be taken by videotape and a court reporter, Lee instructed

Pat Robinson to have the video operator and stenographer ready the following day at 11 a.m. If Judge Platt reversed Magistrate Ross and permitted going forward, they needed all the time they could get.

Wednesday morning, Lee, Steve, Jim, and other members of the Plaintiffs Committee met in a federal courtroom of the Eastern District of New York in Brooklyn. Lee had asked Tom Kettner to come as well. Since he had written the story in *Stern*, he could personally attest to the circumstances of bringing the witnesses to New York. After two good nights' sleep, Tom seemed fully recovered from any jet lag. Like any good reporter, he checked out the décor—the light wood-paneling, the wall with photographs of various judges hanging above the jury box; the lamps hanging from the tall ceiling, the judge's bench and witness box, and the benches for spectators looking like pews in a church.

Lee nodded to Steve Fearon and James Shaughnessy at the other table, representing Alert and Pan Am respectively. Both glared at him. Fearon, though tight-lipped, appeared less hostile. Shaughnessy, more round-faced than Fearon and balding like Lee, looked like Terry Bradshaw, the football player, trying to intimidate his opponent.

Judge Platt arrived briskly from his chamber and wasted no time. Giving Lee a hard stare, he started the hearing. "I want you to explain how, where, and when you learned of the existence of these witnesses."

Lee recounted the story in detail: The original *Stern* article faxed to him, the trip to London, the meeting with Muller Moy, and the many phone calls to Kettner in Frankfurt and Munich. "Your Honor, Thomas Kettner is here in the courtroom with us and can verify the details," Lee said.

He explained how Koch and Schutz had appeared on Munich TV and how Koch's life had been threatened. "Koch and Schutz are sitting in my office now, ready to testify," Lee said. "The stenographic reporter and video operator will be there in half an hour. This is a willful misconduct case, and willful misconduct is difficult to prove. Witnesses are hard to come by, and these two witnesses are here from Germany. As Your Honor knows, there were over two hundred and fifty passengers on the airplane. The future of all their families will depend on whether we can prove the facts."

"Very well," Judge Platt said. "I will now hear from Pan Am's attorney."

James Shaughnessy, lead counsel for the defense, stood up and said, "There's no way we can be ready for these depositions, Your Honor. We have to have time to investigate. We understand Koch, in particular, is a very questionable witness, but we have not had time to talk to his boss, General Manager Weber. We would be prejudiced by having to cross-examine now. Furthermore, we have produced thousands of documents. Plaintiffs' counsels have not even had a chance to read them all, let alone study them for potentially important depositions. If they examine these witnesses now, they will be back later to retake the depositions."

They were the same arguments Lee would have made, and he started to get a bad feeling.

Judge Platt turned to him. "Mr. Kreindler, if I permit you to go forward with your direct examination of these witnesses, on the condition that the defendants can cross-examine now to the extent they want to and defer such parts of their cross-examination as they wish until another date one to two months from now, will you agree to bring the witnesses back at your expense?"

Agree? Lee would have agreed to jump off the building. He answered "yes" immediately.

Shaughnessy harumphed dismissively and whispered something to his co-counsel, who shook his head.

Meanwhile, Judge Platt took his time considering the arguments. Then he said, "In that case, the defendants may cross-examine as they wish now and defer as much as they wish until later. However, they defer examination at their own risk if anything happens to the witnesses. The direct examination will still be usable. Do both sides understand?"

Lee would have loved to do a small victory dance. The relieved look on the faces of his fellow attorneys told him how big a win this was.

The judge then ordered that direct examination would begin at 2 p.m. and would continue until such time as the defendants deferred additional cross-examination.

So, on Wednesday afternoon, May 8, 1989, the testimony of Oliver Koch, the first deposition in the Lockerbie case, took place. Lee examined him, bringing out everything they had discussed the previous day, and the defendants briefly cross-examined. The next morning, the defendants asked a few more questions and then deferred the rest. A brief deposing of Werner Schutz followed, and the defendants deferred all of his cross-examination.

Lee thought it was a good beginning, although he still had to figure out how to connect Koch's testimony to the cause of the disaster.

However, in his June 1989 letter to the families, he wrote:

> *The deposition is spectacular. Our hope was to score a knockout blow in the first round, and we may have done it. The Koch deposition, in particular, will undoubtedly be one of the key depositions in the case. It has made a dramatic difference in our chances for success!*

A week later, Dona Bainbridge called Lee to inform him that she had her baby and named him "Henry Jr."

"Mazel Tov!" Lee exclaimed with genuine affection.

"Thank you," Dona said. "How is the case going? I need to know."

"I am now more than hopeful," Lee assured her. "I am actually optimistic."

8

SHENANIGANS AT THE AIRPORT

June 1989

When the second *Stern* magazine article appeared in Germany, describing Alert Management's security lapses at the Frankfurt Airport, Pan Am vigorously denied the allegations. Its spokespeople, led by Jeff Kriendler, issued statement after statement that the Helsinki warning had been given to screeners in Germany and England and that Koch was a liar. They branded him as an incompetent hanger-on with no serious responsibilities at the airport, a disgruntled employee out for revenge after being dismissed.

Once again, the phones rang off the hook at Kreindler & Kreindler. Newspaper, radio, and television reporters wanted comments and information.

One of the calls came from John Wasley, the producer of "The Reporters" on FOX Television. Wasley said," I am fascinated by the Lockerbie story. Can I see you and talk about the case?"

Lee agreed and invited him to his office. He understood the potential benefit of getting to know a television producer with more clout than frontline correspondents or newspaper reporters. The Australian media mogul Rupert Murdock had bought FOX three years earlier, and the news division's reputation for serious investigative reporting was still intact.

There was another reason Lee agreed to the meeting. During discovery and depositions, the plaintiff's lawyers and investigators were not allowed to contact Pan Am or Alert employees. They could speak with them only while taking depositions with the defense attorneys present and monitoring the proceedings. But those legal constraints did not apply to the news media.

The man who arrived at Lee's office was dressed in conservative business attire—dark gray suit and blue tie—and looked more like a fellow attorney than a media representative. He had a neatly trimmed, salt-and-pepper beard, a friendly face, and a good sense of humor. John Wasley and Lee got along from the get-go.

Because the court's confidentiality order covered all Pan Am discovery documents, Lee could not discuss their content with Wasley. Instead, he told him about what Oliver Koch said in his deposition, that he had found the Helsinki warning on Ulrich Weber's desk and that his boss had backdated the notice to support the lie he had given it to the screeners.

"I want to pursue this," Wasley said with growing excitement. "We'll put Steve Wilson on the segment. He's the ballsiest reporter in the business."

"We can help with background information we got from Koch in his testimony," Lee offered. "By the way, he is due to return to New York in five weeks for the second round of depositions."

Wasley's face brightened. "Could we interview him then?"

"I'd be happy to facilitate that," Lee promised.

Based on their initial and subsequent conversations, Wasley sent Steve Wilson with a camera and sound crew to the Frankfurt Airport to further investigate. Frankfurt was the second busiest airport in Europe after London's Heathrow, and plans were in the works to expand it further. The team filmed the Pan Am premises, both inside the terminal and in the loading areas but found nothing unusual.

Shenanigans at the Airport

Then, Wilson decided to visit Alert Management's offices, hoping to get a closer look at the training facilities there. He took John Jones, a member of his film crew, with him.

When they got there, the blond receptionist greeted them with a big smile and said in perfect English, "We have been expecting you. How was your flight?"

As she led the way inside and he met Alert managers, Wilson realized they were awaiting visitors from the Pan Am office in New York and thought he and John were them.

Deciding to play along, he made sure he did not say anything that wasn't true. He introduced himself, "I'm Steve Wilson from New York, and this is my assistant, John Jones." No one asked for any identification.

They made an odd-looking pair. Wilson, short and heavy-set, wore a dark suit that commanded respect. Jones, tall and slim, was dressed like a cowboy with a Stetson hat, belt buckle, and boots. Wilson could tell by the looks among the Alert managers that they thought, "Those crazy Americans. We'll just have to put up with them." Still, they were polite and eager to please, and invited Wilson and Jones into their offices and showed them everything they wanted to see.

What the supervisors did not know was that Jones had a camera hidden in his Stetson and could film wherever he pointed his head.

When Wilson noticed the security training manual lying on a desk and asked, "Could I have a look at it?" one of the managers said, "Why don't you take a copy with you to lunch, and you can check it out?"

As luck would have it, Alert had recently hired a security company from Israel to train its screeners and X-ray operators. Sessions were in progress and Wilson and Jones sat in on one of them. During a discussion period, Wilson stood up and said, "Can I ask the participants a few questions?"

The instructors were happy to oblige. Most of the screeners understood and spoke English. As everyone introduced themselves by name, Wilson realized that several had been on duty at the time of the Lockerbie crash—Lee had provided FOX with a list of Alert's employees who worked that day.

Wilson focused his questions on them. "Were you on duty at the loading of Flight 103? Did anyone tell you about the Helsinki warning? The Toshiba warning from the FAA?"

They all answered in the negative.

When Wilson asked for a show of hands from those who did not receive the warnings, everyone raised their arms. That completely contradicted what Pan Am had been telling the news media. Throughout the session, Jones kept filming and caught it all on videotape!

As Wilson and Jones left, they had a good laugh, imagining the faces of the Alert managers when the actual Pan Am visitors from New York showed up.

* * *

By agreement with the district court and defense attorneys, five weeks after his first appearance, Lee and the Plaintiffs Committee flew Oliver Koch from Germany to New York for the second round of depositions. This time Oliver brought his girlfriend Andrea with him. He insisted that he couldn't come without her. His mother had died shortly after he had returned to Germany, and Andrea was the only person he trusted. A pretty young woman, she was devoted to Koch, touched him frequently, and tousled his hair. They went out most nights to party accompanied by a staff member who ferried them around and made sure they didn't get into trouble.

One evening, Lee, Jim, Noah Kushlefsky, and Lisa Meacham took Oliver and Andrea out to dinner. Ruth came along, too. They did not discuss any aspects of the case but kept conversation to unrelated and personal topics. Ruth showered Oliver and Andrea with so much warmth and attention that they thanked her warmly when they said their goodbyes.

During the days, Oliver sat diligently for his deposition and answered all questions put to him. This time Shaughnessy and Fearon cross-examined in more detail.

In discussing the FAA's Toshiba bulletin, Oliver insisted the warning that bombs in radio cassettes would be "extremely difficult to detect by normal X-rays" was never given to the screeners. Although it was his responsibility to disseminate such information, he could do so only on instructions from Ulrich Weber. But, just as with the Helsinki warning, his boss at Alert had never shown him the FAA bulletin.

Lee had booked a conference room at the Grand Hyatt Hotel, a block and a half from the Kreindler & Kreindler office, for meetings with the media. Following Koch's deposition, Steve Wilson interviewed Koch on camera for the FOX show. Lee also had Koch talk to William Carley of *The Wall Street Journal* and Richard Whitkin of the *New York Times*. Whitkin was a Pulitzer Prize winning reporter, an expert on aviation space technology, and a good friend of Lee's. But in the face of Pan Am's forceful denials, both papers' editors ultimately decided not to run the story. It was the first hint Lee got about how powerful and influential the airline and its insurers were in controlling some of the news media outlets.

FOX News was an exception. Because Lee provided the background material for Steve Wilson's story, people at the network felt indebted to him. When he asked to view the videotapes to prepare for the depositions of Pan Am and Alert personnel in Frankfurt, he got no for an answer, as expected. Letting lawyers see raw footage before airing a show was considered a no-no. But after pleading with Wasley "in the interest of justice," he got the go-ahead. The following morning,

Lee, Jim, Noah Kushlefsky, and Lisa Meacham were at FOX's New York TV station looking at the tapes.

Lee took pictures of the video screen showing the Alert employees raising their hands to answer Steve Wilson's questions. He was particularly interested in Andrea Schwab Caslis. Several times, she stated clearly that she had not received the Toshiba or Helsinki warnings. Lee knew that she had been on duty at the time of the loading of Flight 103. He took as many pictures of her as possible and had a number of them blown up into eight by 12 photographs.

But before Lee left for Europe, he contacted John Brennan again, this time by telephone, hoping to lay groundwork for negotiations and a settlement.

The president of USAU sounded no less irritated than during their first meeting and stonewalled again. "There is nothing any airline can do to protect itself against such a terrorist attack," he insisted.

"That may have been the case before, but it isn't anymore," Lee responded. "The question now is what Pan Am did or didn't do, and the record is extremely revealing there."

Brennan cleared his throat and said dismissively, "We don't owe any money here. If I change my mind, I'll call you. You don't have to call me."

And he hung up.

Later that morning, Lee received a call from Michael Hughes in Scotland. The USAU and Brennan had instructed a Scottish solicitor to explore settling cases there.

"Are you sure?" Lee asked, surprised.

"Yes, they've definitely made overtures," Michael said.

Lee found it odd. Why would Brennan be so adamant about pursuing the Pan Am litigation in New York and so accommodating elsewhere?

That afternoon, at a pretrial conference at the district court in Brooklyn, Lee happened to meet Robert Alpert, USAU's chief of claims. Flushed with irritation, he cornered him in the hallway. "What are you guys doing in Scotland? What game are you playing?"

Alpert looked startled but made no effort to deny the accusation. "It doesn't affect the passenger cases, Lee," he said appeasingly. "We're just talking about the ground cases." Echoing a comment Brennan had made to Lee during their first meeting, he added, "The passenger cases won't be settled until the Supreme Court of the World denies our last application."

The familiar words startled Lee and gave him pause. Pan Am and USAU certainly had coordinated their public statements so that everybody blew from the same horn. What else were they orchestrating behind the scenes?

9

DOCUMENTARY EVIDENCE

June—August 1989

Because Oliver Koch's testimony revealed serious lapses in Alert Management's security in Frankfurt, Lee directed his team to comb through the discovery documents again. Was there any evidence to tie Pan Am's management to those security failures?

Members of the Plaintiffs Committee met several times a week to go over what they unearthed. Over time, they pieced together the development of airport security protocols and a history of how Pan Am and its leaders dealt with them.

It turned out there were several cases before Lockerbie involving bombs hidden in radios or other electronic devices and smuggled aboard airplanes. Some involved Pan Am directly.

- In 1982, Pan Am was the target of a bomb that exploded on a flight from Tokyo to Honolulu. The captain managed to land the plane safely, but one person was killed in the blast and 16 were wounded. A similar device was discovered on a Pan Am jet in Rio de Janeiro.
- In 1983, authorities found a bomb in an unaccompanied bag, loaded from one airline to another, destined for a Pan Am flight from Rome to New York.
- In 1985, two suitcases containing bombs were checked on Canadian Pacific Air and ticketed to Air India flights. One exploded aboard an Air India 747 jumbo jet, killing 329 persons. The other detonated at Tokyo Airport

while being transferred from one plane to another. Both bombs came in unaccompanied bags transferred from another airline.

Responding to the rise in terrorist activities, in April 1986—two-and-a-half years before Lockerbie—the FAA sent out a series of security measures for airports in the United States and overseas serviced by American carriers. The set of regulations was called the Air Carrier Standard Security Program (ACSSP) and established minimum requirements for U.S. airlines. Pan Am incorporated them into its security manual and disseminated it to its employees.

At ordinary and enhanced security airports, where the terrorist threat was not as great, the ACSSP permitted X-ray examinations of unaccompanied bags. But at "extraordinary security risk airports," like Rome, Athens, and Paris, and at Frankfurt and Heathrow, the two points of departure for Pan Am Flight 103, the FAA had stringent regulations for U.S. carriers operating internationally.

Section XV C.1.(a) of the ACSSP regulations required them to:

> *Conduct a positive passenger/checked baggage match resulting in a physical inspection or non-carriage of all unaccompanied bags. The carrier may use either physical match or administrative match, but in either case, it should be done in a way that passengers are aware of the use of the procedures.*

In effect, Pan Am had to match every checked bag with a passenger who boarded the plane. "Physical match" meant placing all luggage on the tarmac for passengers to personally identify before loading it on the aircraft. "Administrative match" entailed using a checklist, either by computer or manually. Ground crews could only load unaccompanied bags on the plane after a physical inspection, which meant baggage checkers opened the suitcases and searched the contents by hand.

The ACSSP stipulated other measures as well. Certain passengers, termed "selectees" because they were deemed potential risks, had to undergo a more thorough security check. Aircraft parked on the tarmac for loading had to have guards at all times. The operators of X-ray machines needed to "possess sufficient eyesight proficiency to perform their duties." Supervisory personnel had to be familiar with all passenger and baggage screening aspects.

In addition, a Ground Security Coordinator (GSC) had to ensure that all security measures were monitored and met. Before take-off, the GSC had to advise the pilot-in-command of "all pertinent security information" for the flight, including the presence of unaccompanied bags. The ultimate judgment of whether to fly rested with the pilot, who was responsible for the lives of everyone on board.

Pan Am management recognized that it was legally obligated to follow the ACSSP requirements. So, in April 1986, the airline established procedures in Frankfurt and London to perform the required passenger/bag matching. Unaccompanied bags from other carriers, also called "interline bags," were identified and loaded only after a physical search.

At the same time, Pan Am applied to the Transportation Department to approve a $5 surcharge per passenger for trans-Atlantic flights to help cover the cost of implementing the federal regulations. Knowing the extra levy would not be popular with the public, the airline created an ad campaign touting its enhanced security measures—hiring additional personnel, using trained dogs to sniff out bombs in suitcases, and installing state-of-the-art scanners.

One advertisement signed by Ed Acker, Pan Am's Chairman of the Board and CEO, and placed in the *New York Times* and other publications stated:

> Dear Air Traveler, on June 12, 1986, Pan Am will initiate one of the most far-reaching security programs in our industry, a program that will screen passengers, employees, airport facilities, baggage, and aircraft with unrelenting thoroughness.

THE FIGHT FOR JUSTICE

The company also aired television commercials featuring Acker, proclaiming the same message.

At the same time, Pan Am created its separate subsidiary corporation, Alert Management, to provide security for its flights. That way, it kept all aspects of its airport responsibilities in-house and did not have to pay outside contractors.

That was the official version.

Combing through the documents, Lee's team discovered that it was all a charade. The "bomb-sniffing" dogs featured in the commercials were untrained animals rented from a local kennel, the scanners were outdated, and many of the new hires were unqualified "rent-a-cop" workers.

A memo from Alert Management's first president, Fred Ford, to Pan Am senior executives complained that the promised security program was not being implemented. Ford described the creation of Alert as "double dipping." By advertising special security measures, Pan Am attracted more passengers and increased its revenue. But by failing to install them, it bilked the traveling public.

Ford was let go a month later.

Physically matching bags was cumbersome and caused delays, costing the airline money. An accidental miscount of luggage required starting over and could add as much as an extra hour on the ground. As a result, Pan Am, led by its Vice Chairman and COO Martin Shugrue, decided to abandon bag matching and physical search of unaccompanied luggage at airports, flagged as vulnerable, starting with Athens and Rome in 1986, followed by London in 1987, and Frankfurt in June of 1988, six months before Lockerbie.

Instead, Pan Am substituted X-ray examinations for all its international flights. That went counter to FAA regulations, but there was no paper trail proving the involvement of Pan Am's upper management in the decision.

Documentary Evidence

Until Lisa Meacham and Noah Kushlefsky barged into Lee's office one afternoon, waving several documents. "We've found something!" Noah shouted. "We think we have a smoking gun!"

Infected by their excitement, Lee called Jim and Steve Pounian to join them while Lisa laid the documents on the jackscrew table.

One was a telex sent in early March 1988 from Martin Hübner, Pan Am's security director in Frankfurt, to Edward Cunningham, chief of security at Pan Am's headquarters in New York. He questioned management's decision to eliminate positive matching and rely on X-raying for interline bags and begged for more security personnel.

> *At certain times in the morning, there may be a total of five B 727 aircraft parked on open ramp positions at the same time, not including our flights operating to Berlin. There are only two Alert employees assigned to perform the searches and to control access to the cabin and on the ground. This seems to be inadequate, particularly when aircraft are parked at a distance from each other.*
>
> *I have discussed these items in the past with station management in Frankfurt. It has been pointed out to me that for financial reasons the security staff has to be kept to a minimum.*

In response, Daniel Sonesen, acting director of security in Pan Am headquarters in New York, sent a telex that stated:

> *Per message of 10 Mar-88 answer: The Dir. FAA R Salazar has granted X-ray as an alternative to searching pass. baggage. We got the jump on the issue and purchased X-rays for those stations where interline was going to be a problem, i.e., off-loading on the no-show. We have fixed the problem by purchasing X-rays and X-ray interline bags.*
>
> *In the event of a no-show interline pax and his bag is loaded in the belly, we go!!!!!*

The crucial phrase "bag is loaded in the belly, we go!" meant that an interline bag unaccompanied by a "pax"—passenger—put on an airplane without a physical search was no reason to prevent a flight from take-off. That went completely counter to the ACSSP requirements.

Lee and his partners looked at each other in disbelief. Here was direct evidence of Pan Am deliberately ignoring federal regulations.

"What about FAA Director Raymond Salazar granting X-rays as an alternative to physical search?" Lee asked Lisa. "Is there any evidence of that?"

"It is highly dubious," she replied. "We found no correspondence between Salazar and Sonesen or Cunningham in the documents."

"I can't believe they were so brazen," said Jim.

"Or foolish," added Steve dryly.

"It's a game changer," said Lee, rubbing his hands. "Good work!"

There was further evidence, by omission, that Pan Am management deliberately ignored FAA requirements. Following the accidental shooting down of an Iranian Airbus by the U.S.S. *Vincennes* missile cruiser in July, 1988, the FAA issued a security bulletin warning of the high threat of terrorist retaliatory attack against a U.S. passenger air carrier and put the entire aviation community on high alert.

However, Lee's team found no directives from Pan Am's American headquarters or European security heads to beef up security. The principal U.S. carrier in Europe did nothing to raise its relaxed rules of baggage examination. Nor did it follow the ACSSP instructions that the security procedures, including positive matching, be "rigorously applied."

10

DEPOSITIONS IN GERMANY

August 1989

Armed with the knowledge from the discovery documents and Koch's deposition, Lee and his team flew to Frankfurt, Germany, in late August. They planned to examine 16 people, including security screeners, X-ray operators, and duty officers who had worked for Pan Am and Alert Management at the time of the Lockerbie disaster.

Lee also wanted to depose Ulrich Weber, Koch's immediate superior, and Beate Franzki, Alert's acting Frankfurt station manager. However, the defendants were obligated to produce only employees still with the company for questioning. Pan Am had fired both Weber and Franzki after the outrage over Lockerbie, and they were not available to testify.

Lee wanted at least two of the three partners from Kreindler & Kreindler working on the case to be present for every deposition. Steve Pounian was busy in Washington, D.C., on another air disaster trial—Korean Airlines Flight 007, which had been shot down by a Russian missile when it mistakenly ventured into Soviet airspace. So, the team consisted of Lee and Jim Kreindler, Noah Kushlefsky and Lisa Meacham, Frank Granito Jr, and Mitch Baumeister.

Jim was to lead the depositions for the Pan Am employees, and Lee would back him up. Then, they'd switch for the Alert Management workers. Other team members could ask additional questions of the witnesses.

Noah and Lisa took care of essential documents culled from the heaps of discovery material. They had studied, cataloged, and shown them to experts when they needed to have them explained. Then, they recorded them in a computer database to retrieve them quickly when needed.

Everyone stayed at the Frankfurt Airport Sheraton Hotel, which had a large conference room to use for the depositions. Pat Robinson had booked a suite for Lee with a living room that became the "command center." Along with a computer, copier, and fax machine, it had two telephone lines with direct access to the New York office in case they needed backup help or more information.

The conference room was bright and airy, with a floor-to-ceiling glass wall on one side overlooking a runway of the Frankfurt Airport. Lee had hotel staff shut the drapes so the arriving and departing flights would not distract from the proceedings. He was glad the overhead lighting was incandescent rather than fluorescent, creating a warmer, non-institutional atmosphere. Several serving tables lined one of the sidewalls. Covered with white linen cloths, they had a coffee urn, cups and saucers, and silver platters filled with sandwiches, Danishes, and other refreshments.

Lee wanted to videotape the testimony, but the defendants' witnesses all refused. He figured the German attorneys for Pan Am and Alert Management, with guidance from James Shaughnessy and Steve Fearon, had told them to say no.

The deposition process was cumbersome. The American lawyers would ask a question in English, have it translated into German, and posed to the witness. Then, the German answer would be translated into English. Court stenographers would take down both language versions for later use. As a result, the proceedings took about four times as long as in the United States. And they were expensive—the translators charged an exorbitant hourly fee. The plaintiffs' attorneys had to pay for everything. It strained the firm's resources, but Lee knew they had no choice. It had to be done.

Everyone sat at a large conference table in the middle of the room. The plaintiff and defense attorneys lined up on opposite sides, like two football teams for a scrimmage. At the center, facing each other, sat the witness and the lead questioner from Kreindler & Kreindler. Other lawyers flanked them like guards, with aides and paralegals at the ends. Defense attorney Shaughnessy occupied the chair to the right of his witnesses, ready to run interference. He wore a permanent scowl as if determined for everyone to be tense and uncomfortable.

The first Pan Am witness was Herbert Leuniger, Frankfurt's former station manager. He had retired at the beginning of January and was the honoree at the Christmas party on December 21 while Flight 103 was loading. He was also one of three ground service chiefs at the time who supervised security activities. In his mid-60s, Leuniger had graying hair, a hooked nose, thin lips, and a pointed chin, which he stuck out arrogantly.

As he settled in the witness chair, his eyes flashing with contempt, he said, "As far as I'm concerned, this is a complete waste of time."

Jim Kreindler refused to let himself get rattled and proceeded with questioning. It was the first time Lee had seen his son take a deposition, and he was impressed. Jim's experience from the Brooklyn DA's office and at the firm was paying off. He was well-prepared and polite but asked penetrating questions. The one thing that bothered Lee was that Jim often looked at his notes between questions while waiting for the translators to finish.

Lee recalled his first international case in 1972 when he participated in a trial in London for a British Airways Trident crash that occurred after the plane had just taken off from Heathrow Airport. The proceedings were conducted according to the rules of the British legal system by Commissioner Sir Geoffrey Lane, a member of the high court in London who later became the Lord Chief Justice of England. Lee represented the families of nine Americans who died. On that occasion, he was also trying to break the Warsaw Convention.

Lee had felt honored to appear in the English court. He considered British barristers the best trial lawyers in the world. When he finished his first cross-examination of a witness and asked for a moment to review his notes before sitting down, Sir Geoffrey looked at him from the bench with disapproval. "We don't do that here in England. At least not if you are a qualified barrister," he said. "We commit all relevant information to memory and take our seat after we ask the last question."

Feeling like a student humiliated by a teacher, Lee blushed and sat down. He vowed he would not make that mistake again and spent that evening in his hotel room studying for the next day's witness examinations.

Later, he got his "revenge" by introducing American customs into the tight-laced English proceedings. On the last day of the trial, Ruth arrived in the courtroom from the United States with their young children just before the afternoon session. Jim and Laurie had been away from Lee for several weeks, and when they saw him, they ran down the long aisle, shouting, "Daddy, Daddy, Daddy!" Lee scooped them up in his arms and gave them each a big kiss.

The next day, the British papers ran front-page articles with the headline "First Kiss in a British Courtroom."

Still, Lee learned an important lesson from Sir Geoffrey. So, during the afternoon break in the depositions, he asked Jim, "Do you always look at your notes?"

"Of course," Jim answered.

Lee did not say anything but broached the subject again over dinner. "You are doing great, Jim, except for one thing. You don't keep eye contact with the witness," he said. "When your eyes go down to that yellow pad, you lose him. You can't tell if you have him on the hook or letting him get away. Try doing it without looking at your notes."

Jim's lips tightened, and he pushed the peas around on his plate like a teenager enduring a parental lecture.

Undeterred, Lee continued," Study your notes *before* you start and take the whole deposition without looking at them. When you think you are finished, ask for a brief break and review your notes then, before you say, "No more questions." That's okay because these are depositions, not a trial; no judge or jury here. In a trial, you'll have to sit down without as much as a glance at your notes." He added, "I learned about taking depositions that way from your grandfather, who was a great trial lawyer."

Then, Lee told the story of Sir Geoffrey scolding him and reminded Jim of when he and Laurie made a big splash in the British courtroom. Jim chuckled at the memory, but Lee could tell he didn't enjoy being called on the carpet.

The following morning, Jim looked serious and ill at ease. Before resuming his questioning of Leuniger, he took a long look at his notes. Then, he placed them on the table. As he was about to begin, he stopped and put the yellow legal pad in his briefcase, out of sight.

He began, haltingly at first, like someone who broke his leg and takes his first steps without a cane, but he soon gained confidence. His questions flowed from Leuniger's answers. He tracked his every move and never let him get away.

Leuniger acknowledged that, as Pan Am's Station Manager, he was responsible for supervising and monitoring Alert's screeners and ensuring they were adequately trained and qualified. After all, they examined passengers, luggage, and interline bags. But he only communicated with Ulrich Weber, the head of Alert for West Germany. He called Weber "a good man" despite his dismissal by Pan Am.

Jim got Leuniger to admit that he did not have the faintest idea of the Alert employees' qualifications or the training they received. Nor did he know if anyone at Pan Am had ever given Alert screeners instructions concerning the Toshiba and Helsinki warnings. Jim's questioning made Leuniger look like a hands-off manager on the eve of retirement, just putting in his hours and doing little else. Nonetheless, he insisted that security had been up to snuff.

Testifying next, Martin Hübner, Pan Am's director of security for Germany, presented a very different picture. He was in his early 40s, did not smile, and answered questions in a clipped matter-of-fact manner. To Lee's surprise, he was remarkably forthcoming

At some point, Hübner mentioned the letter he had written to Edward Cunningham, Chief of Security at Pan Am's headquarters in New York. He explained that they were short-staffed in Frankfurt and that station management had told him it was for financial reasons. Noah instantly called up the document on the computer. He pulled the physical copy from his file and handed it to Jim, who showed it to Hübner.

After looking it over, Hübner said, "Yes. This is the message I sent to New York. I was afraid of the consequences if security did not improve."

"Did you receive a reply?" Jim asked.

"Yes, but they refused to provide us with the funds to hire sufficient personnel."

Hübner revealed that in June 1988, Pan Am's management instructed Ulrich Weber to severely cut security expenses in Frankfurt. He also verified that the requisite baggage reconciliation—positive match—procedure for interline bags was discontinued when Pan Am started X-raying in July 1988.

Jim showed him the March 1988 "bag is load in the belly we go!!!" telex from Daniel Sonesen.

"Yes, I saw it," Hübner acknowledged. "I was of the opinion this was not a good decision because of the unreliability of X-rays and the need to perform a match. I feared the worst might happen."

"So, Flight 103 never underwent positive checked baggage match and physical inspection of the unaccompanied bags, as required by ACSSP?" Jim asked.

Hübner answered, "No."

Turning to the Helsinki warning of an imminent bomb threat to a Pan Am flight, Jim asked Hübner how he first heard of it.

"I got it from the U.S. Consulate, which had received it from the German Ministry."

"Not from Ulrich Weber?"

"No."

"So what happened?"

Hübner explained that he spoke to Al Kunz, the passenger service manager, and they decided to look out for Finnish women passengers. He also advised Daniel Sonesen in New York who ratified that action. Hübner could not recall who had suggested it, but he was sure Berndt Mayer, the acting station manager for Pan Am in Frankfurt who succeeded Leuniger, notified the screeners.

During his deposition, Berndt Mayer said he had attended the Christmas party and had one cocktail. He also testified that he hadn't done anything about the Helsinki warning, but he thought Monica Diegmuller, the alternate GSC, had handled it. Or perhaps Al Kunz.

When Kunz's turn came, he testified that he was at the Christmas Party for the duration and had "a couple of beers." The red veins around his bulbous nose suggested otherwise, but Jim did not pursue it. Kunz remembered the discussion with Hübner on the Helsinki warning. He verified that Hübner asked him for a suggestion on how to handle it and that he proposed checking Finnish women on the flights.

During follow-up, Lee asked him if he felt qualified to suggest how to handle a bomb warning. When Kunz asked what he meant by that, Lee elaborated, "By virtue of your training, experience, or skill, did you feel qualified to suggest the correct response to a bomb warning?"

Kunz said, "No."

Lee then asked him if he knew that a 100% baggage check had been ordered in Helsinki, and he said yes, he had seen the telexes. The exchange was revealing:

> Lee: Did it occur to you to check with Mr. Fircowicz in Finland to see why he thought a 100 percent check was necessary?
>
> Kunz: No.
>
> Lee: Did Pan Am at the time have any flights from Helsinki to Frankfurt?
>
> Kunz: No.
>
> Lee: So, a 100 percent baggage check in Helsinki by Pan Am couldn't possibly find or stop the bomb referred to in the warning?
>
> Kunz: I guess that's right.
>
> Lee: In fact, a 100 percent baggage check by Pan Am in Helsinki was totally useless in terms of this warning.
>
> Kunz: That's true.
>
> Lee: But in Frankfurt, which is where the bomb was to get on your airplane, all you did was look for Finnish women, and because of your lack of training and lack of qualification, you had no idea if that was an appropriate response?
>
> Kunz: That is true.

Ultimately, Hübner, Leuniger, Mayer, and Kunz all agreed that the responsibility for monitoring the specific security measures for Flight 103 fell to Monica Diegmuller, the alternate GSC in charge.

Mrs. Diegmuller was a statuesque blonde in her early forties who had been with Pan Am for a long time. Until she took maternity leave to have a child and become a stay-at-home mom, for a few years, she had been in charge of the Clipper Club, mainly serving drinks to business class passengers. After she returned to work, she held several positions, but the sum total of her security training consisted of a mere three hours. Yet she was quite indignant that Jim dare challenge her qualifications.

Mrs. Diegmuller did reveal, however, that management had never told her to say anything about the Helsinki warning to the screeners. "That wasn't my job," she said.

In the afternoon, while Flight 103 was loading, Mrs. Diegmuller went to the party in honor of Mr. Leuniger. She was there, she testified, for about a half hour and had a sandwich and some tea. After she left, she did not go directly to Flight 103 because she "had other responsibilities."

When she got to the airplane, she met briefly with the flight crew. The load manifest sheet she gave to the captain had a box checked off, indicating "no security risk on this flight." She said nothing about the Helsinki warning or the notice regarding radio cassette player bombs a month earlier and did not mention any interline bags aboard the plane.

"But didn't the Pan Am Security Manual and the ACSSP require you, as the GSC, to personally give the pilot all pertinent security information for the flight?" Jim asked.

Mrs. Diegmuller glanced at her fingernails. "I understood that it only applied to specific threats to a particular flight," she said.

"Do you know if the captain knew about the Helsinki and Toshiba bomb warnings?"

"No."

Lee leaned back in his chair. He was proud of his son. Jim was performing his job well. And he was pleased to see that, as the day progressed, James Shaughnessy's scowl kept getting grimmer.

What emerged in the course of the depositions was a picture of rampant disorganization. The left hand did not know what the right hand was doing, but there was plenty of finger-pointing and passing the buck. Lee and his team realized that the supervision by Pan Am of the Alert operation was a joke, a comedy of errors that would have made for a great sitcom if it hadn't resulted in tragedy.

The initial impetus for questioning Leuniger, Hübner, Diegmuller, and other Pan Am officials in Frankfurt was to verify various documents mined from the trove of discovery materials. Because of Jim's incisive questioning, the Plaintiffs Committee developed proof that left little doubt that Pan Am's failures were deliberate and willful and that high company officials knew they could result in a disaster.

11

THE ALERT DEPOSITIONS

September—November 1989

Following the Pan Am witnesses, Lee deposed the Alert Management screeners, office staff, and supervisors. Based on public statements that Pan Am had issued, he expected some witnesses would say they had received the Helsinki warning. Koch's testimony and other sources made clear that this was not true, so Lee and his team prepared accordingly.

When FOX Television aired "The Report" on August 26, in the middle of the Pan Am deposition, Lee arranged to have the show taped in New York in a format that would play on a German VCR. Pat Robinson sent copies to Frankfurt, on Lufthansa and TWA, to ensure the legal team would have one to use in time, but both got stuck in transit.

Noah Kushlefsky asked hotel staff to set up a VCR and a large monitor on a TV wagon. He tracked down the tapes at the Lufthansa and TWA cargo depots, dealt with German customs bureaucracy—no small task—and brought them to Lee's suite. During a lunch break from the Pan Am witness depositions, the team gathered over sandwiches for a matinee viewing. Featured in living color was Andrea Schwab Caslis, the screener responsible for the Lockerbie flight, raising her hand and answering Steve Wilson's question if she received the Helsinki warning in the negative.

"I wonder what she'll say when she testifies," said Jim.

But Andrea was not the first Alert witness after the noon break. Oliver Koch had testified that Hans Christ was with him when he discovered the Helsinki warning the morning after Lockerbie. Pan Am had called Koch a liar and incompetent, disgruntled employee. Christ was the Chief Supervisor, and if any other personnel had given the Helsinki warning to Alert Management, he would have known about it. His testimony was crucial to corroborate Koch's. Lee did not know what he could do if Christ denied knowledge of what had happened.

When Christ arrived, he appeared nervous. Not much older than Koch, he had nicotine-stained fingers and looked like someone desperate for a cigarette. Much to everyone's surprise, he confirmed Koch's testimony. He was there when Koch found the Helsinki warning and had not heard or been told about it before then, nor had he seen it posted on office bulletin boards anywhere.

Steve Fearon, as surprised by Christ's admission as everyone else, shot an angry glance at Alert's German attorneys.

Lee felt a surge of relief. So much hinged on Koch's testimony, and Christ had verified it. For the first time in months, he allowed himself to relax for a moment.

After a break, the next Alert witness was Karen Winhold, one of the screeners at Pan Am's main counter, where most passengers had checked in for Flight 103. She was a brunette in her 20s with deer-in-the-headlight eyes and kept looking at the German attorneys as if pleading for help.

When Lee asked her if she had been notified about the Helsinki warning, she said pointedly, "I was told to pay special and particular attention to Finnish women!"

The translator shook her head as she conveyed the answer to Lee in English. Later, during another break, she told him, "That

The Alert Depositions

is unusual language for her. It's high German, which she doesn't speak. I would expect her to use a colloquial phrase like "look out for" or "check on."

The next witness was Ranzon Malik, a cabin checker who cleaned the airplanes during layovers and the only Alert Management employee willing to testify in English. He was dark-haired and olive-skinned and had been on the job for only three months at the time of Lockerbie. Like many working for Alert in Frankfurt, he was paid at a low hourly rate, close to the German minimum wage. Malik testified that he had not received the Helsinki warning. Given his work, he did not need to know about it.

Uwe Schröder, his partner on the cleaning crew, was a few years older. He wore an ill-fitting suit and crooked necktie for his deposition. Certainly, he had seen the Helsinki warning, he said. Wolfgang Schwab, his supervisor, had posted it on the bulletin board in the Alert office, where the duty roster was displayed.

Schröder recalled that it warned "to pay special and particular attention to Finnish women."

The translator shook her head again, gave Lee a meaningful glance, and added in a whisper, "He used the same phrase. No one from his background would say it that way."

Next came Detlef Giertz, a screener at the main counter. His narrow chin and darting eyes gave him a ferret-like appearance. He testified that Wolfgang Schwab, his supervisor, had told him about the Helsinki warning and that anything Wolfgang Schwab said he took seriously.

"What exactly did Wolfgang Schwab tell you?" Lee asked.

"To pay special and particular attention to Finnish women," he answered without hesitation.

Lee nodded. Then, he leaned back and scrutinized the witness. His understanding of German was good enough that he could recognize the pattern. Some screeners denied that they had received any warning. But, a few of the people on duty at the time of the Lockerbie flight insisted they knew all about it and used the same, exact, strange sounding phrase. They had been coached to repeat it either by Alert Management or the company's attorneys.

That made Andrea Schwab Caslis a critical witness. As the daughter of Wolfgang Schwab, the Alert supervisor on duty at the loading of Pan Am 103 in Frankfurt, she had higher standing in the company than the other screeners. Would she tell the truth as she had on FOX's "The Reporters" show?

Andrea wore a simple, dark-green dress and necklace with a small gold cross. She had blond hair, which she occasionally touched as if to ensure every strand was still in place. Her sober, unsmiling expression reflected the seriousness of the occasion, and she took some time getting settled in the witness chair.

After reminding her that she was under oath, Lee started to question Caslis. He employed the exact words Steve Wilson used when his FOX cameraman had secretly filmed her, "At any time on or prior to December 21, were you advised of the bomb threat delivered to the U.S. Embassy in Helsinki stating that a Pan Am flight from Frankfurt to the United States would be blown up?"

Caslis shifted in her seat and glanced down at the table. Then she said, "Yes, I was told to pay special and particular attention to Finnish women by Pan Am supervisor Vanderberg the morning of Lockerbie."

The members of the Plaintiff team traded glances. She had decided to lie!

A witness committing perjury is a grave matter, especially when the examiner is in a position to prove it. It is serious for the witness lying under oath and for the party under whose auspices the witness appears.

Lee proceeded cautiously. He took the still pictures of the training class from a folder in his briefcase, which showed Caslis with her hand raised. "Mrs. Caslis, I want to give you every opportunity to tell the truth," he said, laying them on the table before her. "Don't you remember a training class earlier this month attended by two gentlemen from New York? Don't you remember telling a man in a dark suit named Mr. Wilson that you had not received the warnings?"

Andrea Caslis glanced at the photos indifferently. "No, I didn't say that," she said. "That's my picture, and my hand is up, but I didn't say that."

"Are you aware that the visitors had a hidden video camera?"

"I didn't know it then, but I know it now," she replied. "My husband is in the United States and has seen the show. He called me and tried to play the audio over the telephone, so I could hear it."

In that case," Lee said, "when Steve Wilson visited your training class, didn't he ask the following questions and get the following answers?"

He picked up a sheet of paper from the table and read the exchange from the broadcast tape word for word:

> *Steve Wilson: Now, this is very important. Andrea, you say it was after the situation happened; what do you mean?*
>
> *Andrea Caslis: Well, after the Lockerbie accident.*
>
> *Wilson: After the Lockerbie. But there was no warning before the Lockerbie accident?*
>
> *Caslis: No warning before the Lockerbie.*
>
> *Wilson: Is that correct, Andrea? No warning about the radio device? No warning about people from Finland? Is that correct?*
>
> *Caslis: Yes!*

When Lee looked expectantly at Caslis, she did not meet his eyes but doubled down, "I did not say that!"

Lee signaled Noah, who went to the cart parked in the corner of the room with the VCR cued up. He rolled it to the head of the table so everyone could see the monitor.

Then Lee played the tape twice. The words he'd just read rang out loud and clear. After the second time, the silence in the deposition room was deafening. The lawyers for Pan Am and Alert were gaping in shock. James Shaughnessy stared straight ahead, the muscles in his clenched jaw working overtime.

Andrea Caslis kept touching her hair. But her voice had a nervous edge when she said, "That tape was edited. Parts have been cut out. That is not what I said."

Lee looked at her kindly. "Mrs. Caslis, I don't want to hurt you. I simply want the truth," he said. "I must tell you that four of us in this room, Jim Kreindler, Noah Kushlefsky, Lisa Meacham, and I, have all seen the original, unedited tape in which you said several times that you never got the warning." He paused to let his statement sink in. Then he continued, "I will ask you once again, 'Did you say that?'"

Shaking her head vehemently, Caslis insisted, "No."

Lee had the tape marked for identification. Then he turned to Steve Fearon and Jim Shaughnessy, whose eyes shot daggers at him. "I think the fair thing to the witness is to suspend the deposition, to return to New York, and to attempt to get the entire unedited tape."

By then, it was late afternoon, and both sides were eager to adjourn the session. Lee and his team went to a pub to celebrate and consumed entirely too much German beer, as he admitted to Ruth in a phone call later that night.

The following morning, the defense lawyers agreed to suspend Caslis' testimony until a later date. They also agreed to Lee's demand to defer the deposition of her father, Wolfgang Schwab. He seemed to be a key player in the little clique of Alert screeners who were on duty when Flight 103 loaded and insisted they received the Helsinki warning. Lee wanted him to know about the supporting evidence on the unedited tape before he took his testimony.

The next witness was Hans Franke, the duty officer at the time of Lockerbie. Smoothing out the lapel of his long-sleeve shirt, he said there had never been a Helsinki warning posted on the bulletin board, but there was an oral warning. On December 8 or 9, Ulrich Weber received a telephone call from Wolfgang Schwab during a supervisors' meeting. Weber handed him the phone, and Schwab told Franke about the Helsinki warning. He instructed him to go to the counter and tell the screeners, who were there at the time, which he did.

Lee asked, "Was Oliver Koch at that meeting?"

"Yes," Franke answered, "But I'm not sure if he heard the conversation or ever knew about it."

Franke was the last witness to claim he had received the Helsinki warning. The rest, both in Frankfurt and later in London, affirmed that they were not made aware of it. Lee felt satisfied that he had enough testimony to prove that no such warning had been issued.

But there was more to come. Beside Andrea Caslis, the witness Lee wanted to depose most urgently was Stella Schneider, Ulrich Weber's secretary and bookkeeper at the time of Lockerbie. Having been promoted to chief duty officer in charge of administration, a significant step up, Schneider was at the center of operations and knew what was going on. She was also a key witness in corroborating Oliver Koch since he had testified that she was present when Weber back-dated the stamp on the Helsinki warning.

But the defense kept making excuses why Stella Schneider could not come. Despite repeated requests, she still hadn't made an appearance as the deposition period neared an end. Even when Lee became adamant, Shaughnessy, Fearon, and the German lawyers continued to drag their feet. Finally, in exasperation, Lee called the Federal District Court in Brooklyn. When Judge Platt directed the defense attorneys to produce Ms. Schneider without further delay as the next witness, they caved.

As Lee and his team waited for her to appear, one of the local media people reported that Hans Christ had just received notice from Alert Management that he was fired! The man who had testified two days before and told the truth about the Koch discovery of the Helsinki warning was unceremoniously dismissed. Lee took it as a message to other witnesses of what would happen if they didn't play ball. He hadn't expected such strong-arm tactics so soon, and it made him angry.

Stella Schneider arrived for the deposition, preceded by a cloud of perfume. She was an attractive woman in her early forties, heavily made up and with her blonde hair elaborately coiffed. She had insisted that her new boss, Kurt Warschauer, be present, apparently determined to show him how much of a team player she was.

Yet, it soon became evident that she would confirm Oliver Koch's testimony. Yes, she was present when Weber back-dated the Helsinki warnings. There were several copies of the altered document, and Weber had her initial every single one. When Lee showed her one of the copies, she identified her initial, S, near the bottom.

While Schneider did not agree right away that she was present in the office on December 22 when Koch first discovered the Helsinki warning, she did so later when Jim asked her a follow-up question.

Meanwhile, her testimony highlighted the dichotomy concerning the Helsinki warning. Schneider confirmed that the document languished on Weber's desk until after Lockerbie and then was falsified

The Alert Depositions

to fool the FAA. But she also corroborated the telephone call on December 9 from Wolfgang Schwab to Hans Franke and the oral instruction to inform the screeners on duty.

So far, Lee was satisfied with the outcome but could not figure out why the Pan Am and Alert lawyers had been so reluctant to produce Stella Schneider as a witness. That emerged in the examination of the working conditions under Ulrich Weber.

Lee knew from Koch that the 29-year-old Weber was a promiscuous bisexual who had given promotions based on personal favors and relationships rather than merit or professional qualifications. Stella Schneider confirmed it all. More damning, she insisted that it was common knowledge.

According to her testimony, there were frequent conversations among the Alert employees and managers about Weber and his "extra-curricular" activities. Yes, there was a celebration when Alert opened its Munich office. Yes, Weber took four screeners to Salambo, the well-known brothel there, for a long weekend, although Schneider could not say if he charged the bill to Alert. Yes, there was an occasion when an airplane cleaner, after he and Weber spent a weekend away together, returned to work on Monday in the upgraded position of a screener. And, yes, a secretary received a promotion to supervisor of supplies, and from that to acting chief station officer for Frankfurt, without any training or experience in security whatsoever.

It was truly extraordinary testimony to wrap up the depositions. Even one of the younger German defense lawyers was astonished, commenting to Lee during the noon break, "Well, that was an interesting morning!"

Lee could not help by chuckle. No wonder the defense attorneys had dragged their heels in delivering Stella Schneider as a witness. All the salacious information she provided was significant for the case because Pan Am had the duty of supervision. Pan Am was damned if it knew about Weber's shenanigans and equally damned if it didn't.

* * *

Two months later, in early November, Lee and his team returned to Frankfurt for the second round of depositions. They brought along the unedited tapes of "The Reporters" show, but they didn't need to play them. By then, Andrea Caslis and her father, Wolfgang Schwab, had a change of heart. Both testified that they did not receive the Helsinki or Toshiba warnings until after the Lockerbie disaster. No doubt, a consultation with their attorneys about the seriousness of lying under oath led to their miraculous memory recovery.

While their testimony tied up one loose end, the attorneys for the Plaintiffs Committee pursued others as well. They had found three former employees of Alert Management who had been discharged. No longer under the threat of being fired, they were extremely forthcoming and agreed to be videotaped. The lawyers for Pan Am objected at the last minute to deposing "non-party" witnesses in Germany, claiming it was against German law and invalidated any testimony given, but Lee insisted on doing it anyway. Judge Platt later ruled that the depositions were admissible evidence.

Beate Franzki, the Frankfurt station manager at the time of the Lockerbie disaster, was in her early 40s and elegantly dressed. She corroborated what Lee and his investigators had discovered in the meantime: Ulrich Weber, the director of security for Alert Management, Germany, had a criminal record. He had been convicted of passing bad checks in the United States and had received a dishonorable discharge from the U.S. Army.

Sabine Fuchs, a screener, spoke English well and did not require a translator. A petite brunette, Weber hired her when they had met at a nightclub. She was working as a beautician at the time. He assigned her to the main counter to screen passengers for Pan Am 103 and identify "selectees" that required special security attention.

Lee asked her, "Did you identify any selectees?"

She answered, "Mr. Kreindler, I couldn't. I didn't know what a selectee was."

Simone Keller, another screener, was a pretty 18-year-old with curly blonde hair and no security experience either. Undeterred by Lockerbie, Weber hired her a few days after the disaster. After five days on the job, he promoted her to supervisor.

"What happened at the job interview where Mr. Weber hired you?" Lee asked.

She answered, "Herr Weber, he looked me in the eyes, and he said, 'I can tell from your eyes you are qualified.'"

"Why did he promote you only five days later?"

Without embarrassment, Keller said, "I slept with him over that weekend."

Another important finding that Lee coaxed from the witnesses was that Pan Am's Frankfurt station management always received advance notice of FAA inspections. On several occasions in 1988, Herbert Leuniger ordered adding personnel to create the appearance of adequate security staff for the visiting inspectors, which otherwise did not exist.

Once, while the inspectors were en route, Weber reported to Leuniger that Alert did not have enough guards and screeners to satisfy FAA requirements. Leuniger told him to place the guards at the front of the aircraft where the FAA inspectors would come down the air stairs upon arrival. When they had passed through the door into the airport, the guards were to run around to the back of the airplane and line up for duty at the rear door when the inspectors left. The Marx Brothers could not have concocted a better routine to delude the visitors.

A year after the Frankfurt depositions, Lee's investigators tracked down Ulrich Weber to Rockford, Illinois. He was eager to talk, as if he had nothing to lose, and confirmed the story in a video deposition.

Perhaps the most crucial witness Lee deposed on the second trip was Alert's X-ray operator, Kurt Maier. Since Pan Am no longer performed the required passenger/bag matching, the company had only one arguable defense against a bomb in an unaccompanied interline suitcase—his testifying that he saw no radio cassettes in any of the suitcases he X-rayed.

Maier was a nondescript man in his mid-sixties. He had thin lips, and graying hair combed over his balding forehead. His hands trembled as he sat down, so much so that James Shaughnessy patted his arm to give him confidence.

At the time of Lockerbie, Maier had been an Alert Management employee for only seven weeks and an X-ray operator for less than a month. He had received no formal training and had not seen the standard training videos. He worked alone in a trailer near the cargo doors to the airport building.

Lee asked him, "Were you ever given the warning that bombs were found in Toshiba radio cassette recorders?"

He answered, "No."

"Were you ever instructed to stop a bag containing a radio or radio cassette?

"No."

"What were you told?"

"To look for electronic devices that were suspicious.'"

"How many bags did you X-ray?"

"Thirteen."

"Did you find any such devices?"

"No."

The Alert Depositions

Lee felt that his testimony was vague enough to neutralize any contention that there had been serious screening of Flight 103's baggage.

Overall, the first two trips to Frankfurt were a success. Lee and his team amassed damning evidence of Pan Am's security lapses. The depositions confirmed Koch's testimony. As an added bonus, the evidence revealed that those at the higher levels of corporate management in New York had little regard for security. They thought it was a waste of time and money. Their contemptuous attitude trickled down to those in charge of the Frankfurt station, resulting in everyone there treating security as a joke.

In his clients' newsletter of September 12, Lee wrote:

> *You may not have to wait until the trial to see what these witnesses look like. Just as Oliver Koch was interviewed by FOX Television and the BBC following his deposition, Franzki, Fuchs, and Keller were filmed following theirs. ABC is doing a documentary on Lockerbie, and I believe others are also. Between them, the world is getting a pretty good look at what was going on at Pan Am-Alert Frankfurt!*
>
> *We have accumulated incredible proof of gross misconduct in Frankfurt. If we were dealing with a normal insurance company, I would expect to get a call about now inquiring if we wanted to settle our cases. But Mr. Alpert is so stubborn and so arrogant that I won't believe it until I see it.*

Little did Lee know that Robert Alpert, senior vice president and chief of claims at USAU, would soon resign. His stated reasons were his frustration with the company's handling of the Lockerbie case and because of its refusal to make fair settlement offers to the Lockerbie families.

Meanwhile, Lee turned his attention to another crucial aspect of the case. He knew that Pan Am and its defense attorneys counted on

THE FIGHT FOR JUSTICE

him and the Plaintiffs Committee not being able to prove when and how the bomb that destroyed Flight 103 made it onto the airplane. Without that evidence, the defense could claim that all the security lapses were irrelevant.

12

DISINFORMATION CAMPAIGN

November—December 1989

Lee knew he had Pan Am and Alert Management on the ropes regarding airline security at Frankfurt and London airports. But he also knew that he was dealing with large companies determined to limit their exposure and expected them to mount a counter-offensive. He called it the "Star Wars" phenomenon, after the popular sci-fi movie saga that had premiered in 1977, and often quipped, "What follows 'A New Hope' is that 'The Empire Strikes Back.'"

While Lee and his team were on their second round of depositions in Frankfurt at the beginning of November, a front-page article appeared in the well-known London daily *The Independent*. "Dramatic news," it trumpeted under an enormous banner headline, "CIA CAUSED LOCKERBIE":

> *Lawyers for Pan Am and its security firm are taking action to prove that the Israeli secret service, Mossad, warned the U.S. authorities of a terrorist attack on Pan Am Flight 103 a full 24 hours before the plane exploded over Scotland, and that West Germany's BKA criminal police warned U.S. officials of "suspicious activities" in the baggage area 90 minutes before the plane took off from Frankfurt.*
>
> *The subpoenas issued against the United States government's most secret agencies by lawyers for Pan Am and its security*

> *subsidiary, Alert Management Systems, Inc., represent an effort to broaden the argument over responsibility for the Lockerbie air crash and to explore a world of Middle Eastern espionage and mutual terror that has so far eluded the disaster inquiry.*

By November 3, the *New York Times*, *USA Today*, the *Guardian*, the *International Herald Tribune*, and other newspapers worldwide published similar articles, claiming the involvement of various intelligence agencies in the Lockerbie disaster.

The telephone in Lee's Frankfurt hotel room rang in the middle of the night, waking him from a deep sleep. It was Elizabeth Dix, one of the Lockerbie clients. The death of her husband on Flight 103 had left her and their young son, Dermot, destitute and scrambling to make ends meet.

"Is it true, Lee, that the CIA is involved? Did the CIA have something to do with killing my husband?" she burst out hysterically. "If it is, I want you to help me renounce my U.S. citizenship!"

Lee did his best to calm and reassure her, promising to look into the rumor and take care of it.

The calls kept coming into the morning and throughout the next day. Reporters and clients gushed with additional rumors and bombarded him with questions.

But that was only the beginning.

The following morning, James Traficant Jr, a Congressman from Ohio, held a televised a press conference on the U. S. Capitol steps. Glaring at the cameras, he looked like an angry pit bull. With his signature nest of hair piled high on top of his head, flashing eyes, and furrowed eyebrows, he projected outrage personified.

Waiving five pages from a supposedly secret document, the Interfor Report, he fulminated, "This says that the CIA was responsible for the Lockerbie bombing because it permitted the switching of a suitcase in Frankfurt during a protected drug delivery operation.

Disinformation Campaign

I believe the CIA used very weird means to a tragic end. I'm charging the CIA for turning their backs on heroin shipments from Frankfurt.... I'm determined to get to the bottom of this!"

The next day, on November 4, *The Independent* carried an article entitled "CIA Failed to Act on Lockerbie Tip-off" that fleshed out the details of the accusations. The story became the lead article in virtually every newspaper and television newscast worldwide.

Lee suspected that the USAU and John Brennan were behind leaking the report. The Plaintiffs Committee had demanded all documents and information supporting the notices and subpoenas when they first filed for discovery. At that time, the lawyers for the defendants did not mention the report. Either they had lied then, or this dramatic "new" information was a fiction concocted to muddy the waters.

In response, Lee held a press conference and conducted numerous interviews with newspaper reporters and all the major American and international TV networks. He didn't mince words. "The CIA story is nonsense," he said. "I am sure the insurer of Pan Am has cooked it up to deflect attention from what is coming out of our depositions here in Frankfurt."

Lee's comments were carried all over the world, too.

That evening, after conducting depositions and interviews, reassuring clients that the Interfor Report was bogus, and fielding what felt like hundreds of news media calls, Lee crawled into his hotel bed, exhausted. Suddenly, his whole body shivered as he experienced a moment of doubt. Congressman Traficant was telling everyone that the CIA was involved in Lockerbie and that he was asking for a congressional investigation. Lee knew that four CIA officials had been aboard Flight 103, although it was doubtful that any terrorist would have been aware of that. Could it be that Traficant was right and he was wrong?

He shook off the notion but could not fall back to sleep. So, he called home to Chappaqua. Ruth had just finished dinner, and they talked about all that had happened. She agreed that all the hoopla was lies and fabrications. Hearing her reassuring voice was like a soothing balm. After they hung up, he finally drifted off to fitful sleep.

By the time he returned to New York, Lee had seen the five pages of the Interfor Report himself and reviewed Pan Am's efforts to subpoena high-level U.S. government witnesses. The report was written by an Israeli agent using the pseudonym "Avner," but it soon became known that his name was Yuval Aviv and that USAU had hired him. Pan Am officials claimed its lawyers in the case did, but Lee's investigators verified that the insurance company's officials were responsible.

In his report, Aviv charged that a switch was performed at the Frankfurt Airport by a Pan Am baggage handler. He exchanged the Samsonite suitcase containing the bomb for the bag of a passenger, whose name was Khalid Jafaar. This supposedly occurred during a "CIA-controlled delivery" drug operation. The baggage handler's supervisor was also part of the operation. Aviv recommended that they both undergo polygraph tests.

Pan Am's attorneys used the accusations as grounds to subpoena various CIA and other U.S. government officials for depositions.

A few days later, Lee received a call from John Merritt, the chief investigative reporter for the *Observer* in London. He had met him briefly at a press conference after the initial news of the Interfor Report broke. As Lee was leaving, Merritt approached him, introduced himself, and asked him to comment on the report. When Lee told him he had not read it yet, Merritt said, "I'll get back to you."

Even though they'd chatted for less than 30 seconds, Merritt, who had fiery red hair, probing blue eyes, and an ingratiating smile, had impressed Lee. He was glad to talk with the reporter again. Perhaps the journalist had dug up information that would be valuable for the case.

"Have you had a chance to look at the report?" Merritt asked.

Lee answered, "I have only seen the five pages released by Congressman Traficant."

"I'll send it to you," Merritt promised. "Then, perhaps you will comment."

Within half an hour, Lee had faxed copies of the 24-page Interfor Report in hand and studied them with great interest. As far as he could tell, they were full of spurious claims, dressed up with names, dates, and places to make them appear authentic and factual.

In their follow-up phone conversation, Lee told Merritt what he knew was untrue, avoiding any information protected by the district court's confidentiality order. Merritt, in turn, explained how fabricated and false the rest was. He had checked the sources and was sure the entire account was phony.

On November 16, in a blistering front-page story in the *Observer*, John Merritt exposed the Interfor Report as a big lie. He called it "rubbish" and characterized as a sham the claim that the CIA let a bomb on Flight 103. He had traveled to the United States and met with Aviv and Traficant. The congressman had thrown him out of his office. Merritt revealed Aviv as a grifter and Traficant as a willing dupe. It was a charitable label for a corrupt politician. A decade later, he was indicted in federal court for making personal use of campaign funds. Convicted of 10 felony counts, including bribery, racketeering, and tax evasion, he served seven years in a federal prison.

When the Plaintiffs Committee met at the Kreindler & Kreindler office to strategize about what to do regarding Pan Am's claims, everyone around the conference looked grim-faced and tense. They knew the situation was dire. Suppose Pan Am managed to depose CIA and State Department officials. Their testifying would open up a whole other line of explanation for why the disaster happened, seriously crippling the willful misconduct case.

Looking around at the glum faces, Lee realized he had to do something to lighten the mood. He took the 24 fax pages from Merritt, tossed them on the conference table, and said, "Well, the good news is that it's all bullshit."

Everyone burst into laughter and relaxed.

"So, what do we have to deal with?" Lee asked, inviting them to brainstorm.

"I don't think they'll get government officials to testify," Mitch Baumeister offered.

"But Judge Platt will be reluctant to deny discovery to Pan Am if it looks like he is doing it without cause," Frank Granito Jr said.

"Pan Am is doing everything they can to slow the case down and prevent it from going forward," his son, Frankie, chimed in.

Twirling his mustache absentmindedly, Jim Kreindler asked, "So, what do we do?"

Lee stared at the pages on the table and said, "If Judge Platt needs a reason to reject the defense claim, then we'll have to give him one. The best way to demonstrate that there is nothing to these rash allegations is to take the testimony of Aviv himself."

On December 15, the plaintiffs gave notice for Aviv to be deposed. That led to considerable legal wrangling. The defense attorneys claimed that Aviv was a "non-testifying expert" retained by the defendants and that he was not subject to being deposed. They also said that his report was privileged. Lee and the plaintiffs' team answered that publicly leaking his report, either by the defendants or Aviv himself, waived any objection to his being forced to testify.

To resolve the issue, Judge Platt ordered an evidentiary hearing. Merritt's article, which Lee brought to his attention, made enough of an impact that he granted a subpoena for Aviv and set a date for the hearing before Federal Magistrate Allyne Ross in early February of the following year.

Disinformation Campaign

Lee used the time to initiate a background investigation of Aviv in Israel. That yielded some interesting facts, notably that he had never been a Mossad agent, let alone an officer in the Israeli Army. It was more evidence that Aviv was a pathological liar.

In the meantime, Steve Pounian and Mitch Baumeister returned to Germany for another round of depositions. The most important witness was Kiling Tuzcu, the handler Aviv claimed had switched the suitcases. Tuzcu, one of many Turkish employees of Pan Am at the Frankfurt airport, had the job of picking up the luggage as it arrived in the trays of the automated conveyor system. He would separate out suitcases that came from other airlines. Fifteen minutes before a flight's departure, he drove them for scanning to the Alert X-ray machine operated by Kurt Maier. Then, he took them to the aircraft for loading. In the late afternoon of December 21, 1988, he had been stationed at Gate B 44 to receive the interline bags for Flight 103.

But the first witness was Tuzcu's supervisor, Roland O'Neil, whose title was baggage master. When Steve questioned him, O'Neil said everything regarding the loading of Flight 103 proceeded according to standard, routine procedure.

The depositions over the following days brought no unexpected revelations.

Kiling Tuzcu was the last witness on that trip. After that, Steve and Mitch would head to London to examine the Heathrow baggage handlers. But when the lawyers assembled in the Sheraton Hotel conference room for the deposition, James Shaughnessy was not present, although he had attended all sessions until then. His stand-in, Nancy Cohen, another lawyer for Pan Am, announced that the witness was not available. She was unsure where he was, but he would not be there until the next day.

The following morning, Tuzcu appeared with Shaughnessy by his side. He was in his mid-20s and had a shaven head and goatee. He seemed nervous and frightened. His eyes kept darting to the Pan Am lawyer.

At the start of the deposition, Steve asked routine questions: What is your job? Were you on duty on December 21, 1988? What were you doing that day?

Suddenly, the conference room door burst open. Three men wearing dark blue jackets, like FBI agents during a raid, barged in. One of them shouted in German. "I am Inspector Fuhl of the Federal Criminal Police. Stop this deposition! You are all violating German law! Charges of kidnapping will be filed against you. This man, Tuzcu, was taken out of this country and polygraphed, which is against the law in Germany. Stop this deposition immediately!"

The translator for the plaintiffs did her best to keep up with the barrage of accusations. Steve and Mitch were baffled. Tuzcu ducked low, head between his shoulders as if he wanted to hide under the conference table.

It took several days to get things sorted, including an emergency conference call with Judge Platt in the United States. A series of conversations and follow-up depositions revealed that Tuzcu, O'Neil, and a third Pan Am employee were brought to the deposition conference room in the Sheraton Frankfurt Hotel three days earlier. There, they faced James Shaughnessy, a German lawyer for Pan Am, and a man named Keefe, whom Yuval Aviv had employed to administer polygraph tests. Shaughnessy and the German attorney asked the three employees to consent to the examinations. Afraid of losing their jobs, they agreed.

Following the polygraphs, Keefe announced that O'Neil and Tuzcu lied when asked if there was a bag switch. When they both denied it, Shaughnessy ushered them from the room and put them on an airplane to London. There, with Aviv present, he attempted to have Scotland Yard detectives examine them further. That was the reason Tuzcu

Disinformation Campaign

had been a day late for his deposition with Steve Pounian. Aviv asked Shaughnessy to prepare and sign a statement of what the investigation uncovered, which he did.

But Scotland Yard had informed the Federal Criminal Police in Germany, which did not take kindly to the actions of Pan Am's lawyers. That led to the BKA inspectors storming into the conference room threatening arrests. Ultimately, they calmed down and did not make good on their threat to bring kidnapping charges against the Pan Am attorneys and Aviv.

It turned out that Aviv had instigated the whole charade, making Shaughnessy an unwitting accomplice. The Pan Am lawyer apparently thought he was charging to the airline's rescue on a white horse by exposing two liars. Instead, he was caught with egg on his face.

When Steve and Mitch finally deposed Kiling Tuzcu, he vehemently denied switching interline bags on Flight 103.

* * *

While these defense shenanigans were damning enough, Lee wanted to make sure he could prove that the entire Interfor Report was a pack of lies. Although he could depose Aviv under oath, he was sure the Israeli con man would lie through his teeth. How to cut through his web of falsehoods and fabrications?

Lee decided he needed John Merritt to testify, but when he called London, the reporter was on assignment in Tangier, Morocco. By then, it was Friday, and the evidentiary hearing before Magistrate Ross would begin in New York the following Monday. Lee finally got hold of Merritt, who agreed to act as a witness, although he first had to get permission from his newspaper. It was unheard of for a reporter to testify on the subject matter of one of his stories, but he would do it if it would help the Lockerbie victims. He felt it was his duty. The following day, he called to say his editor and publisher had agreed.

The next challenge was getting him from Tangier to London to pick up his files and then to New York to meet with Lee before he took the stand in court. Pat Robinson worked her magic. She found a flight that got Merritt to London Saturday night in time to gather his documents on Aviv and then catch the Sunday morning Concorde to New York, a four-hour trip. Lee had him picked up at JFK Airport and driven to his house in Chappaqua.

After Merritt arrived, they had a light lunch, prepared by Ruth, and spent the rest of the day working on his testimony. Then Merritt brought out notebooks, in which he had recorded his observations from the interviews with Yuval Aviv, James Traficant, and others. He impressed Lee again with his keen mind.

On Monday morning, both sides assembled at the Brooklyn Federal Courthouse for the evidentiary hearing, and Lee got his first look at Yuval Aviv. The Israeli was in his early forties and had close-cropped, military-style black hair. He chatted with the Pan Am lawyers standing at their table as if he didn't have a care in the world. Occasionally, he looked at Lee with an arrogant smirk on his face.

When Magistrate Allyn Ross arrived, she was all business. She gaveled the hearing to order and asked Lee to proceed and make his case.

Lee called Aviv as his first witness. Aviv stood up from behind the defense table and strutted across the courtroom like a peacock. After taking his seat, he swore to tell the truth and nothing but the truth and looked at Lee expectantly, almost taunting him.

Lee approached and led him through a series of general questions.

"Are you a former agent of Mossad?"

"Yes."

"What rank did you attain in the Israeli Military?"

"Colonel."

"How did you come by the information contained in the report?"

"Through my many Mossad contacts."

Disinformation Campaign

Happy to brag about his achievements, Aviv continued to answer, leaning comfortably back in the witness chair.

But then Lee asked him, "Did you leak the Interfor Report to Congressman Traficant?"

Aviv's eyelids fluttered, and he glanced toward the defense table. Then he said, "I plead the Fifth Amendment."

"Did you leak the report to any media organizations?"

"I take the Fifth."

And so it went, Aviv not realizing that taking the Fifth in this kind of hearing was tantamount to admitting guilt.

After he finished with Aviv, Lee called John Merritt to the stand. The reporter was a marvelous witness, an animated storyteller, and with a good sense of humor. Magistrate Ross fell in love with him, British accent, fiery red hair, and all.

At some point, John recounted how he had taken along his assistant, Simon de Bruxelles, to interview Aviv. Contrary to John's instructions, Simon had a small tape recorder in his pocket, which he triggered accidentally. "Suddenly, Simon's right trouser pocket started to talk!" John said with pretend bafflement and the courtroom exploded with laughter.

But John also had the goods to expose Aviv's lies. Lee let him reveal the truth about Aviv's Mossad and military services. By the time John finished his testimony, Aviv was a dead duck. John had blasted him out of the water.

In her 27-page opinion, Magistrate Ross found that Aviv had lied repeatedly during his testimony and that he, and possibly Pan Am's officials, insurers, and lawyers, had leaked the Interfor Report to Congressman Traficant and the media. John Merritt's revelations, taken together with Magistrate Ross' opinion, convinced Judge Platt that the allegations concerning CIA and other governmental agencies' involvement in Lockerbie were phony. He told Pan Am's

THE FIGHT FOR JUSTICE

lawyers that unless the defendants could make a prima facie (evidential) showing of some substance to Aviv's analysis, there was no reason to justify going forward with testimony along this line of inquiry.

When they did not, he struck down the defendants' subpoenas and deposition notices. The CIA and other government agencies and departments would not have to testify.

Pan Am's and USAU's delaying tactic and attempt to muddy the waters had failed. As for Yuval Aviv, Pan Am eventually fired him.

13

SECOND ATTEMPT TO SETTLE

February—August, 1990

Taking depositions continued for months in Frankfurt, London, Dumfries, Washington, New York, and other places. The cost of discovery worldwide—for travel, venues, translators, and stenographers to prepare transcripts—was enormous. Lee began to worry about the financial impact on his law firm. Their accountant had informed him privately that they were spending two-thirds of the firm's resources on the Lockerbie case.

Fortunately, the concerted efforts brought results. In New York, questioning Pan Am officials at the company headquarters verified much of the documentary evidence Lee's dogged researchers had unearthed in the discovery files.

In London, depositions of ground personnel and Pan Am station officials revealed that security measures at Heathrow Airport were as lackadaisical as at Frankfurt. Lee and his team proved that, despite the Helsinki and Toshiba warnings, the bags from Frankfurt were loaded into an aluminum container and placed aboard the 747 aircraft with no additional security measures taken. The Ground Security Coordinator was not there on December 21. The passenger service agent who acted as GSC in his stead had zero security training and was unaware of the ACSSP requirements.

With evidence of Pan Am's security failures continuing to mount—in documents, depositions, and widespread news coverage—Lee thought it was time to propose settling the case again. So, in March 1990, he called John Brennan and suggested they talk. Brennan agreed.

Lee sent him a detailed 11-page letter in preparation for the meeting. He reviewed the facts of the case as established in discovery and depositions, discussed the phony claims of Yuval Aviv and the Interfor Report, and mentioned the defendants' illegally administering polygraphs to the Frankfurt baggage handlers Tuzcu and O'Neil.

This time, Brennan was more polite. The USAU president didn't barricade himself behind his desk but invited Lee to join him in the lounge area of his spacious office. Lee sat down on the tan leather sofa. Brennan took the power position in the armchair at the head of the low table.

"Would you like a cup of coffee?" he asked graciously.

"Yes," Lee accepted. "Black, please."

After the secretary brought in the china cups on a silver tray, with cookies and muffins for refreshments, Lee and Brennan got down to brass tacks and discussed various aspects of the case. By then, the bellicose chairman of USAU had changed his tune. He no longer claimed airlines had no defense against terrorist attacks. He conceded that the proof Lee and his team had assembled was damning.

"But you can't show that it had anything to do with Lockerbie," he insisted. "None of it proves how the bomb got aboard."

Lee took a sip of coffee. "That remains to be seen."

Brennan leaned toward him with eyes narrowed. "Even if you can get a jury to find willful misconduct, you'll never sustain it on appeal."

Lee realized that Brennan was not ready to settle. The bullheadedness surprised him. If the defendants lost the case, the insurance company would have to pay the victims' families hefty damage compensation. By the normal rules of the game, USAU could negotiate a much better deal now.

The day after the meeting, Brennan called Lee. The testimony of Kurt Maier, Alert's X-ray operator in Frankfurt, had piqued his interest, and he suggested bringing Maier to New York for a second deposition. "If his testimony is clarified, there might be a greater chance of settling the case," he promised.

Lee continued to be skeptical of Brennan's motives. The man seemed happy to string the plaintiffs along while ferreting out what evidence they had and how it might affect their strategy in a trial. Because Maier would be a defense witness, Brennan probably figured he could improve on his earlier testimony.

Still, Lee acquiesced, even though Maier had seemed tentative and unreliable. But he stipulated to videotaping the testimony, and Brennan agreed.

Maier arrived two weeks later, and the deposition occurred in a large conference room at the insurance company's offices. Since this was the defendants' proceeding, their attorneys went first.

Lee thought Maier seemed more confident, especially when they got to the crux of the case, the Toshiba radio bomb. To James Shaughnessy's question, "How many bags for Flight 103 did you X-ray?" Maier answered as before, "Thirteen."

"What did you discover?"

"There were no radio cassette recorders in any of the thirteen bags."

His response was cut and dried, and Shaughnessy nodded, pleased. He'd gotten the answer he wanted.

But when Lee's turn came to cross-examine, the X-ray operator was less certain. Lee asked Maier about the notes he made when he inspected the bags. "Your summary shows nothing about radio cassette recorders," Lee said. "Can you be certain there weren't any in those thirteen bags?"

"I don't remember if there were any," Maier hedged.

"What would have happened if you had seen any?"

"That would depend."

"On what?"

"If they looked suspicious."

Lee paused to let that statement sink in. Then he asked, "Are you saying you sometimes let radio cassette recorders go through unchecked?"

"Yes."

Later, in discussing the deposition with Brennan, Lee pointed out that Maier reversed himself. His testimony left open the possibility that a radio cassette recorder with a bomb inside could have slipped past.

Still, Brennan refused to discuss any settlement. "I don't agree with your interpretation," he said obstinately.

So, Lee and his team redoubled their efforts to track down evidence of who was responsible for getting the bomb on Flight 103.

* * *

On May 15, 1990, the Commission on Aviation Security and Terrorism, appointed by President George H. W. Bush after persistent and effective lobbying by the victims' families, issued its report. It described the lapses in security by Pan Am and the FAA and denounced the lack of "national will" to fight terrorism. The report made over 60 recommendations that became the basis for the Aviation Security Improvement Act of 1990, passed by Congress later that year.

While the findings supported many of the Plaintiffs Committee's conclusions, they did not put additional pressure on the defendants to settle. So long as no evidence existed of where and how the bomb

Second Attempt to Settle

made it onto Flight 103, Pan Am and the USAU were willing to bide their time.

Lee would have liked to know what the criminal inquiry in Scotland had discovered. Unfortunately, a tight fence continued to surround the investigation, and the Plaintiffs Committee was not permitted to get near the evidence.

However, in June, Peter Fraser, the Scottish Lord Advocate in charge, announced that a Fateful Accidents Act Inquiry (FAAI) would convene in Dumfries. It would start on October 1, 1990, but its duration was uncertain. Fraser estimated four to five months, with a Christmas and New Year's break. Attendees would include the Scottish, American, and German governments and attorneys for the American and Scottish victims' families.

According to Scottish law, the FAAI had to happen in the district where the deaths had occurred. But there was no building in Lockerbie large enough to accommodate the expected attendees. So, the authorities located a public mental hospital in Dumfries, about 12 miles from Lockerbie. It had a large gymnasium, which the Scottish government converted into an auditorium at a cost of more than $200,000. Security police would patrol everywhere, and only people they cleared would be allowed in.

Although it was a long wait until October 1, Lee felt that the FAAI offered the best opportunity to discover how the bomb got aboard Flight 103. The criminal investigation had pursued witnesses and avenues of inquiry unavailable to the plaintiffs' attorneys and might reveal significant information they did not have. As representatives of the largest group of victims' families, Lee and his team would have a prominent role.

Lee planned for Michael Hughes to be in attendance throughout the inquiry to maintain continuity. Members of the plaintiffs' team would participate on a rotating basis and question important witnesses.

Expenses had become matter of great concern. Michael's four-month fee, travel costs, and accommodations for the American attorneys would become a heavy financial burden.

The Scottish Lockerbie Disaster Group, which handled about 50 passenger cases, applied for a million-dollar grant from the U.K. government. The funding would pay for the attendance of all their solicitors at the FAAI, as well as their junior and senior advocates.

The Plaintiffs Committee decided to ask for British government assistance, too. Its attorneys represented 22 of the U.K. passengers' families, more than a third, and had done virtually all the work in putting the civil litigation together. They knew the facts better and were familiar with many witnesses who would be called to testify.

Michael worked tirelessly to get at least half of the Lockerbie Disaster Group's funding. He made numerous telephone calls and traveled to London several trips. But the Scottish group and its solicitors in England had too much political clout and got all the money. The Plaintiffs Committee would have to cover all the costs for participating on its own.

Lee and the other attorneys decided to appeal to the plaintiff's families for help. They did not take that step lightly but felt they had no other option. Many of the families were financially strapped. But some had the wherewithal because of their corporate jobs or businesses, and they agreed to help pay for attendance at the inquiry. Lee was once again impressed by how committed the families were to seeking justice and the truth about what happened, and it made him more determined to see things through to the end.

In August, about two months before the FAAI started, Lord Advocate Fraser held an orientation and coordination meeting in Edinburgh. He invited all parties to become familiar with the rules under which the inquiry would be conducted. Lee attended on behalf of the Plaintiffs Committee.

Second Attempt to Settle

Michael Hughes suggested that the trip should accomplish more than familiarizing Lee with FAAI procedures. He urged him to visit Lockerbie, tour the auditorium in Dumfries where the authorities would hold the inquiry, and meet with the important officials and participants in the investigation. Michael arranged everything to ensure Lee's trip went smoothly. He even familiarized himself with the side streets and traffic shortcuts in Dumfries so there would be no time wasted getting around.

When Lee arrived in Glasgow the following week, Michael met him at the airport and drove him to stay at One Devonshire Gardens, Glasgow's newest and best hotel. The following morning, he and Lee enjoyed a Scottish breakfast together, with tattie scones made from potatoes and butter, black pudding, baked beans, fried eggs, and bacon. Then, they set out in Michael's Ford Escort for a full day of meetings.

They drove to Lockerbie, and Michael showed Lee the disaster's impact on the town, especially the Sherwood Crescent neighborhood. Workers had removed all the rubble from the burned houses and filled in the long crater where a section the airplane's fuselage had plowed into the ground, but the area still looked like a ragged, unhealed scar.

From there, they went on to Dumfries to meet John Dunn, Procurator Fiscal, the equivalent of an American district attorney, who was prosecuting the Lockerbie crimes. At the hospital gym where the inquiry would take place, Michael pointed to the location of the Plaintiffs Committee's table, where Lee and his team would sit. It was the best spot in the auditorium for attorneys representing victims' families.

What surprised Lee most was seeing the hospital patients outside walking around the grounds, some alone, some accompanied by nurses. What a strange place to hold the inquiry.

In Airdrie, they met with Hugh Findlay, the clerk of the sheriff principal in charge. Findley would play a significant administrative role in the hearings. His reputation as a punctilious attorney preceded him. He had joined the Civil Service in 1952, the same year Lee joined his father's law firm in New York. After working at the Admiralty for four years, Findlay became a sheriff clerk at Dumbarton, Glasgow, Stornoway, Airdrie, and Lanark. He was an important figure in the Scottish Rules Council and, at some point, visited every court in Scotland as a staff inspector. Lee took an immediate liking to him.

"We will do everything we can to help with your inquiries," he assured Findlay.

"We appreciate anything you can do," the sheriff principal's clerk said warmly.

Back in Glasgow, Lee called Ruth at their home in Chappaqua and told her about his day. "Next time, you must come with me. It's very beautiful here, and everyone is very friendly. They're treating me like I'm the King of England," he said elated, unaware of the mixed feelings many Scots had toward the British monarchy.

The following day, Lee and Michael took the train to Edinburgh for the Lord Advocate's meeting. It was a misty morning. Catching glimpses of several lochs—lakes—and lush green meadows and hills dotted with sheep and crisscrossed by stone walls, Lee asked, "How is the weather this time of year?"

Michael grinned and answered with a favorite Scottish saying, "If you can see the mountains on the other side of the loch, it's going to rain. If you can't see them, it's raining."

That warning did not dampen Lee's desire to bring Ruth along for the start of the inquiry.

When they got to the courthouse in Edinburgh, all the major players in the civil suit were there, including James Shaughnessy,

Second Attempt to Settle

Steve Fearon and Jeff Kriendler for Pan Am and Alert Management. John Connors, a Department of Justice attorney, who represented the U.S. government in both the criminal and civil case, showed up. Lee had met him during the Yuval Aviv hearing when Pan Am claimed federal agencies were involved in the bombing. Lawyers from different countries on behalf of victims' families had come as well. However, only a few reporters milled about outside the building because the meeting was limited to participants in the inquiry.

Lord Advocate Peter Fraser, wearing a black robe and yellow curled wig, welcomed them from a podium in the conference room. He was a middle-aged man with fleshy cheeks. Michael had done his homework and briefed Lee on him ahead of time. Fraser had been a conservative politician, and Margaret Thatcher appointed him Solicitor General for Scotland in 1982. Seven years later, just after Lockerbie, he became Lord Advocate. That same year, he was made a life peer as Baron Fraser of Carmyllie and appointed to the Privy Council, which advises the British monarch.

For a man of such standing, Fraser did not put on any airs, however. He had a no-nonsense manner and succinctly outlined the scope of the inquiry. They all would receive their turn to ask questions of the witnesses. Certain queries, such as those involving interline baggage, would not be permitted. Fraser did not offer an explanation other than that he would not allow any airing of unsubstantiated conspiracy theories during the hearings.

After the session ended, Michael and Lee went to Fraser's chambers for a private meeting. Dark wooden bookcases filled with law books lined the walls. The two windows were tiny, and several desk lamps provided illumination. Away from his public role, Fraser was much more personable. He had removed his wig which revealed graying hair and allowed himself a smile. "I am delighted to meet you, Lee," he said. "Sir Geoffrey Lane speaks very highly of you."

Lee was surprised that the judge from a case nearly two decades ago remembered him. Fraser had done his homework as well.

With the meeting off to a good start, Lee outlined the extensive work he and the Plaintiffs Committee had done documenting Pan Am's and Alert Management's security breaches at Frankfurt and London airports. He promised, "We will cooperate in every way we can to make the inquiry a success."

The Lord Advocate was pleased and surprised Lee again when he said, "I think you should go first in examining the witnesses."

Things were off to an excellent start.

14

INQUIRY AND TRAGEDY

October—December 1990

Lee could not attend the opening day of the FAAI because he had to participate in a hearing regarding punitive damages for an earlier case at the United States Court of Appeals for the Second Circuit in New York. Fortunately, he was first on the calendar and left immediately afterward for JFK airport, where he met Ruth to catch the Concorde to London. They overnighted at a hotel in Heathrow and caught the 7 a.m. shuttle to Glasgow.

Throughout his career, Lee's cases took him all over the United States and to other countries, as far away as India and Japan. As he became recognized for his expertise in aviation law, invitations to speak at international conferences came from Britain, France, and even South Africa, China, and Thailand.

For someone who dealt daily with airplane accidents and disasters and clocked scores of miles by plane, he was not afraid of flying. He considered air travel one of the safest ways to get around. "I'm a very relaxed passenger," he once told a reporter. "Flying is extremely safe. An accident happens only when there is an extraordinary coincidence of a number of things going wrong."

In fact, Lee loved to fly. One time, he traveled to Florida for a deposition. When he returned, Ruth went to the airport to pick him up, but the flight was inexplicably late, and she became worried.

After the plane finally landed, Lee came out of the arrival gate with a beaming smile.

Ruth ran up to him and said, "Oh honey, I was so worried!"

Lee kissed her and jokingly explained, "The pilot knew who I was and invited me into the cockpit to fly the airplane."

Until they had children, Ruth accompanied Lee on many of his travels. Because he was busy during the day, she went sightseeing and shopping alone. Over the years, she walked along the banks of the Loire, Seine, Po, and Arno rivers and saw the statue of David in the Gallery of the Academy in Florence many times. But she and Lee spent the evenings together, enjoying good food and allowing him to unwind from his hectic, stressful schedule.

When Jim and Laurie were too small to travel, Ruth stayed home, and phone calls had to suffice. No matter how busy he was, Lee called every night to talk with his children.

Because Lee's depositions and cases took up most of his time, Ruth arranged with her mother, who lived nearby in Mount Kisco by then, to keep a supply of gifts for the children—toys and knick-knacks. Lee would stop by her house on his way to the airport and collect already-wrapped presents to surprise Jim and Laurie when he returned. If Lee had time off during conferences, he bought gifts for Ruth. He brought home a silk shawl from India and a rug from Pakistan, which became the centerpiece of the living room floor of their home, and many other beautiful objects.

As soon as the kids reached school age, Lee wanted them to experience the world and learn to appreciate other cultures. So, they came along on many of his trips. Ruth always packed apple sauce, bottled water, and dry cereal for the children. She and Laurie ate practically nothing their hosts offered, but Jim ate everything put in front of him.

In Singapore, they visited "death houses," which had small, open areas where cancer patients could congregate and play mahjong with their families. Although they were terminally ill, they were not isolated from their community. When Lee worked in Gabon in Africa, they went to Lambarene, the hospital Albert Schweitzer founded. There, too, sick patients were not separated from their families. This was long before the hospice movement took hold in the United States.

In the evenings, they talked excitedly about their adventures, and Lee shared what happened during his day.

There were dangerous times, too.

On a trip to East Africa to scout potential meeting sites for the annual International Academy of Trial Lawyers convention, Lee and his family stayed at Governors' Camp in the Maasai Mara National Reserve in Kenya. Located by a bend in the Mara River, the accommodations consisted of large, luxury tents.

The morning after arrival, they all went for a game walk to look at wild animals. Along the way, they inadvertently woke a sleeping hippopotamus, which came roaring out of the bushes and took off after them. When Jim ran behind a large tree, the hippo charged after Lee. Laurie pushed her father out of the way to safety and distracted the angry creature. When it came after her, she climbed a tree to safety.

Ruth watched the scene from afar, terrified. Fortunately, the hippo soon lost interest and trotted away. After everyone hurried back to the camp and calmed down, they all had a good laugh about it.

"Quick thinking," Lee complimented Laurie. "Thank you."

On another occasion, during the international conference in Ghana, a high court judge hosted the Kreindlers. He arranged for Ruth and the children to tour the countryside around Accra, the capital. At some point, Jim got very sick. When they rushed him to a clinic, the French-speaking doctor was away, and they could not understand his colleague's native tongue. Jim was lying on a cot next to the operating room, where a patient was screaming. At some point, Ruth heard the doctor say "Morphine" for treating Jim and knew they had to get away. Using a diamond ring her mother gave her, she "bought" their way out of the clinic and back to their hotel. From there, they rushed to the airport and got on a flight to Germany. When they reached Frankfurt, they knew they would be all right.

As soon as they reached New York, they went to the Travel Medicine Clinic in Greenwich Village for people who had returned from abroad with unusual diseases. After a thorough examination, the doctor there told them that Jim had a 22-foot-long tapeworm, probably from eating raw wildebeest.

Ruth looked at Lee and said, "Honey, I love you with all my heart, but if you ever ask me to go back there, I swear to God, I will kill you."

Lee nodded, knowing how close they had come to tragedy.

So, he and Ruth were seasoned travelers when they went to Scotland for the Lockerbie FAAI. After their night flight from London, they arrived in Glasgow early in the morning and took a taxi to Dumfries, one of those black English town cars known as a hackney carriage. The ride took two hours, much of it along the M74 Motorway, Britain's equivalent of the American Interstate. It was a bright, sunny fall day, and they enjoyed the view of the rolling green hills of the Scottish countryside.

They planned to check in to their hotel and for Lee to change clothes and be there for the opening of the second day of the inquiry. Michael Hughes and Steve Pounian would meet him at the entrance to the hospital's auditorium.

When they got to Dumfries and arrived the Cairndale Hotel, Lee received a call from the office in New York on his cell phone. He asked Ruth, "Why don't you go in and register while I take this?"

The family-run hotel, made of large brownstones, had a stairway leading up to the first floor and entrance lobby. When Ruth introduced herself to the middle-aged manager behind the counter, his welcoming smile vanished, and he grew ash-faced. "I am so very sorry about your husband," he said. "It was a dreadful accident."

Puzzled, Ruth started to ask what he meant when Lee came up next to her, looking shaken. "I just heard Michael Hughes was killed in a car accident last night on his way home," he said.

Ruth gasped and clutched his arm.

The manager became very flustered and red-faced. "Oh, I am so sorry, Mrs. Kreindler, Mr. Kreindler. They told us it was you."

Lee waved him off. He felt like a hammer blow had struck him.

In a small voice, Ruth asked the manager, "Do you know what happened?"

He shook his head apologetically.

By the time they got to their room, they were calmer. Lee called Steve Pounian, who was also staying at the hotel. They all met in the bar room downstairs.

According to Steve, the first session of the FAAI had gone smoothly. Michael had represented the Plaintiffs Committee well. Pleased with his performance, he left to drive home to his family in Glasgow. Along the way, he stopped to call his office and his wife, Felicity. Ten miles from Glasgow, the driver of a huge lorry heading south lost control. The semi-trailer truck barreled through the median barrier and struck Michael's car. He was beheaded on impact.

Because of the tragic accident, the Lockerbie inquiry adjourned until Friday. Lee and Ruth drove back to Glasgow to be with Felicity. Lee had not met her or the children before. Though devastated, she welcomed him and Ruth into her home as if they were family. Lee was glad to have Ruth along. Her warmth and compassion offered more comfort than he could have provided alone.

Over the following days, they accompanied Felicity and her five children to the funeral ceremony at church and the cemetery. They attended the family purvey, held in a hotel meeting room, along with their son Jim, Steve Pounian, Mitch Baumeister, Frank Granito Jr, and Frank Granito III.

Liquor flowed freely, according to local custom. Lee was not a Scotch whiskey connoisseur, but he learned to drink Glenmorangie straight. He heard many stories about Michael, whom everyone liked. He had been thrilled when offered the job representing the Plaintiffs Committee and felt honored to work with Lee, a famous attorney. This was his great moment, his opportunity to shine on the world stage. What a terrible shame that he had been deprived of that chance.

When Lee finally got to his hotel room, he took a moment to remember Michael's infectious excitement, his animated expressions, his dry humor. Michael had dedicated himself to the Lockerbie case, and now he was gone, the light in his eyes forever extinguished. Lee felt his loss deeply, both on a human and a professional level. Sharing his worries with Ruth about the future of the case without Michaels' expert guidance, he said, "It feels like there's a curse on Lockerbie!"

Yet, when they visited the town the next day, they found the people generous and open-hearted, going out of their way to make them feel comfortable and welcome. They saw the Memorial Garden at Dryfesdale Cemetery, where three stone tablets stood surrounded by tranquil greenery and well-kept flowerbeds, with the names of the 270 victims carved into the granite.

On the outskirts of town, a farmer showed them the meadow on his property where a section of the plane's fuselage had fallen. The grass had grown back, and sheep were grazing peacefully, but the ground's contours were still rugged and pitted. It was hard to believe that such a horrific act of mass murder had occurred in such a charming, bucolic place.

For Lee and Ruth, it was a quiet interlude, a rare opportunity to enjoy stillness and beauty in hectic, unhappy times.

Inquiry and Tragedy

When the FAAI resumed, they went to the auditorium in Dumfries together. As Lee joined Steve Pounian, Ruth saw Jeff Kriendler talking with a member of the Pan Am delegation. Their eyes met and they hesitated for an instant. It felt to her as if, arising from all the contentious antagonism of the case, an insurmountable chasm separated them. But she started to walk across the parquet floor, and Jeff left his party. Lee looked up and watched them meet in the middle of the room. Ruth kissed Jeff on the cheek, and he hugged her, setting aside for a moment all the disagreements that divided them to affirm their human and family ties. Then, they went back to their respective sides.

* * *

In the midst of the inquiry, word reached Lee of another media tempest brewing in the United States. Pierre Salinger, who had served as President Kennedy's press secretary, was now a commentator for ABC television. Promising extraordinary news, "one of the biggest stories of the century," he announced that the Lockerbie disaster had occurred during a Drug Enforcement Agency delivery operation.

Not to be outdone by a rival network, Brian Ross of NBC, in a featured news broadcast, reported that officials of a DEA division were conducting an inquiry into top-secret undercover heroin operation in the Middle East to find out whether it was used as a cover by the terrorists who blew up Pan Am 103.

According to law enforcement and intelligence sources, the Pan Am baggage area in Frankfurt was a key to the operation. Informants would put suitcases on the Pan Am flights apparently without the usual security checks, according to one airline source, through an arrangement between the DEA and German authorities.

When Lee arrived for the inquiry the following day, a phalanx of reporters confronted him, shouting questions at him and the other attorneys. Lockerbie clients telephoned at all hours, asking

THE FIGHT FOR JUSTICE

if the reports were true and what Lee planned to do about them. It took great effort to remain even-tempered and not let the media frenzy become a distraction.

Over the next several days, both television reports were the major news items in Scotland and worldwide.

As far as Lee was concerned, the story was complete nonsense, no different than the Yuval Aviv CIA scenario. This time the source was a former DEA official named Lester Coleman, who switched careers. He became an investigative journalist and did some work for a Connecticut television station.

It came as no surprise that Pan Am's defense team used the "revelations" to ask Judge Platt again that the U.S. government be made a third-party defendant in the case, and to grant subpoenas to depose various federal agencies' personnel. John Connors expressed outrage and promised the DOJ would move for sanctions when the case was over.

Lee and the Plaintiffs Committee also objected on the grounds that Coleman was probably another shill for the defense. Judge Platt demanded an accounting from the defense lawyers about their relationship with Lester Coleman.

In a letter by James Shaughnessy to the court, he admitted that Coleman was a consultant for the defense and that the Pan Am legal team had paid his "expenses." In addition, Shaughnessy had met with him in the Hyde Park Hotel in London during the depositions of Heathrow Airport ground personnel. Those admissions were enough for Judge Platt to deny the subpoena request, although he continued to let stand the claims Pan Am brought against the U.S. government.

For Lee, the strategy pursued by Pan Am and USAU was clear now. Whenever there were significant revelations offered to the public—in the Frankfurt depositions and now at the inquiry in Dumfries—someone at Pan Am or its insurer planted a story casting doubt with made-up alternative theories. It was patently unfair and potentially

Inquiry and Tragedy

illegal for defense attorneys to generate false stories in the media. While Lee wished that he had more evidence to show their wrongdoings, he made sure that his investigators were on the case. He did not think this was the last time Pan Am's attorneys would try to pull a fast one.

Sure enough, as more information about the Lockerbie disaster came out during the FAAI in Dumfries, the phony story concocted by Yuval Aviv resurfaced.

On December 17, *Barron's* magazine featured a cover story with the headline, in bold print: PAN AM FLIGHT 103: WHO'S COVERING UP WHAT? Subtitled "Terrorist-Drug Link Alleged by Private Probe," the eight-page account repeated information from the Interfor Report. It also mentioned Pan Am filing a claim against the U.S. government, asserting it was responsible for the Lockerbie disaster because it permitted a bag switch during a protected drug "delivery" operation in Frankfurt.

In discussing the polygraph examinations administered to Tuzcu and O'Neil, the *Barron's* article strongly suggested that the witnesses lied, claiming that Tuzcu, at O'Neil's prodding, switched a luggage bag at Frankfurt. That information could have come only from the Pan Am and Alert defense team.

This time, Lee was not blindsided. The writer of the *Barron's* article, Maggie Mahar, had called him for comment before publication. Lee got the impression that she was talking to him only for the record but that the gist of her account was preordained—she seemed determined to write a tall tale filled with lies.

Although the story was a big distraction, it could not diminish the importance of the public inquiry in Dumfries. Running for over 55 days, from October 1990 to February 1991, and hearing evidence from more than 130 witnesses, it was a significant event in the Lockerbie story. The FAAI marked the release of material and information in the criminal investigation, including the possible origin of the suitcase containing the bomb in Malta. It also gave the Plaintiffs Committee their first look at some of the principal witnesses, notably Inspector John Boyd and Detectives Derek Henderson, James Russell, and John Bell. Lee made sure he talked with them afterward, hoping to establish relationships that would be beneficial in the future.

He had already met John Boyd, the original head of the Lockerbie investigation. As chief constable for Dumfries and Galloway, he had never dealt with an air disaster, but he organized a superb search effort, utilizing police emergency powers, calling in the army and air force, and requisitioning all the private helicopters at the Glasgow airport. His attention to detail and insistence on the highest standards of evidence gathering, as well as his sympathetic treatment of the victims' families, earned him everyone's respect. Five months later, Boyd became the Inspector of Constabulary in Scotland. He had close-cropped, grayish hair, wore gold-rim glasses, and was unpretentious and soft-spoken. Lee liked the way he paid careful attention to his questions before answering them.

Detective Henderson lived in Lockerbie within 100 yards of Sherwood Crescent, where a section of the aircraft had caused a firestorm of destruction, and he had barely managed to spirit his wife and young child to safety. He and James Russell struck Lee as salt-of-the-earth policemen—honest and competent.

John Bell drew Lee's attention because he had gone to Malta to trace the origin of the unaccompanied suitcase. But he did not testify at the inquiry and refused to talk about what progress he had made. The Lord Advocate did not allow it.

Still, there was plenty of new information that would prove helpful to the plaintiffs' cause. Lee was satisfied that attending the FAAI had been a good idea. He only wished that Michael could have been with him to share in the discoveries.

15

STEPS TOWARD PROVING CAUSATION

December 1990 to September 1991

On December 14, an article appeared on the front page of the London *Independent*, written by David Black. It included photos of a computer printout copy supposedly establishing that a piece of luggage had originated in Malta, gone through the Frankfurt Baggage Conveyance System (FAG), and ended up on Pan Am Flight 103. The article raised more questions than it answered and did not prove the Air Malta connection. However, when Lee checked with several reliable news media sources, they confirmed that the essential claims of the story were valid.

Lee called Black in London and asked if he could have hard copies of the original printout and any other documents or information he might have.

Black wanted to be helpful. "I'd love to," he said. "But in this case, I can't say more than what was in the article or give you any documents. It would jeopardize my source, and I promised him I wouldn't."

Although Black and the *Independent* turned out to be a dead-end, Lee kept at it. He and his team mentioned the FAG computer printout to every reporter sniffing around the criminal inquiry who called them, hoping for a break.

In January 1991, Pan Am declared bankruptcy. Much of the news coverage portrayed the Chapter 11 court filing as a protective measure to avoid liability for Lockerbie and suggested that the litigation and financial exposure brought down the airline. But there were other factors. The first Gulf War, after the Iraqi invasion of Kuwait in 1990, caused fuel prices to skyrocket at a time when worldwide air travel experienced a severe downturn. In addition, Pan Am's fleet mainly consisted of many older, less fuel-efficient aircraft, which added to operating costs. Increased competition as the FAA awarded routes to other airlines also reduced the number of passengers Pan Am carried and shrank its profit margins.

Lee knew that blaming the Lockerbie litigation for Pan Am's woes was nonsense since any damage payments to the victims' families would come from the airline's insurance company, and he said so publicly. As far as he was concerned, the rot started with management at the top. Even if Lockerbie hadn't happened, it was just a matter of time before Pan Am went belly-up.

Meanwhile, the pursuit of the FAG computer printout paid off. Lee and his team found an English reporter, Charles Lane, who knew about the document. Lee arranged to meet him for drinks at the Berkeley, a five-star luxury hotel in London's Knightsbridge district, just south of Hyde Park. Although the building was a massive old sandstone edifice, the bar inside had modern décor with several alcoves that allowed patrons to talk privately.

Lane was a chubby man in his forties with watery eyes and hair graying at the temples. "I'm not sure I can help you, Lee," he said reluctantly. "I wanted to go public myself, but I needed more proof and made the mistake of showing some of the material to David Black. You know what happened next."

He left unspoken that Black misappropriated the documents and scooped him.

"That must have seriously pissed you off," Lee commiserated. "I would have felt the same way." Then, he pleaded with Lane to let the Plaintiffs Committee have the documents and any related information. "I promise we will not use them without your express permission," he said.

Several drinks later—Lee knew from experience that many reporters liked their whiskey and kept the liquor flowing—Lane became more amenable. He agreed to come to New York, all expenses paid, to share what he knew. Lee's ability to establish rapport with people once again met with success.

Two weeks later, Lane arrived at Kreindler & Kreindler with a worn leather briefcase containing his entire file on the case. It was detailed and voluminous. Lane had done an outstanding job of securing information. Over several hours, he laid out to the Committee members what he had managed to piece together. How and where Lane got all the material, he never revealed. It was clear, however, that some of it came from files of the official criminal investigation in Scotland.

The key documents were copies of the computer printout indicating all bags delivered to Pan Am 103 in Frankfurt and the worksheet of Station 206 that showed the unaccompanied suitcase had come from Air Malta Flight KM 180. The computer printout had notes and scribbles in the margins. It was attached to a report by the German Federal Criminal Police (BKA), which said that it belonged to Kurt Berg, a supervisor in the computer department of the FAG.

"The BKA found this shortly after the flight crashed," Lane explained. "They've been sitting on it since late 1988. The person who gave it to me thought there was a German cover-up of what happened. He wanted the story to come out!"

That revelation generated a great deal of excitement around the conference room table. Here was the first physical evidence tracking the suitcase originating in Malta at the Frankfurt Airport.

"This is almost as good as a smoking gun," Steve Pounian said, smiling.

As the others nodded, Frank Granito Jr rubbed his neck, said, "I hate to rain on our parade here, but how are we going to authenticate these documents so we can use them in court?"

He had put his finger on the nub of the problem. Copies of papers from a reporter who wouldn't name his source were not admissible in a trial.

Lee got up and walked to the window to think. The printout and worksheet originated in Germany. Following the normal procedure of taking testimony would require an application to the District Court in Brooklyn for "Letters of Request for Judicial Assistance" addressed to the German Ministry of Justice and German courts. But because the U.S. government was a party to the case, any deposition notice also would go to the attorney for the Justice Department. Lee felt sure the DOJ would move to quash the depositions on the grounds that they could jeopardize the criminal investigation.

Looking at the traffic below, he mused, "Why don't we proceed the way we did with Oliver Koch? Once we establish that airport witnesses will qualify the documents, let's have them come to the United States for depositions."

"Better to apologize afterward than get a flat-out No asking for permission," Frankie said, grinning.

Jim added, "Yes. If we get them here and hide them until their depositions, it might be possible to get the testimony we need."

But Mitch Baumeister seemed reluctant. "How do we do this? How do we know how to approach the right people in Frankfurt?" he asked.

For a moment, there was an awkward silence in the room. It seemed like an insurmountable undertaking.

Steps toward Proving Causation

Then Lee remembered one of the Lockerbie family members. "Why don't we ask Frank Rosenkranz? He is fluent in German and knows his way around the Frankfurt Airport."

Everyone thought that was a good idea.

When they contacted Rosenkranz, he immediately agreed to help. He had lost a daughter in the crash and was active in the Victims of Pan Am Flight 103 group. A middle-aged businessman, he had grown up in Germany and come to the United States as a teenager. His import-export company frequently took him to Europe, and he was familiar with the cargo holds and shipping practices of airlines at all the big international airports.

Lee, Jim, and Steve spent several days preparing him for his mission. They gave him copies of the FAG printouts to read and digest so he could discuss them intelligently with the witnesses. They also provided him with a list of questions to ask.

Rosenkranz did an excellent job. He flew to Frankfurt and located a FAG employee who confirmed the authenticity of the computer printout and the essence of the story behind it. He was willing to come to New York to testify, but only with the approval of his superiors. Rosenkranz stayed in close touch with Lee and Jim by telephone as he spoke to the higher-ups at FAG. Several managers were inclined to grant permission, but when they kicked the decision upstairs, the FAG board of directors refused permission.

Lee tried another track. He enlisted the support of a prominent German lawyer, Gerhart Baum, who had previously been the German Minister of Justice and knew several FAG board members personally. Lee had met him at an aviation law conference in Paris and established a good relationship with him. But when Baum tried to intercede on the plaintiffs' behalf, the FAG board remained adamant: it would not allow its employees to travel to the United States to give testimony.

Fortunately, Gerhard Baum was a man cut from the same cloth as Lee—determined and persistent, who refused to give up in the face of obstacles and adversity. He continued to lobby the FAG Board members he knew personally and obtained a significant concession. In a phone call to Lee, he reported, "They assured me that if we follow the procedures of the Hague Convention on the taking of international testimony, they will cooperate if and when the matter comes before a German Court."

That was a positive development. But it did not solve the problem of revealing that the Plaintiffs Committee possessed the documents when they served Pan Am and Alert's attorneys with copies of the Letters of Request for deposing witnesses in Germany.

During one of the Plaintiffs Committee strategy meetings, Mitch Baumeister proposed a solution. "If we can't keep it a secret that we have them, why don't we let the cat out of the bag and go public with it now?" He smiled at Lee. "As lead counsel, you should do the honors."

Lee took off his glasses and twirled them in his fingers. It was not a bad idea. He was giving a speech at the Aviation Law Symposium at Southern Methodist University in Dallas the following week. Several important USAU officials would be in attendance, including Russell Mirabile, who had replaced Robert Alpert as chief of claims.

He put his glasses back on, looked at the others, and grinned. "Okay, let's have some fun."

When his turn came to speak at the conference, Lee first discussed general developments in the Lockerbie case. Then he sprung his surprise, "We have in our possession documentation that will prove the bomb was in an unaccompanied bag interlined from Air Malta KM 180 in Frankfurt to Pan Am 103 in Frankfurt."

There were gasps from the spectators.

Lee singled out Russell Mirabile in the audience and continued, "I predict that the first person indicted for the crime will be a Libyan intelligence agent who bought clothes and other material from a shop in Malta."

As soon as Lee got back to New York, Pan Am's defense served him with a notice to produce all the documents he'd referenced in his SMU speech. Lee decided to have more fun and called Mirabile at the USAU office. When the chief of claims picked up, he said, "Russ, why didn't you simply ask me for the papers? I'm glad to give them to you."

Mirabile was not amused.

Although the Plaintiffs had yet to qualify the documents in admissible form, they made copies and provided them to the lawyers for the defendants and the U.S. government. Lee figured their DOJ attorney, John Conners, had seen them already.

* * *

On May 20 and 21, 1991, Lee and Jim took three important depositions of Scottish police officers and detectives in Dumfries. The witnesses arrived wearing their dress uniforms. They laid their caps with checkered bands on the table next to the notes they brought along. The depositions proceeded in the usual oral question-and-answer format.

John Boyd, by then the Inspector of Constabulary of Scotland and highest police officer of the country, had headed the original criminal investigation. He testified to its enormity and thoroughness. The searchers collected 319 tons of wreckage and debris scattered over 845 square miles—more than 4 million pieces, which they tagged and entered into a computer tracking system. Accident investigators and engineers reconstructed the plane's fuselage, exposing a 20-inch hole indicating an explosion in the forward cargo hold. The baggage containers nearest the hole had sustained severe damage consistent with a bomb going off inside. The investigators conducted test explosions to confirm the precise location, amount, and type of explosive used.

Detective Constable Derek Henderson and Detective Sergeant James Russell had been tasked with tracing all the checked suitcases on the airplane but had pursued different paths. Sergeant Russell testified that the lock on the brown Samsonite suitcase that held the Toshiba radio cassette bomb was recovered. His team tried every key carried by every passenger in that lock to see if it would work, but none fit. That represented significant evidence that the suitcase did not belong to any passenger on board the flight.

Constable Henderson set out to determine the identity and origin of every suitcase in the container that held the bag with the bomb. He and his team obtained information worldwide on all passengers. Using a sophisticated computer program, they found 66 suitcases and traced all but one to passengers. When they could not match it with anyone, Henderson concluded it was therefore "unaccompanied."

These findings were all significant evidence that could be used at the civil trial. While they did not explain how the bomb got on Flight 103, they made clear that none of the passengers were responsible. The bomb had to be hidden in an interline bag that made its way on board.

Just as revealing were the conversations Lee had during recesses in the hallway of the Dumfries auditorium. At one point, James Shaughnessy took him aside and said, "You know, if the Scottish or American government prosecutors provided us with some evidence of how the bomb got on the airplane, the defendants might be inclined to talk settlement."

When Lee shared the offer with John Connors, he received a surprising answer. "The U.S. government has already supplied information along those lines to Judge Platt," Connors said. "If we involve the

Steps toward Proving Causation

court, perhaps the defendants can be satisfied and come to the table for settlement."

Lee felt that Shaughnessy had made the proposal in good faith. By the time the depositions ended, he, the defense lawyer, and Connors agreed to request a meeting with Judge Platt.

But before returning to New York, Lee flew to Atlanta for an American Bar Association Forum discussion of punitive damages in accident litigation. Sitting next to him on the panel were Robert Alpert, USAU's former chief of claims, and Greg Buhler, assistant general counsel of Pan Am. Once again, Russell Mirabile sat in the audience, along with Dominick Alfieri, vice president of USAU claims. Both were in charge of the Lockerbie cases under John Brennan.

Lee decided to go for the jugular. In his opening statement, he said, "The defendants' refusal to settle Lockerbie is irresponsible. There is no way to deny exposure. Whatever the reason for their not settling, it has nothing to do with the facts of the case."

At a cocktail party afterward, Alfieri came up to Lee and said, "That was an interesting new twist."

Joining them, Mirabile insisted, "The case isn't settled because the plaintiffs can't prove causation. You can't show how the bomb got on the airplane."

Lee smiled to himself. They were ganging up on him. He'd touched a nerve! "We have made substantial progress on causation," he said. "I would welcome the opportunity to show you the evidence."

Back in New York, Lee requested an in chambers conference with the court following the next court session. The meeting with James Shaughnessy and John Connors occurred in Judge Platt's office in the morning. Lee related the conversations in Dumfries mentioning evidence that he knew the government had already provided to Judge Platt about how the bomb got onto the airplane.

Platt looked at Lee and said, "Give me fifteen minutes to speak with John Connors alone."

Lee left with Shaughnessy and went outside the building. He bought a cup of coffee from a sidewalk vendor and sat on a bench near the fountain in Walt Whitman Park, enjoying the late spring sunshine.

When he returned to the courthouse, feeling refreshed, the clerk invited him and Pan Am's lawyer back to the judge's chamber. As Lee entered, John Connors gave him a slight nod.

After they had settled in their chairs, Judge Platt took an official looking document from his desk and read it out loud. The statement clearly implied that the bomb had been in an unaccompanied bag loaded onto Flight 103 in Frankfurt. He took off his reading glasses and looked Lee and Shaughnessy. "The issue of the trial will be, first, did Pan Am, in its inspection and screening in Frankfurt, use due care in permitting that to happen," he said. "Second, did Pan Am use due care in London in relation to how the bomb got on the airplane."

Lee leaned back in his chair and slowly expelled his breath. This was better than he had expected, supporting the claims he and the Plaintiffs Committee had made all along. James Shaughnessy kept picking at the crease in his trousers.

At the conclusion of the meeting, he said to Lee, "I'll report to the insurance carrier immediately and get back to you as soon as possible." But then he added, "I still don't believe that's how the bomb got on the plane."

Following the conference, Lee had several telephone conversations with Russ Mirabile in which he reviewed the evidence and related it to what Judge Platt had said.

Mirabile kept quibbling, "Judge Platt did not say that the bomb bag was an unaccompanied bag that got on the flight in Frankfurt."

Steps toward Proving Causation

On July 1, 1991, Lee wrote him, "If there is any doubt about what Judge Platt said or its import, I suggest we have another meeting in chambers with you and John Brennan present."

Mirabile never responded.

Lee concluded that the defendants wanted to drag out the proceedings, hoping to bankrupt the plaintiffs' law firms. For a large insurer with big pockets, this was child's play. For Kreindler & Kreindler and the other law firms representing the victims' families, it was a tremendous financial burden. None of the attorneys on the case earned a cent while expenses for depositions, travel, and support personnel kept mounting.

The pressure weighed heavily on Lee. He lost plenty of sleep worrying over his firm's finances. They had to make cutbacks, and the other partners were not happy that three of their best attorneys were generating no income.

* * *

Toward the end of September, Thomas Plaskett, the CEO of Pan Am, resigned. He left with a golden parachute, a million-dollar severance payment that was considered hefty at the time. Lee received a number of calls from the Lockerbie victims' families, expressing their frustration and outrage. It bothered him enough to write a letter to the *New York Times*, which was printed the week after Plaskett's departure:

> *The resignation of Thomas Plaskett as CEO and President of Pan American World Airways and the payment to him of $1.2 million in severance pay is unthinkable when contrasted with the fact that the families of Lockerbie victims have not yet received a cent in damages for the deaths of their loved ones.*
>
> *Mr. Plaskett was CEO of Pan Am on December 21, 1988, when the Lockerbie bombing occurred. He was ultimately responsible for Pan Am's abysmal "security" at that time.*

> *Should corporate managers responsible for security failures, causing hundreds of deaths, receive million-dollar severance pay when victims' families still have not been compensated?*
>
> *Airline insurance, airline travel, and our legal system all have one thing in common. They are supposed to serve the public. Something is missing in the translation.*
>
> Lee S. Kreindler
> Chairman, Plaintiffs' Committee,
> and Lead Counsel
> Lockerbie Federal Court Litigation

Lee had no expectations that Pan Am officials, including his own cousin, would respond or attempt to justify the company's action, and they never did.

16

FURTHER STEPS TOWARD PROVING CAUSATION

October—November 1991

Lee had filed letters of request with Judge Platt to depose the FAG workers in Frankfurt, Germany, in June of 1991. The defendants countered with letters for four additional German witnesses, Pan Am employees whose testimony they wanted to preserve for the trial. Lee had expected John Connors to object on behalf of the U. S. government and was pleasantly surprised when he didn't.

It took four months to process the Letters of Request. The German courts were nothing if not thorough and moved at a snail's pace. When they finally approved, they made arrangements to schedule the testimony. The process was not completed until October 14, 1991.

Steve Pounian went to Frankfurt for the defendant's depositions, and Lee joined him at the end of the week for the start of the FAG testimony before a different judge. When he arrived, Steve told him, "If you thought the depositions at the Sheraton Hotel were slow, just wait. It's like wading through molasses."

The next morning, it took just a few minutes for Lee to understand Steve's warning. The hearing occurred in a small courtroom on the third floor of the administrative courthouse in Frankfurt, a nondescript, modern concrete-and-glass building. The presiding judge was Paula Hecker-Hafke, a stern-looking woman with blonde hair under a red cap that matched the color of her robe. She wore steel-rimmed glasses. Her single pearl drop earrings were the only jewelry she wore.

She welcomed the American attorneys representing the plaintiffs, the defendants, and the United States government in English and explained how things would proceed. Lee had no idea what to make of her.

First, Lee would ask a question in English, which the English court reporter would take down.

Then, the translator would render it into German, and Judge Hecker-Hafke would put the question to the witness, who answered in German.

Everyone had to wait while the judge dictated the witness' answer to the court stenographer, who recorded it on her computer.

Finally, the translator would convey that version into English, which the plaintiffs' stenographer would take down.

Needless to say, it took seemingly forever to get an answer to a question and have it recorded. The result was a pair of transcripts, one in German, the official record of the German court, which the German Ministry of Justice transmitted to the Federal Court in Brooklyn, New York. The other version, prepared in English by the American court reporter, was also legal and sufficient for Lee's purposes and could be used as testimony during the civil trial.

The first witness was Gunter Kasteleiner, the baggage traffic controller in charge of the section of the airport, which included flights departing from Gate B 44, where Pan Am Flight 103 to London had been parked. He was in his late 30s, formally dressed in coat and tie, and had intelligent blue eyes. He understood the questions in English and answered without Judge Hecker-Hafke having to prompt him. Lee thought Kasteleiner was an excellent witness.

The primary purpose of the proceedings was to authenticate the copies of documents the plaintiffs had obtained through "unknown

Further Steps toward Proving Causation

sources." The most important was the computer printout of the baggage delivered to Pan Am 103.

Lee showed Kasteleiner the document and asked, "Do you recognize this?"

Kasteleiner said, "Yes." He pointed to the scribbles in the margins. "These are the notes of Kurt Berg. I recognize his handwriting. They are accurate representations of what I told him."

"Does it look authentic to you?" Lee asked.

"Yes, it appears authentic to me."

Lee felt a warm prickling well up in his chest. They had just proved that the printout was real.

But when the judge heard the answer, she turned to the witness and said in German, "Look at it carefully. How do you know it's not a forgery?"

Lee could not believe his ears when the translator rendered her words into English. He stared at Steve in shock.

Kasteleiner said, "Your Honor, now that you point it out to me, I don't know that it is not a forgery. I did not print it out and don't know who did. I cannot swear that this printout is authentic."

Lee sat at the plaintiffs' table, his hand on his chin, feverishly thinking about how to salvage the deposition.

But Judge Hecker-Hafke was not done. She asked the witness, "Where do you think the original is?"

Kasteleiner replied, "I'm not sure, but it is a FAG document. The FAG probably knows."

The judge turned to Jürgen Göb, the FAG attorney attending the depositions, and asked him to find out if his company still had the printout and, if so, to produce it. The lawyer, who looked the image of a blond-haired, bureaucratic lackey, bowed smartly and said, "Yes, Your Honor, I'll make some calls," and left. Lee almost expected him to click his heels.

When Göb returned, he reported that the FAG had given the original documents to the BKA. Judge Hecker-Hafke then picked up the pushbutton telephone on the court bench and put in a call to Inspector Fuhl of the BKA in Meckenheim.

Steve whispered to Lee, "That is the guy who interrupted the Tuzcu deposition. He's a piece of work. I took his testimony last week along with the other Pan Am witnesses, and he refused to answer any questions."

With Judge Hecker-Hafke, Inspector Fuhl was apparently more forthcoming. After asking if the BKA had the document, she listened for some time and hung up. Then, she reported her conversation to the courtroom. Fuhl told her that the BKA did, indeed, have the documents. But he could not give them to her because of an ongoing international investigation. He also insisted that they were the property of the FAG, not the BKA, and releasing them would require their approval.

Judge Hecker-Hafke stared at the Jürgen Göb and said, "Will you please obtain the approval of FAG for the BKA to turn over the documents? I consider them to be highly relevant and important."

Lee and Steve were speechless and amazed. The German judge had taken over the proceedings! Maybe there was hope, and they would get the original documents after all.

When Göb reported that there was no objection to the BKA producing the documents, the judge telephoned Inspector Fuhl again.

Apparently, he protested that there was an international investigation going on, and he could not release the documents unless the State Prosecutor in charge of prosecuting Lockerbie crimes on behalf of the German government told him to do so.

The judge hung up and dialed another number, this time to the Chief Prosecutor for the State of Hessen. As it happened, he had his office two floors above in the same building.

Further Steps toward Proving Causation

"Herr Oswald, please come down here," Judge Hecker-Hafke said, "I want to talk to you."

Two minutes later, Chief Prosecutor Oswald appeared in the courtroom. He was a corpulent man in his 50s and seemed somewhat put out. The judge explained in rapid-fire German that the documents were essential to the case before her, and she wanted them delivered. Oswald spread his hands in a helpless gesture and said, "There is an international criminal investigation going on. I must know under what authority you are directing me to produce these documents."

The judge leaned down toward him and said stern-faced, "Under the authority of the United States District Court for the Eastern District of New York, which has issued Letters of Request for Judicial Assistance, and my own authority as the German Court with jurisdiction, Herr Oswald. "

Unfazed, Oswald asked, "May I see the Letters of Request from the American Court?"

When the clerk handed him the documents, he read them carefully.

Lee caught Steve Pounian's eye. He felt like they had front-row seats at a melodrama, a legal thriller, with unexpected twists and turns, setbacks, and successes. Here they were in a tiny German courtroom, and a German judge, chosen at random, was about to tell three countries that they had to divulge the documents they'd been keeping under wraps.

A glance at James Shaughnessy told him the Pan Am lawyer was just as fascinated and bewildered.

Oswald finished reading and looked around at the assembled lawyers, the witness, and finally the judge. Then he said, "All right, you can advise the BKA that I have no objection."

Judge Hecker-Hafke immediately picked up the telephone and called Inspector Fuhl. When he answered, she said pointedly, "Both the FAG, which owned the documents, and the Prosecutor for the State of Hessen, who had German jurisdiction over prosecuting Lockerbie crimes, have consented. Now, Inspector Fuhl, may I have the documents?"

After she hung up, she told the courtroom that Fuhl would fax them immediately. Lee imagined he'd agreed in a tight, clipped voice.

An hour later, Judge Hecker-Hafke's secretary walked in with copies of the originals of all the documents Lee wanted. The cover letter from the BKA indicated that the attached were true copies of originals in possession of the BKA, which should not be released because of the pending investigation.

James Shaughnessy then objected to using the documents because they were not the originals.

The judge looked at him like someone wanting to swat a fly. "Mr. Shaughnessy, these documents are now as well authenticated as any documents in history," she said. "I rule under German law that they are usable in this case. I hereby inform my colleague, Judge Platt in New York, that these documents, which we shall now use in lieu of the ones we started with, are admissible in evidence under German law and, in my opinion, should be accepted by the United States Court as well."

That's when the realization hit Lee. Despite the constraints of the criminal investigation, he and the Plaintiffs Committee had in their hands the hard evidence that would enable them to prove how the bomb got on the airplane! They now had an authentic copy, not from the *Independent* or an unidentified Scottish detective whistleblower, but from the FAG and the BKA!

The two documents, taken together, established that an unaccompanied interline suitcase went through the baggage conveyance system in Frankfurt from Air Malta Flight KM 180 to Pan Am 103. The computer printout provided detailed information about the

Further Steps toward Proving Causation

time the bag was coded in at Station 206 (code number S0009), the route that it took to the early baggage store holding loop, the time that it left the holding loop, and the time it arrived at Gate B 44 where Pan Am Flight 103 was parked.

The other was a worksheet for Station 206 that the two coders, Mr. Koca and Ms. Candar, used to write the flight number of the aircraft from which bags came and entered them into the system. It showed that between 1:04 p.m. and 1:10 p.m. they only received and coded in baggage from Air Malta KM 180.

Because Lee knew that the passenger manifests of Pan Am 103 and KM 180 showed no passenger from Air Malta to Pan Am, he now had proof that the bag had been unaccompanied.

However, he needed a witness to explain it all in detail. Gunter Kasteleiner, who was in charge of directing the movement of the baggage and was knowledgeable about the entire system, was that witness. When questioning resumed, Lee went through the computer printout and the worksheet with him step by step.

Toward the end, Lee asked him to look at the worksheet again, with Air Malta KM 180 coding listed for 1:04 to 1:10. "Is there any way, considering this record, that that bag, coded in at 1:07, might not have been from Air Malta?" he asked.

Kasteleiner answered, "Yes, there is. It is always possible that a late bag from an earlier flight arrived and was slipped in at that time and that the coder failed to note it. You would, of course, have to ask the coder. But I consider it highly likely that the bag was from Air Malta."

He became even more definite when Shaughnessy attacked him on that point during cross-examination. "No, it is highly likely that the bag was from KM 180," Kasteleiner insisted.

By then, it was late Friday afternoon, and everyone agreed to postpone the deposition until after Kurt Berg testified. The BKA, in its

February 1989 report, had listed him as the source of the computer printout. His handwriting was on it. He was a key witness. But Berg was going into the hospital for surgery late the following week, so he would testify for the three days before the operation, after which Kasteleiner's deposition would resume.

From his hotel room, Lee called Lord Advocate Fraser in Scotland. He had informed him of significant developments since their initial meeting in Edinburgh. Fraser was very interested when Lee reported on Kasteleiner's testimony and the release of the documents. It turned out the criminal investigation had not taken the testimony of any FAG witnesses. They had relied on the German BKA.

A thought crossed Lee's mind: Was this why the United States government had not interfered with the depositions? Perhaps the investigators welcomed getting these German witnesses under oath.

He called Ruth with the good news and they celebrated his success in getting the documents authenticated. For the rest of the weekend, Lee tried to catch up on sleep while prepping for the day ahead. Under different circumstances, he might have done some sightseeing.

On Monday, the depositions resumed with Kurt Berg. A slight man with a sour expression, he looked ill at ease. At first, Lee thought it might be because of his upcoming surgery. But all his answers were cautious and qualified. Something bothered him, but it was impossible to guess what that was. Steve Pounian handled the bulk of the deposition, and John Connors asked questions on behalf of the United States, as did James Shaughnessy for the defense.

For Lee, the most important thing was for Berg to qualify the printout, which everyone thought he had made. That was what the BKA reports implied: he had discovered the information in an FAG computer a month after Lockerbie and printed it out.

But when Lee asked him, Berg said, "I did not produce the printout."

Further Steps toward Proving Causation

Stunned, Lee said, "Well then, who did?"

"I don't know," Berg replied. He looked at his lap, contemplating, and added, "I think Frau Erac might have produced it."

Bewildered, Lee asked, "Who is she?"

"She works in the FAG central computer control room."

Judge Hecker-Hafke, who had followed Berg's testimony with great interest, cleared her throat. When she had everyone's attention, she said, "Well, I guess we had better get Frau Erac in here to testify."

That turned out to be quite a challenge. Depositions in a foreign country were directed under Letters of Request from the American Court. There was no such letter for Frau Erac because no one on the Plaintiffs Committee had heard of her. To facilitate the process, Lee enlisted the help of Gerhart Baum. The German attorney once again proved his worth. Over several days, with Judge Hecker-Hafke's help, he managed to persuade the Ministry of Justice to issue a subpoena for Frau Erac without going through a long, drawn-out international back and forth.

Meanwhile, Kurt Berg's deposition concluded on Wednesday, followed by the resumption of cross-examining Kasteleiner. The end of that week marked the completion of three weeks in Frankfurt for Steve Pounian, so he headed home. Jim joined Lee the following Monday for a tour of the FAG facilities and the continuation of the depositions.

Near the conclusion of the Kasteleiner testimony, John Connors, representing the United States, started to examine the witness. His questions were long and detailed. The process was agonizingly slow for Lee and Jim, who wanted to get to Frau Erac.

During a break, Lee asked Connors why he was going into such excruciating detail and received an interesting answer. "My charge is to eliminate any doubt," he said. "When we finish here, it has to be clear that that bag went through the X-ray machine."

For Lee, that was an important clue why the U.S. government had not objected to deposing the FAG witnesses. It seemed the German government had been less than helpful in assisting the criminal investigation. Connors, wearing his hat as a government attorney in the civil litigation, was the first American criminal lawyer who had been able to question any German witnesses at all!

To test his hypothesis, Lee asked, "Why did the U.S. government permit us to take the FAG witnesses' depositions, given its previous opposition to any invasion of the criminal investigation?"

Connors answered, "Because it has been a German show."

With German witnesses being examined under the direction of a German court, the Germans called the shots on what testimony they would permit. It taught Lee something he had not known: While the Anglo-Saxon legal traditions paid great deference to a criminal investigation, this was not true in Germany. Under German law, a judge had broad discretion and could deny calling witnesses at will. Thus, a combination of German legal traditions, the desire of the U.S. government to gain more information on what had happened in Frankfurt, and one judge's curiosity led to the Plaintiffs Committee being able to take vital testimony.

Between Shaughnessy and Connors and some additional questions from Jim and Lee concerning the newly discovered worksheets, Kasteleiner finished his testimony Wednesday afternoon.

That night, Lee could hardly sleep, awaiting the deposition of Frau Erac, potentially the most crucial witness for the civil case.

17

FRAU ERAC

Bogamira Erac was an attractive woman in her late 30s with Slavic features, a friendly smile, and personality to match. She had medium-length, ash-blond hair and wore no jewelry other than a wedding ring. She had two young daughters in school and worked as a supervisor in the *Gepäckförderanlage* (*GFA*), the Central Computer Control Room of the Frankfurt Baggage Conveyance System.

Frau Erac seemed unaffected by the tense atmosphere in the courtroom that greeted her in anticipation of her testimony and was happy to provide any information asked of her. She spoke German, Serbo-Croatian, and a bit of English. First, she described her background. She had worked at a tech company that helped design the Frankfurt baggage computers. When that system started to operate, she joined FAG.

In those days, Frankfurt was Europe's most automated airport. With a sophisticated system of conveyor belts that resembled a miniature roller coaster, more than 20,000 pieces of luggage moved with German clockwork precision through the FAG every day. After entering the system at passenger check-in or staging stations for arriving aircraft, suitcases traveled in coded plastic tray containers along 20 miles of underground tracks. Some bags went to holding areas. Others progressed directly to the stations where the ground crew took them to be X-rayed or loaded onto departing planes.

The Central Control Room, where Erac worked, had three colossal mainframe computers. G1 controlled the movement trays with bags in them. G2 managed the movement of empty trays, and R-0 was a backup error system that would take over in case of any failure or mistake by the other two.

A smaller computer, the KIK, had no monitors but two keyboard stations and a dot matrix printer on a nearby table to generate printouts when directed by an operator. The KIK's job was to keep track of what the other computers were doing and, at any point in time, locate a bag in the system.

The KIK computer could also provide a detailed listing of all bags for a particular flight, including where they were coded into the system, where they had gone for holding purposes, and when and where they were finally delivered and exited the baggage conveyance system.

An operator could call up all this information in seconds with a few simple command strokes.

Lee showed Erac the copy of the printout and asked, "Did you, at any time after the Lockerbie disaster of December 21, 1988, obtain a printout of the movement of baggage to Pan Am 103, the Boeing 747 that left Frankfurt on the first leg of the flight to London."

Erac answered, "Yes."

She explained that she had been on duty, monitoring the computer functions of moving the bags to load the flight. After she finished the day at about 10 p.m., Erac left her office and drove home. When she turned on the car radio, she heard about the Lockerbie crash. "I was horrified and distraught," she testified. "My first concern, frankly, was that something might have gone wrong in loading the baggage that was my responsibility."

When Erac got to work the next day, everyone talked about the disaster. One of her colleagues was very upset because he had once been a passenger on the Boeing 747 that blew up over Lockerbie.

During a lull in work, she went to the KIK computer and got a listing of the movement of all bags for Pan Am 103. She reviewed the printout carefully and was relieved that nothing had gone wrong. "There were no discrepancies in the baggage movement," she said.

"What did you do next?" Lee asked.

"Well, I showed it to some of my associates in the control room," Erac answered.

"Then what did you do?"

"I took the printout I had prepared and put it in my locker."

"This was the day after the Lockerbie disaster?"

"Yes."

Lee adjusted his glasses. "What happened next?"

"Nothing happened."

"Nothing happened?"

"No."

Perplexed, Lee asked, "What do you mean?"

"I thought someone would come around asking me about it," Erac explained. "The KIK computer automatically records over the old data after eight days. I figured someone else might try to do a printout before that happened or ask me for mine, but no one ever did."

Lee shared a meaningful glance with Jim sitting next to him.

Erac continued, "A few days later, I went on vacation to Yugoslavia. When I returned in mid-January, I asked my colleagues if anybody had inquired after me, but no one had. Another week passed before I decided to tell my boss, Kurt Berg, what I had done. By then, everyone knew that a bomb had caused the disaster. When I went to see Berg, I told him I had a printout of the baggage for Pan Am 103. He was surprised and said, 'Give it to me.'"

The courtroom had gone quiet. Everyone's eyes were on her.

"What did you do then?" Lee said carefully.

"I went to my locker and got the printout to give to Mr. Berg," Erac said matter-of-factly. She furrowed her brows as if remembering and continued, "Then I decided that maybe I should make a copy."

For the first time in his life, Lee stood up and applauded during a deposition. The others in the courtroom were startled. Judge Hecker-Hafke looked at him with disapproval, but a small smile played at the corners of her mouth. Jim looked down to hide his grin.

Lee took a moment to collect himself and asked, "What did you do with the copy?"

"I put it in my locker."

When Erac gave the original printout to Kurt Berg, he did not say anything. But the next day, he asked if there were any other records concerning Pan Am Flight 103. She checked the office and computers and reported that she found nothing.

Lee looked at her over his glasses and asked, "Did you have any further discussions concerning the printout with Mr. Berg?"

She answered, "No."

"You never discussed it at all with Mr. Berg?"

"No."

"Did the BKA come around to interview you?"

"No."

"Did the Scottish police interview you?"

"No."

"Did the American FBI interview you?"

"No."

"Has anybody interviewed you about this?"

"Only you, Mr. Kreindler. Today."

The impact of what he had just heard struck Lee with full force. The woman in the witness chair was the only person in the world who could authenticate the most crucial evidence of how the bomb got on the Pan Am flight, and the criminal investigation in Scotland did not even know she existed! James Shaughnessy stared straight ahead, looking like a block of petrified wood. John Conners glanced up at the ceiling. Jim kept shaking his head in disbelief.

Lee took a deep breath. Then he asked, "The copy of the computer printout you made when you gave the original to Mr. Berg—do you have it with you here today?"

"No," Erac said.

"What happened to it?"

"I guess it is still in my locker."

Lee wanted to applaud again, but he turned to Judge Hecker-Hafke and said, "Your Honor, in light of this extraordinary testimony, I would like to suggest that we suspend court so that Mrs. Erac can go to her office and see if the copy is still in her locker."

The Judge agreed. "Why don't we all take extra time for lunch to allow representatives of all the parties to accompany Mrs. Erac to her locker," she said.

So, Erac, Lee, Jim, John Connors, Jürgen Göb from FAG, James Shaughnessy's assistant, and an interpreter drove to the airport. They took separate cars. Along the way, Lee stopped by his hotel room and picked up his camera.

Then, everyone convened in the lounge of the Frankfurt Airport administrative office building. From there, they all went to a small room with tan-colored, vertical lockers on three sides, two sinks for washing up, and a long, narrow seating bench attached to the floor in the middle.

Erac pointed to one of the lockers. "This is mine."

When Lee asked, "Could I take pictures of you opening your locker," she blushed.

"I'm a little embarrassed because it's not cleaned up," she said, wrinkling her nose.

"That's okay, don't worry about it," Lee assured her. "It's just to document for the record."

Erac opened her locker as Lee snapped pictures. On a shelf at the top were Coca-Cola bottles, a thermos, and a salami. A light blue smock and a change of clothes hung from hooks on the sides. At the bottom, buried under an extra pair of shoes and a button-up cardigan sweater, was a foot-high stack of papers. Erac took them out, hefted them onto the bench, and started going through them.

Watching her getting close to the bottom, Lee had a sinking feeling that he was on another fool's errand.

Suddenly, Erac cried out, "Aha! Here it is." With a triumphant expression, she handed Lee a piece of paper, crinkled and curled at the edges. It was the copy of the computer printout she'd made when Berg asked for the original.

Lee showed it to the others, who looked at the sheet of paper incredulously. It had been lying hidden in her locker for almost three years!

The group then visited the FAG control room. As they entered, two coders looked up briefly from their stations and returned to monitoring their computers. They seemed to be used to visitors gawking at the marvels of German engineering.

Lee took pictures of the G1, G2, and R-0 computers. The displays reminded him of the New York subway map with bags moving along the lines from station to station. He also photographed the video monitors throughout the room tracking bags as they were being moved through the Frankfurt Airport.

Erac showed Lee the KIK computer where she had generated the printout for Flight 103. Without monitors and its two terminals and keyboards, it looked like the ugly duckling among swans.

Lee asked, "Does it have the capability to do the same thing for the flights being loaded now as on December 21, 1988?"

She said, "Yes. Or, if you prefer, I can print out all the information from any flight in the last eight days where loading has been completed." She indicated a monitor that displayed airplanes that were about to take off and had departed earlier that day.

Lee pointed to a Delta flight to London that had left an hour earlier. "Would you print out all the baggage that was moved to this flight?"

Erac sat down at the KIK computer terminal, and Lee took pictures as she tapped a command on the keyboard. Immediately, the print head of the nearby dot matrix printer went into action, clacking loudly and making a high-pitched whine as it generated the information. Erac tore the fanfold printout from the machine, removed the tractor holes on both sides, and made copies for everyone on a Xerox machine in the corner of the room. The papers listed all the details of where and when the bags were coded in, where they went, and when they left the system, just as for Pan Am Flight 103 on December 21, 1988.

Lee took his copy back with him to the courtroom. He entered it as a plaintiff's exhibit in the record, along with Erac's copy of the printout for Flight 103 that had languished in her locker all this time.

The next morning, when Lee continued Erac's deposition, he showed her prints of the photographs he had taken at the airport. She identified them all: the equipment in the control room, her sitting at the KIK computer to provide the printout, her opening the locker—salami and all—and her locating the printout in the big stack of papers.

While waiting for his flight, he telephoned Lord Advocate Fraser at his home in Scotland and reported Erac's spectacular testimony. When he told him about the printout she'd made the day after the Lockerbie disaster, he was dumbfounded.

"My Lord!" he exclaimed over the telephone. "How did we not know that?"

He thanked Lee for his extraordinary efforts and congratulated him on tracking down such a crucial piece of evidence.

As Lee left Frankfurt for New York on Friday evening, he was so happy he felt like dancing on the tarmac. Against all odds, they had found an unimpeachable witness who qualified the piece of evidence they needed most to make their case.

Jim stayed on in Frankfurt to conclude Erac's deposition and to take the important testimonies of Yasar Koca and Mehmet Cander, the two coders at Station 206 who entered the Air Malta bag flight number into the FAG system.

During follow-up, Erac expressed concern about having her name published. "I'm worried about terrorists targeting me when the news about this gets out," she said. By then, she realized what she'd done was a big deal!

Accordingly, Judge Hecker-Hafke directed all parties not to divulge her name and to alter all photographs to disguise her identity. For the next two years, everyone referred to her as Mrs. X, and Judge Platt gave her the pseudonym "Mrs. Schmidt" for the trial. Shortly after it concluded, she decided it was safe to use her real name in public again.

The day after Lee returned to New York, he received a telephone call from Jim MacDougall, the chief prosecutor of Lockerbie crimes. Lee had come to know him well during the FAAI meetings. MacDougall worked closely with the investigation coordinator, Norman McFadyen, who assisted the Lord Advocate.

"Peter Fraser told me about your call last night," he said. "We are deeply appreciative of your assistance, as always. Would you be so kind as to let me have the lady's name and address and provide me with as detailed an account as possible of her testimony?"

Lee gave MacDougall a full report and sent him a copy of the deposition transcript as soon as he received it. He felt proud that he and his team had found Erac. If and when the Libyan terrorists were ever brought to trial in a Scottish or American court, she would be the only person in the world who could authenticate the computer printout for Pan Am Flight 103 on December 21, 1988. The document would be a significant piece of evidence in the criminal case.

It had taken nearly three years after Lockerbie to get legally qualified proof linking a suitcase from Air Malta to the disaster. Yet, the evidence had been available, not just eight months after the plane exploded in mid-air when the Scottish police received it, but the next day!

That fact raised serious questions about a possible cover-up by German authorities. After all, the BKA knew about the printout and related worksheet in early February 1989, less than two months after the disaster. They even sent investigators to Malta but sat on the documents for five months before telling the Scottish police, who in turn informed their American counterparts.

The fact that the KIK computer would wipe itself clean after eight days was well-known to everyone who worked for FAG. In all likelihood, the BKA knew it, too, or should have known. Did they really ignore this obvious source of vital information until late January when Kurt Berg forwarded Erac's printout?

What about Berg himself? Why didn't he extract a printout during the first eight days? Surely, he knew that the KIK computer contained a record of every bag that had traveled through the system and onto Flight 103.

Erac had made no secret of her printout, telling her associates as well as Berg. Why didn't the BKA interview her? Why was Lee the first to formally ask her questions almost three years after the event? It was evident from the BKA documents that the Scottish-American investigation had been misled and misinformed regarding the identity of the person who had produced the printout and when it had been generated.

Lee surmised that high-ups in German government agencies hoped no one would ever find out that the bomb had come through Frankfurt. They wanted to be spared the embarrassment of admitting to it.

Whatever the reason, eight valuable months were lost to the investigation. Had that not happened, the Lockerbie crime might have been better understood earlier, and other culprits could have been identified.

18

HELP FROM THE CRIMINAL INVESTIGATION

November 1991—February 1992

On November 15, 1991, the United States and Scottish governments indicted two Libyan intelligence agents, Abdelbaset al-Megrahi and Lamin Khalifa Fhimah, for the bombing of Pan Am Flight 103. The evidence also pointed to the involvement of aides of the Libyan leader, Muammar Gaddafi. A little more than two months later, the U.N. Security Council approved a resolution demanding the surrender of the two suspects for trial. Because they were living in Libya, there was little hope that would ever happen.

Lee continued to make every effort to cooperate with Lord Advocate Fraser, Chief Prosecutor MacDougall, and Norman McFayden in Scotland, updating them frequently on the developments of the civil case.

Though he was performing a noble and patriotic service, Lee hoped to benefit in return. He had already received permission to depose John Boyd, the original head of the criminal investigation, and Detectives Henderson and Russell. There would come a time when Lee would ask the Lord Advocate to allow other key witnesses to testify, even if he did not want them to come forward. Fraser rarely granted such authorization to civil litigants, and Lee wanted to put him in a position where he could not say no.

Meanwhile, he and the Plaintiffs Committee had almost closed the gap on proof of causation. Through their factual depositions, they had tracked the movement of the unaccompanied suitcase on flights from Malta via Frankfurt to London and from there onto Pan Am Flight 103 to New York.

For purposes of the civil litigation, they needed to prove only two more things: that the unaccompanied bag contained the bomb and that it originated in Malta.

To accomplish the first required testimony from scientists of the Aircraft Accidents Investigation Board (AAIB) and the Royal Aeronautics Research and Development Establishment (RARDE). They could identify the explosive, the explosive residue, and the clothing surrounding the bomb in the suitcase.

The Plaintiffs Committee identified two experts, Mick Charles and Peter Claydon, who were investigators of the AAIB. They had analyzed the wreckage and overseen the reconstruction of the mockup of the 747. The third, Alan Feraday, Chief Forensic Scientist of RARDE, could speak to the nature of the explosive.

However, getting them to testify proved to be a formidable challenge. Unlike the detectives and policemen Lee, Steve, and Jim examined in Dumfries, they were "crown servants." Under U.K. law, attorneys could not depose them without the consent of the government departments for which they worked. That meant seeking permission from the British Defense Department for Feraday and the Department of Transportation for Charles and Clayden. In addition, everything had to be cleared through Norman McFadyen and Jim MacDougall to preserve the integrity of the criminal investigation.

Getting an answer from either department turned into a Herculean task. Lee had to negotiate with the general counsel for each agency,

Help from the Criminal Investigation

who seemed to take forever to reply. When they finally did, they insisted that the witnesses not appear in person but give their testimony based on written questions. James Shaughnessy objected, and Lee was not happy about it either, but Judge Platt approved the process.

In due course, the attorneys for the U.K. Embassy in Washington, D.C., contacted Lee and presented him with a choice. Agree to take the testimony via written questions or don't take it at all. Neither plaintiff nor defense attorneys could be present during the depositions, but U.K. lawyers in Washington, D.C., would be. Lee and the Plaintiffs Committee would submit direct questions. Shaughnessy and his team would submit cross-examination questions. After a tight review, some of the questions would be allowed. On top of it all, Lee and the Plaintiffs Committee had to pay $70,000 in fees for lawyers they did not want or need.

Feeling like the British government had put a gun to his head, Lee agreed to all terms. Somehow, he and his colleagues would get what they needed. The depositions would sound stilted when read to the jury but would go a long way to prove the plaintiffs' case.

Mick Charles and Peter Clayden's testimony established that the explosion's center was located in the second level of bags of container 4041. That proved the bomb had been in one of the Frankfurt interline bags.

Feraday reinforced that conclusion and provided additional information: the bomb was a plastic Semtex material. More significantly, he helped identify the clothing and other materials in the bomb suitcase, which he had given to Detective Chief Inspector Harry Bell.

That established the link to the second point Lee and the Plaintiffs Committee needed to prove. Bell was the detective who took bits and pieces of the clothing to Malta and traced them to a small retail shop named Mary's House in Sliema, a seaside suburb of the capital Valetta. Two weeks before the bomb exploded, Tony Gauci, the owner, sold an assortment of clothes and an umbrella to Abdelbaset Al-Megrahi, one of the defendants named in the Scottish and American indictments.

Because of his critical and sensitive role, Bell had not been called as a witness at the Fatal Accidents Act Inquiry. Although Lee had requested him when he and his team took the deposition of Russell, Henderson, and Boyd in Dumfries, Lord Advocate Frazer had not allowed it.

Lee felt that his testimony was crucial. But getting permission for him to be deposed would take another two-and-a-half months.

19

ANOTHER ATTEMPT TO SETTLE

December 1991—February 1992

On December 4, 1991, Pan American World Airways ceased operation for good. Following the bankruptcy filing, it sold its routes, planes, and ground equipment to other airlines. It was a sad day for the United States and its premier transatlantic carrier. An American brand name as familiar as Kodak and Coca-Cola, Pan Am had been the flagship of U.S. air travel, leading the world into the jet age in the 1950s and launching Boeing's iconic 747. And now it was gone.

Many of the victims' families called, worried about the impact on the case. Lee had to repeatedly explain that the bankruptcy would not affect their suit. The airline and its subsidiary, Alert Management, were still defendants in the civil case, and any money paid to the victims' families would come from the coffers of USAU, Pan Am's insurance company.

On January 10, 1992, Lee and members of the Plaintiffs Committee attended a pretrial conference in Brooklyn before Judge Platt to discuss the upcoming trial and jury selection. James Shaughnessy brought his team of lawyers on behalf of the defense. John Connors, representing the United States government, also appeared.

The gathering was too large for the judge's chambers, so the conference took place in one of the smaller courtrooms. After consulting his calendar, Judge Platt informed everyone that the trial would begin on April 27, 1992, a little over three months from then. He would assemble a pool of 550 jurors, from which the plaintiffs' and defendants' attorneys would select a jury.

At some point, he looked at James Shaughnessy and said, "The plaintiffs' attorneys have filed considerable additional evidence. Based on that and other considerations, I will not take the case away from the jury. I urge you to consider other ways of settling this matter."

Shaughnessy clenched his jaw. Then he announced, "Your Honor, until there is a finding of willful misconduct which caused this crash, there will be no settlement."

Lee rose from his seat and, choosing his words deliberately, said, "Your Honor, given the preponderance of evidence, I want to note that the defense's attitude is unreasonable."

As expected, he received a quick, nasty glance from Shaughnessy. Lawyers generally have thick skins, but impugning their ability to reason or be reasonable does not sit well with them.

Satisfied that he had provoked a reaction, Lee returned to the Kreindler & Kreindler office to strategize with the team on how best to prepare for the trial. Everyone agreed that the testimony of Detective Harry Bell was crucial. So, Lee took it upon himself to telephone Lord Fraser in Edinburgh. After exchanging pleasantries about each other's families and discussing what it would take to bring the two Libyans to trial, Lee turned the conversation to Detective Bell.

"We really need his testimony," he said. "He is the linchpin in our chain of causation."

The line went silent for a moment. Then Lord Fraser said, "I will think about it."

Lee thanked him and hung up. He told Jim who was in the room with him, "At least he didn't say no."

* * *

Another Attempt to Settle

On January 15, 1992, James Shaughnessy sent a letter to the Federal District Court indicating that John Brennan would like to meet with Judge Platt and Lee to explain the defendants' position. Brennan asked that no other lawyers be present. That was an unusual request and revealed to Lee another layer of Shaughnessy's reaction during the pre-trial conference. It was obvious that like a puppet master Brennan was running the show from behind the scenes, and Shaughnessy resented it. This begged the question: Had something happened to change Brennan's attitude? Could the case finally be settled?

Pleased that poking the bear had roused the USAU president from his lair, Lee wrote a note to Judge Platt applauding the move. He also sent a personal letter to Brennan, thanking him for suggesting the meeting.

Lee compiled a list of the victims' families, breaking them down into dependency and non-dependency cases. If Brennan or Judge Platt were inclined to settle, he was ready to suggest numbers. Lee was confident that the cases could be resolved at a reasonable level if Brennan responded positively.

A week later, Lee arrived for the meeting at the U.S. District Courthouse in Brooklyn. It was a bitterly cold day, and a freezing wind greeted him as he got out of the taxi at Cadman Plaza. He was glad to get inside and take the elevator up to Judge Platt's office. John Brennan arrived while Lee was hanging up his scarf and overcoat. He greeted Lee curtly, and the clerk ushered them into the judge's chambers. As in many New York City buildings, the central heat was turned up high, making the atmosphere stuffy and uncomfortably warm. Lee felt the sweat build up inside his shirt and jacket soon after he entered the room. He and Brennan sat at opposite ends of the plush sofa in a nook surrounded by mahogany bookcases filled with leather-bound law books.

Judge Platt sat in a straight chair opposite them, just a few feet away. He looked at Brennan, and said, "You called for this meeting. You have the floor."

The head of USAU leaned forward and smiled cordially. "Lee and I have a long professional relationship and have settled many cases amicably. I have even turned over sensitive material voluntarily to him."

He mentioned the Applegate memo in the 1974 Turkish Airlines disaster, when the rear cargo door of a DC-10 jet blew open. The crash had occurred near Paris, killing all 346 people aboard. Two years earlier, a General Dynamics product engineer named J.D. Applegate had warned in a memo that such a disaster was "inevitable" unless the company redesigned the cabin floor of the plane it manufactured for McDonnell Douglas. His warning was ignored, and that memo became a crucial factor in the liability suit. The case was eventually settled for more than $60 million paid to 1,123 claimants worldwide.

Brennan cleared his throat and addressed Judge Platt, "I want to correct the impression from the January 10 conference that the defendants acted unreasonably."

He proceeded to justify not settling, relying mainly on the testimony of Kurt Maier, the Frankfurt X-ray operator. "Maier was warned to look out for Toshiba bombs. He did not see a radio cassette player that day," Brennan said. "All experts agree that X-ray search is the most effective means of detecting a bomb." He concluded, "My refusal to settle is not capricious. There is good reason for it because the plaintiffs can't prove a case. If I were shown evidence that the plaintiffs could, we would settle immediately."

Lee nearly fell off the sofa. It was a brazen performance of misrepresentation and deception, worthy of an Academy Award. But he contained his indignation and addressed Judge Platt calmly, "I am amazed by what Mr. Brennan stated about Kurt Maier's testimony and the capacity of X-rays to detect a bomb. Both are contrary to the evidence.

Maier, on cross-examination, clearly testified that he did *not* remember if there were any radio cassette recorders in the Pan Am 103 bags that day. He was not given either the Toshiba or Helsinki warning. He did not routinely stop bags with recorders, only if they 'looked suspicious.'"

He faced Brennan. "You know as well as I that no experts agree that X-rays are the best means of detecting a bomb. The FAA Security Bulletins for the Toshiba and Helsinki warning pointed out that a radio cassette bomb would be very difficult to detect by normal X-ray inspection. That's why ACSSP XV C(1)(a) requiring positive match and removal of an unaccompanied bag had to be 'rigorously applied.' Pan Am did not do that."

He took a folder from his briefcase and spread the contents on the coffee table before him—Bogomira Erac's computer printout, the Station 206 worksheet, and photographs of the Frankfurt FAG facility. Then, he carefully explained what the plaintiffs would prove at the trial.

When Lee finished, Judge Platt examined the assembled evidence. Then he looked up at Brennan and said, "I urge you to consider settlement. From what I've seen here, the case will go to the jurors, and I will not interfere in their deliberations. If I tried to take the case away from them, the Second Circuit would reverse me." He stared hard at Brennan. "From my experience, the jury will find for the plaintiffs, and the verdicts for damages will be very high."

Flushing red, with beads of sweat pearling on his forehead, Brennan responded, "I'd like to review everything Lee has outlined and discuss it with my lawyers and advisers. If I have missed anything, I am prepared to settle." He turned to Lee. "Please send me your supporting material. Based on my review, I think another meeting like this is desirable."

Judge Platt nodded and said, "Let's talk about specific settlement numbers. How many cases are there? What are they worth?

Lee took off his glasses and leaned back. "The collective value of the jury verdicts is likely to run at least two to three hundred million dollars." He glanced at Brennan sitting close-lipped at the other end of the sofa and continued, "I would recommend three-quarters of that if the cases could be settled now."

The judge said, "I think these numbers are reasonable. However, if you agree to settle, I will try to get the plaintiffs to take less."

Brennan replied, "Thank you, Your Honor. I will take it into consideration."

After the meeting adjourned, Lee took a cab back to his office. Once again, he was perplexed. Brennan's obstinacy made no sense, not in the face of the overwhelming evidence of Pan Am's willful misconduct. There had to be something else at play.

But, as promised, he faxed a letter to Brennan, attaching the pages of Maier's deposition that showed he did not remember whether or not there were radio cassette recorders in the luggage he X-rayed.

He followed up the next day with a detailed letter, providing additional relevant Maier testimony. He attached the computer printout of Flight 103's baggage in tray 8849, clearly marking the thirteen interline bags, including the unaccompanied suitcase from Air Malta. He also enclosed Detective Henderson's report, which showed twelve identified interline bags plus the unidentified bomb bag. Finally, he appended FAA Security Bulletin 88-19, which warned that "it would be extremely difficult to detect a bomb by use of X-ray."

In his cover letter, Lee stated:

> *If I may be candid, John, the statement you made that all experts agree that X-ray was the best means of defense against a bomb is nonsense in the face of the warnings by the FAA in November 1988 that X-ray was ineffective. Reconciliation of bags to passengers was the best defense against a bomb, and the FAA required it!*
>
> *Pan Am's failure to perform the mandatory positive match procedure in the face of these specific directions and its*

> *reliance on X-ray in the face of specific notice that it was extremely difficult to detect Toshiba-type bombs by normal X-ray constitutes strong evidence of willful misconduct.*

A week later, Lee sent Brennan another letter enclosing documents from Pan Am witnesses James Berwick and Martin Hübner, the security directors at Heathrow and Frankfurt. They both stated that X-raying was unreliable and that positive match shouldn't be abandoned. Lee included deposition testimony from Hübner that "the decision by management to discontinue completely all interline baggage reconciliation was not a good decision." In addition, he provided a five-page narrative of how the bomb got on the airplane, identifying the evidence that proved each point, and concluded, "I would like to sit down with you personally to discuss settlement of these cases."

On February 6, John Brennan telephoned Lee and said bluntly, "The bottom line is that I am not able to settle. The case will have to be tried. I believe the jury will find for the defense." He added, "I'm sorry, Lee, but I don't have an alternative. The deaths were caused by a crime. I will not pay more than $100,000 for any passenger."

Lee had expected this outcome. So, when Brennan suggested they should meet again before the judge, he agreed but insisted, "I think this time Jim Shaughnessy should be there."

Three weeks later, Brennan, Shaughnessy, and Lee met with Judge Platt in chambers. This time, the USAU president and Shaughnessy occupied the sofa, and Lee sat on his own chair. The air was as suffocating as before, and Lee felt ill at ease.

Brennan started in right away. "I won't settle. I have met with the witnesses. I did my own investigation. Mr. Kreindler won't prove that anything Pan Am did caused the bomb to get on the aircraft."

Shaughnessy chimed in, "The problem with the plaintiffs' evidence is Maier. We will prove that Maier did not see a radio cassette player. They won't be able to prove otherwise by admissible evidence."

Judge Platt sighed and looked at each of the participants in turn. Then he reiterated what he said in the earlier meeting, "I won't take this case away from the jury."

An awkward silence descended on the room. Lee rubbed his forehead. Although he had not expected a settlement, he was disappointed. Brennan and Shaughnessy sat with their arms crossed in defiance, staring straight ahead.

After a moment, Judge Platt continued, "Let's turn to the testimony of the experts. I have read the reports of the plaintiffs' experts but have not seen any by the defendants. They were due today."

Shaughnessy spoke up. "We just served them and filed them with your clerk, Your Honor. We will –"

Lee interrupted, "We received the reports and looked them over, Your Honor. None of their witnesses is an airline security expert. None has any knowledge of the facts of Lockerbie. They intend to testify that terrorism is war and that only governments can fight wars, propositions that are irrelevant to any issues pertaining to the case."

Judge Platt seemed taken aback. He addressed Brennan directly, "If that is so, we may have to take their testimony outside the presence of the jury."

The USAU president looked as if he was about to explode. "Your Honor –"

The judge held up his hand, silencing him. "I will review your reports and make my decision later," he said curtly. "In the meantime, the 550 potential jurors will report tomorrow to fill out questionnaires. The trial will start on April 27, as scheduled. That will be all."

That concluded the last attempt to reach a settlement, three years after the case had been filed! Lee felt that he and the Plaintiffs Committee had gone out of their way to be reasonable, doing everything possible to prove their case while the defense kept stonewalling. It was time to go to trial and to win.

20

MONEY ISSUES

March—April 1992

Meanwhile, Lord Fraser telephoned Lee about his request to depose Detective Constable Harry Bell. "I'm willing to allow some form of testimony," he said. "You must write a letter to Norman McFadyen, suggesting a procedure that will protect the criminal investigation and set forth the precise scope of the testimony you want."

Lee notified James Shaughnessy of his intent to depose Bell and proposed they work out the terms with the Lord Advocate's assistant. His opponent, recognizing the importance of the testimony, demanded broad and unrestricted cross-examination.

When Lee contacted McFadyen, it quickly became apparent that the Lord Advocate would not agree to those terms. It didn't help that Jim MacDougall, the main prosecutor of the Lockerbie criminal case, was appalled at the prospect of allowing Bell to testify.

With a firm trial date of April 27, 1992, time was running out, and Lee was starting to despair. Unable to get agreement from all parties, he proceeded under the Hague Convention rules and sent Letters of Request for Bell's testimony to Scotland. He kept things simple and limited his questions to the essential information for the trial.

Shaughnessy filed his own request asking for a broad range of cross-examination questions.

It was less than a month before the start of the trial, and Lee was busier than ever. Not only was he preparing his opening statement and trial book, but he also had to field an increasing volume of phone calls from the victims' families who were getting anxious and needed his reassurance.

On top of that, the delaying strategy of USAU and Pan Am's defense attorneys put severe financial pressure on his law firm.

One morning, Pat Robinson came into Lee's office. Her pursed lips told him that something was up.

"I have bad news, Mr. Lee," she announced. "Our bank accounts are running so low that they won't cover payroll at the end of this month. We tried some other banks again, but none of them will come to our rescue."

Lee surprised her with grim chuckle. Then he said, "Ah, the curse of Lockerbie continues." It was gallows humor in the face of yet another impending disaster at the worst possible time.

"I'm glad you can laugh about it," Pat said. "But this is serious."

"I know that," Lee replied.

Everyone at the firm had been tightening their belt for the past three years, limping along financially, laboring under the constant tension of the ongoing litigation. While three partners and several associates, paralegals, and secretaries worked on the Lockerbie case, the rest of the legal and non-legal staff carried the burden of the firm's remaining caseload. They had to bring in the fees to cover the cost of lawyers and staff traveling back and forth to other cities and countries to attend hearings and take nearly 180 depositions, which ran to more than 22,000 pages. Lee alone had flown to Europe 25 times. Altogether, the firm had laid out more than $3 million.

The strain on everyone's workload and the financial struggle took their toll. Not only did Lee have to ask the staff to put in long hours, but the partners could not give annual raises or bonuses.

They could not even promise to reward the exceptional service at some point in the future. The firm had to rely on loyalty and dedication to keep people aboard.

One newly minted partner, who had earned over $100,000 a year as an associate, made only $10,000 in 1990, his first year in his new position. He borrowed money against his life insurance policy to make ends meet.

For some employees, it was asking too much, and they quit.

In time, additional staff reductions were inevitable, requiring painful, distressing decisions. The meeting where the partners voted to dismiss the bookkeeper was especially gut-wrenching. Everyone liked her, and she had a family to support.

The departure of some administrative aides and word-processing personnel put an extra burden on the remaining staff. Someone had to type up the briefs and correspondence and make copies for the other trials besides Lockerbie. No one got paid for the additional work.

Lee bore the brunt of many of those cost-cutting decisions personally. He felt it was his duty to participate in the exit interviews, explain the situation to people who had been loyal to the firm, and thank them. Most said they understood. None blamed him. But he felt their dejection and disappointment, which added to his already heavy emotional burden.

As Kreindler & Kreindler found it increasingly difficult to pay bills, its excellent reputation with financial institutions deteriorated. The firm's primary bank converted its line of credit into a loan. Other banks denied any requests for additional funds. The company's money manager had to rely on promissory notes. Once a note was paid back, he would request another. The banks required stringent oversight. They wanted to be appraised of disbursements and potential fees, questioned every expenditure, and demanded quarterly financial statements.

When the firm could no longer meet its commitment to its vendors, it engaged in "creative" accounting, robbing Peter to pay Paul. Many of them dropped their accounts. Others hung in based on good past relations and long-term friendships. Lee and the partners promised partial payment as soon as fees came in from successful litigations.

The kitchens on the two floors stocked only the most basic supplies—salt, pepper, sugar, plates, and cutlery. Soap bottles in the ladies' rooms and tissue boxes on everyone's desk were amenities of the past. Office supplies and materials were curtailed. There were no new magazine or legal journal subscriptions for the library. As equipment began to break down, it became impossible to replace it. Essential purchases were restricted to the cheapest products available and had to come from vendors that would still do business with the firm.

There were additional cutbacks. The firm eliminated staff benefits and raised its health insurance deductible. Monthly luncheons for lawyers to gather and exchange case information were a thing of the past. If people wanted to attend professional conventions or bar association meetings, they had to pay their own way. Weekly attorney lunches at 60 East Club were canceled or held in the conference room. The monthly staff birthday parties were discontinued. The annual Christmas gathering took place at the office rather than at a restaurant.

With every senior partner working overtime on litigations, day-to-day management disintegrated. Major decisions were put off or postponed indefinitely. "After we settle Pan Am" became the stock answer to all pressing issues.

Office morale sunk to an unprecedented low, even among people determined to see things through. The staff felt neglected and cheated. They congregated at photocopiers and in the two kitchens —water coolers were things of the past, too—sharing worries about their jobs and wondering if they would ever see the end of the firm's financial woes.

Lee did his best to keep up everyone's spirits. He knew that, as the captain of the ship, he had to set an example for everyone. If they thought his determination flagged, they would give up. So, he remained optimistic, joked with people, thanked them frequently for their efforts, and showed his appreciation.

At night, on the train home to Chappaqua, he felt bone-weary. Ruth could tell by the set of his sagging shoulders how trying his day had been and worried about the harm to his health. When Lee shared his despair with her, she did her best to cheer him up, and he always returned to the office with an upbeat, cheerful attitude.

So far, Kreindler & Kreindler had muddled along willy-nilly, weathering every financial challenge. But their remaining bank refusing to provide money to cover payroll was a crisis of a different magnitude.

As Lee digested the bad news, Pat asked, "What do we do now?"

"Get me an appointment with Kathleen Tarbell at Chemical Bank this afternoon," he said. Kathleen was a senior vice president with discretionary decision-making power.

After lunch, Lee took a taxi uptown to the bank's headquarters at 277 Park Avenue and announced himself to the receptionist in the lobby. Kathleen met Lee as he stepped off the elevator and invited him into her office.

As Lee explained the situation, she listened sympathetically—they had a good working relationship going back more than a decade —but she kept her arms crossed in front of her. Finally, she said, "Lee, you know I'd do anything I can for you, but I need some collateral. Without that, I can't help you."

On the way back to the Kreindler & Kreindler office, Lee reviewed his options. He could not solicit the victim's families again.

It was one thing to have asked them to chip in $5,000 apiece to cover the cost of the FAAI in Scotland. It was another to seek their help to keep the firm afloat for the trial and the inevitable appeals process.

When he got to his office, he told Pat, "Call a partners meeting."

As everyone assembled in the conference room, the air was charged with tension. By then, all the partners were aware of what was going on. When Lee explained that their bank would not give them anymore credit without collateral, he encountered a wall of silence.

"I know this is difficult and unprecedented, but I need your support," he said. "We're in desperate straits. The bank demands assurances before extending our credit. Who here can help and provide collateral?"

The silence deepened.

Lee looked around the room. None of the partners would meet his eyes. He felt a ringing in his ears.

Looking around at the exhausted, pained faces, Lee realized that most of them wanted to help but were too young to have the kind of assets required by the bank. They felt as helpless as he did. At least they did not challenge his determination to see the case through to the end. Folding his hands in front of him, he reached a decision. "Very well," he said. "I'll take care of it myself."

He got up and left the room.

That evening, when he arrived at his home in Chappaqua, Ruth immediately knew that something was wrong.

After a brief dinner, during which Lee poked at the food, they went into the living room and sat next to each other on the sofa. Lee told her all about what happened during the day. Then he took her hands and said, "I'm going to have to put up our house as collateral."

Ruth didn't pull back from him, but she felt a knot of fear tighten around her heart. The announcement did not come as a complete surprise. Because Lee always shared the bumps in the road, she knew all about the setbacks in the case and the firm's ongoing financial woes. But it upset her that Lee was the only one to bear the financial burden. The prospect of losing their home frightened her.

She had designed and built the house. Her children grew up in it. She remembered young Jim gingerly making his way down the cliffs in the rear of the property and, as he got older, practically leaping over the rocks as a youngster.

It was the house where her children brought all their friends, convened Boy and Girl Scouts meetings, and held just about every high school party, including after the senior proms. It was the place for large family get-togethers, gatherings of international visitors who attended conventions in New York, and fundraising parties for community projects. Jimmy and Laurie helped move all the furniture out to accommodate everyone and acted as junior hosts and hostesses at some of the tables.

She recalled climbing on the flat roof to retrieve a baseball one of the youngsters had hit there. Once up there, she was afraid to come down alone. Fortunately, the milkman arrived and steadied the ladder for her. He'd grinned and said, "Wait until I tell my boys I helped Mrs. Kreindler down from the roof."

A sigh escaped her lips. The Lockerbie litigation had already taken over their lives. What little socializing they did always related to the case. But this was about their home, and Lee was asking too much. Ruth did not want to do it. She would rather see the firm dissolve.

"Say something," Lee pleaded.

He looked so crestfallen that, despite her reluctance, Ruth could not deny him. "Honey, I love this house, but I love you more," she said. "Do what you must. But I am not happy about it."

"I'm not happy about it either, Ruthie," Lee replied. "But I've got a tiger by the tail, and I can't let go."

THE FIGHT FOR JUSTICE

The next day, Lee met with Kathleen Tarbell at Chemical Bank and restored the firm's credit line. Two weeks later, an aviation case was settled out of court, and the fees allowed the firm to keep going without any further liens on Lee's residence. But the atmosphere around the office remained strained.

21

PROVING CAUSATION

April 1992

There was one positive development among the setbacks, financial challenges, and day-to-day frustrations. Word came that the Scottish Court of Records agreed to let the deposition of Detective Constable Bell go forward. By a stroke of luck, Norman McFadyen was the official who dealt with Letters of Request under Scottish law. Knowing the urgency of the case, he expedited matters, agreed to Lee's terms, and denied Pan Am's request for unlimited questions.

Through Scottish counsel, James Shaughnessy appealed to the Court of Records for review. Over the objections of the Lord Advocate, that court permitted some of his wider ranging questions. It further ordered that the approved list of questions be put to the witness in Dumfries by Sheriff Jack Mowat, who had presided over the Fatal Accidents Act Inquiry.

Lee was delighted and eager to proceed. Although he could not ask the questions himself, he was determined to attend the hearing in Dumfries. He had worked to get this testimony for well over a year. He also wanted potential jurors for the civil trial to know he went there. The deposition would get international coverage, and Lee figured that many in the jury pool would hear about it.

On April 14, he flew to Glasgow. He rented a car and visited Felicity Hughes, as he always did when he was in Scotland. She invited him for dinner—haggis, mashed potatoes, and neeps (turnips). She and the children were coping with Michael's death as well as could be expected, although the lines etched on her face had deepened. "I think of him every day," she admitted, tears welling in her eyes.

Lee reached out and covered her hand with his in sympathy. "It will take time," he said, "but things will be all right." He wished he could give her more than boilerplate reassurances.

In the morning, Lee drove to the Sheriff's Court in Dumfries. It was rainy and windy, and Lee had to pay special attention during the two-hour journey because he was unfamiliar with roundabouts and driving on the "wrong" side of the road.

A slew of reporters and television trucks milled near the entrance of the municipal building. Some shouted questions at Lee as he walked up the steps to the entrance, but he ignored them and went straight inside. Sheriff Principal Mowat was already in the room, poised to preside and present the questions. He and Lee greeted each other with a formal handshake.

Detective Constable Bell arrived wearing his dress uniform. He was in his late 30s, with reddish brown hair, hazel-colored eyes, and a ready smile. Lee had met him at the inquiry and liked him immediately. He understood why Bell had been chosen to go to Malta and to get the people there to cooperate.

As Mowat asked the questions Lee had submitted, he allowed Bell to elaborate and embellish. His testimony was stellar.

The detective described how he had taken bits and pieces of clothing and other materials from the wreckage to Malta and visited different manufacturing plants. For example, he brought remnants of a shirt with a "Yorkie" label to the Yorkie factory, where a manager confirmed that it had been made there. No one had interviewed him before, and he wanted to be helpful. Combing through company records, he matched the items to a particular job lot. That allowed Bell to trace it to a retail shop called "Mary's House" in Sliema. The same thing happened with clothing items at other manufacturing companies as well.

Bell then described his interview with Tony Gauci, the proprietor of Mary's House, who had sold the goods to a Libyan man, later identified as Abdelbaset al-Megrahi, one of the two terrorists indicted for the bomb attack on Pan Am Flight 103. Gauci remembered the transaction as unforgettable because the buyer did not care about the size of the items and made his choices indiscriminately.

It all added up to an undeniable fact: The bomb had originated in Malta!

The cross-examination questions from James Shaughnessy did nothing to undermine that finding.

When Bell finished his testimony, Lee felt like doing a jig for joy. He imagined that, for once, he would have rivaled Ruth's elegant, energetic dancing at a ballroom competition.

The timeline was now complete. The plaintiffs had proof that the unaccompanied bomb bag originated in Malta and arrived in Frankfurt on Air Malta Flight KM180. Coded into the FAG baggage conveyance system there, it was delivered to Pan Am Flight 103's staging area. From there, baggage handler Kiling Tuzcu took it to Kurt Maier's X-ray machine and later loaded it onto the Boeing 747 bound for London.

At Heathrow Airport, the suitcase was transferred without any inspection onto the second level of bags in Container 4041 of the Boeing 747. The bomb inside exploded over Lockerbie at 7:02 p.m., destroying the 747, killing all aboard and 11 people on the ground.

Lee knew that, without Lord Fraser's help, the plaintiffs would never have gotten this critical testimony, and he conveyed his appreciation in a phone call afterward.

Back in New York, as he prepared for the opening day of the trial, Lee was as confident as he had ever been that he would win this case.

* * *

Meanwhile, an important development occurred in the District Court in Brooklyn. John Connors made a Rule 56 motion asking for a summary judgment to remove the U.S. government as a third party from the defense.

When Pan Am's lawyers were unable to present any concrete evidence of the government's involvement in the Lockerbie disaster, Judge Platt granted the motion.

The civil case was now an exclusive contest between Lee and the Plaintiffs Committee and Pan Am and USAU.

22

MORE DISINFORMATION

Late April 1992

The *TIME* magazine cover was dramatic on a black backdrop. A stacked headline in bold blue letters appeared next to the image of the battered cockpit section of a Boeing 747 crashing to Earth. It read:

**THE
UNTOLD
STORY OF
PAN AM
103**

"Maid of the Seas" was visible above the blue stripe of the windows section. The lead article, "PAN AM 103 Why Did They Die?" promised a new explanation of how the terrorists' bomb made it onto the airplane.

The issue was dated April 27 but came out a week earlier. Anticipatory coverage appeared on all major television networks over the weekend prior to April 20. Someone had gone to great lengths to make sure the magazine received maximum promotion before hitting the newsstands.

The timing could not have been worse for Lee and the Plaintiffs Committee. The start of the trial was just a week away, and the

TIME article exposed the 550 prospective jurors to a slew of half-truths and outright lies.

Although Lee felt outraged, he was not surprised. He expected something to happen close to the start of the trial to distract the public. He was certain that Pan Am's defense team—with James Shaughnessy acting at the behest of John Brennan—had planted news stories before. But this scheme was more blatant and shameless than he'd imagined, a deliberate attempt to prejudice the jurors ahead of time.

There had been warnings as early as November the year before. One came when Lee received a telephone call from Jeannine Boulanger. In her characteristic brusque manner, she came straight to the point. "Is it true that *TIME* magazine has hired Yuval Aviv?" she asked.

"That's news to me," Lee told her, surprised. "But I'll look into it."

In December, Lee got a call from a reporter working on a story for *TIME* magazine. Roy Rowan, the former editor-in-chief of *Life* magazine and a respected journalist, was doing research for a substantial piece on the Lockerbie disaster. Did Lee have a few minutes to talk to him? Lee immediately thought of the conversation he'd had with Boulanger.

Rowan arrived at the Kreindler & Kreindler offices two hours later. Tall and thin, he cut a suave figure. Under his Harris tweed jacket, he wore a stylish argyle sweater, looking like someone on holiday in the Scottish Highlands.

As Lee shook his hand, he said, "I heard that *TIME* has employed Yuval Aviv. "

Rowan immediately became defensive. "Well…I have interviewed Aviv," he said warily. "But we haven't employed him…as far as I know."

"Why would you even talk to him?" Lee challenged as he gestured to the chair in front of his desk. "He's a proven phony and a liar."

More Disinformation

Taking a seat, Rowan ventured, "Oh, I think that remains to be seen. Nobody really knows how the bomb got on the airplane."

"That's nonsense, Mr. Rowan."

Facing the reporter across the desktop, cleared of all documents, Lee outlined what the plaintiffs would demonstrate at the trial: that the bomb bag was an interline suitcase from Air Malta delivered to Pan Am 103 in Frankfurt.

Rowan asked a lot of questions based on information that could only have come from Yuval Aviv and Lester Coleman. That indicated to Lee the reporter was up to no good.

Another warning bell went off when Rowan wanted to know when the trial would begin. Lee told him, "If you publish Aviv's theories or Lester Coleman's garbage, it will be a very serious matter."

After Rowan left, Lee said to Pat Robinson, "Keep an eye and ear out for him. If that bastard calls again and asks about the start of the trial, please put him on the phone with me. I think he's in cahoots with the defense. Knowing them, they will try to do something devious."

Then, he got busy with the case and forgot all about it.

But Pat did not. She made a note of it. When Rowan called Kreindler & Kreindler again on April 6 and asked, "Is the trial date still April 27?" she said, "I think Lee would like to talk to you about that."

When Lee got on the line, he asked, "Why do you want to know the trial date?"

Rowan said, "Well, I'm just curious."

Lee pressed, "Are you going to go forward with your phony story?"

The reporter wavered, "Well, I don't know."

Lee said pointedly, "Mr. Rowan, you had better get your ass over here right now. There are some documents I am going to show you! Our trial starts in three weeks, and the publication of your article will ruin it. I will show you documents and testimony to make clear to you that Aviv is a liar, and you must not go with that story."

"I'll be there in half an hour," Rowan promised.

Lee called Jim and Steve Pounian on the intercom and asked them to join him in his office. When they got there, he told them what was happening. "I want you as witnesses to the fact that *TIME* knows the truth, no matter what they print," he said.

Rowan arrived, looking spiffy. He was surprised to face a reception committee but recovered quickly. By then, Lee had the key documents for the trial spread out on the table—the computer printout from Frankfurt, the worksheets for Station 206, the code sheet, and the testimony of the coders. He invited Rowan to look them over while he and the others hovered in the background.

By the time Rowan finished reading, his complexion had turned sallow. "It's impressive evidence," he admitted.

"Okay, are you going to print the story?" Lee asked.

"It's not up to me," Rowan said, raising his eyebrows apologetically.

"Come on, Rowan, you know that your story is phony."

Red-faced, the reporter reiterated, "It's not up to me."

He left, casting a final glance at the documents on the table, like someone who knows he's about to commit a wrongheaded act.

When he was gone, Lee, Jim, and Steve looked at each other.

"Trouble brewing," Steve said tersely.

Two weeks later, Lee was at his computer in Chappaqua, working on his opening statement to the jury, when the father of one of the victims telephoned from England. Robert Dorchester had heard about an upcoming cover story in *TIME* magazine and gotten hold of a copy of a rough draft.

To drum up advance publicity for the article, *TIME* had sent an early version of the article to the CBS Television office in the U.K., along with a press release titled "Wrong Suspects May Be Sought in

More Disinformation

Pan Am 103 Case." The finished piece would become available on Saturday, April 18, for the magazine's release on the newsstands the following Monday.

Lee immediately dropped what he was doing and paced around his home office until a fax from Dorchester arrived. As expected, the article was written by Roy Rowan and promised, "A four-month investigation by *TIME* has uncovered evidence that raises new questions about the case."

When Lee read the piece, he was appalled. As a *TIME* cover story, it was extremely damaging to the plaintiffs' case.

Rehashing the Yuval Aviv-Lester Coleman conspiracy fairy tales about Syrian arms traffickers, Palestinian terrorists, and American hostages in Lebanon, it did not contain a kernel of truth. Rowan ginned up the story by introducing an American CIA-operated unit known as COREA, which supposedly trafficked in "drugs and arms to gain access to terrorist groups." He mentioned several mysterious Americans, including a possible double agent named David Lovejoy and a Pan Pam pilot flying to Pakistan whose two suitcases ended up on Flight 103. Except that one was switched during loading with a "rogue bag" originating in Cyprus.

What happened to the displaced suitcase? And how did the rogue bag containing the bomb elude the Frankfurt Airport security system? Aviv had no idea. However, the article repeated the lie detector incident with the Frankfurt baggage handlers, Kiling Tuzcu and Roland O'Neil, and concluded that there was enough evidence to support the rogue bag theory.

Lee was astonished. The polygraph episode was one of the most incredible in the whole case. The German government had threatened to arrest James Shaughnessy on criminal kidnapping charges for what he did. And there was simple proof that the accusations were just so much hot air. Both Tuzcu and O'Neill went back to work for Pan Am and continued in their jobs loading baggage onto passenger flights after Delta purchased the bankrupt airline's routes, hangars, and terminals.

Afterward, Pan Am's defense attorneys never claimed a suitcase had been switched. They stated on the record that they did not know how the bomb got on the airplane.

Lee imagined that Rowan must have been paid handsomely to produce such a thorough hack job. The reporter even mentioned him by name: "Lee Kreindler, the lead attorney for the victims' families, is suing Pan Am for $7 billion." That claim was especially galling. Lee had explicitly told Rowan that the total value of the cases had been variously estimated from $250 to $500 million. Pan Am's insurance policy protected the airline up to a maximum of $750 million.

There was one new item regarding Lester Coleman. The article suggested that the former DEA spy had spotted a newspaper picture of one of the Pan Am Flight 103 victims, a young Lebanese American, and recognized him as one of his drug-running informants. That gave him the idea to approach Pan Am—he was looking for work—and led to the affidavit claiming a narcotics sting operation. James Shaughnessy had used that to subpoena FBI, CIA, DEA, and other government agency officials, although without success.

While Lee had suspected for some time that Coleman was the source of much of the conspiracy nonsense, Pan Am had repeatedly denied it had anything to do with him. Thanks to *TIME* magazine and an apparent slip by Shaughnessy, there was no longer any doubt. He and his client, USAU, planted the lies in the media, using Lester Coleman as their key witness. The lengths to which the defense manipulated matters a week before the trial began were shameless and obscene.

By the time he finished reading the article, Lee was so furious that he wanted to crumple up the pages and throw them against the wall. But he channeled his anger and wrote a letter to Judge Platt to address the bogus claims and seek redress for the victims' families:

> *Dear Chief Judge Platt:*
>
> *In* TIME *magazine, dated April 27, 1992 (the opening date of our trial), which reached the newsstands today but was highly publicized on radio and TV starting Saturday afternoon, April 18, there appears a long cover story. It contains the most shocking and most prejudicial false information about the Lockerbie story that one can imagine. Bearing directly on the upcoming trial, it appears to have been given to* TIME *by the defendants.*

Lee attached two copies of the magazine. One was a clean issue. In the other, he marked specific sections of the article and referenced them for further discussion. He also attached an annotated copy of the press release *TIME* magazine had sent out on Saturday to publicize the piece.

In a detailed 46-point analysis, Lee refuted each phony claim. He did not hide his disdain for the defendants and their unethical behavior. For the page that contained the blatantly false assertion that the U.S. government was responsible for the bombing, he recommended that the court consider asking Shaughnessy to autograph a copy for John Connors.

The letter continued:

> *And now: on the very eve of trial, after the jury panel of 550 men and women have filled out lengthy questionnaires, and after a tremendous amount of time and money has been spent by plaintiffs' counsel in studying the panel and striking many of them, this article appears containing inadmissible and highly prejudicial evidence that is bound to poison the mind of every juror picked.*
>
> *The plaintiffs do not want to give up the April 27 trial date. We have been worn out physically and financially drained by*

> *the unconscionable conduct of the defendants. But we don't see how we can get a fair trial from a jury taken from this panel.*
>
> *Plaintiffs, therefore, move, through this letter, to strike the jury panel and convene a new panel as soon as possible, hopefully within two weeks.*

Lee further called for an evidentiary hearing on leaking information to *TIME* magazine and Roy Rowan, requiring all the parties to testify—Yuval Aviv, Lester Coleman, James Shaughnessy, John Brennan, Russell Mirabile, and others. He wanted the hearing to look into the origins of the article and its promotion, any compensation paid for it, and the timing of its publication coinciding with the beginning of the trial.

Plaintiffs also moved for sanctions, payable immediately, to partially defray past and present preparation and out-of-pocket expenses of $2 million.

The letter concluded,

> *We further request an order of the Court instructing the defendants that they are precluded from advancing any of the arguments in the* TIME *article that lack evidentiary basis, and a further instruction that they not be mentioned in opening statements, unless there be a prior proffer of proof.*
>
> *Plaintiffs request that this motion be set down for a hearing, at the convenience of the Court.*
>
> *Respectfully yours,*
>
> LEE S. KREINDLER,
Chairman, Plaintiffs Committee

Lee cc'd James Shaughnessy, John Connors, and all members of the Plaintiffs Committee.

When the *TIME* magazine issue hit the newsstands on April 20, it caused a media uproar. Once again, all major television news channels carried it, including CNN. Some showed the provocative cover on air. The outrageous claims of the story were debated at length with no acknowledgment that their author, Ron Rowan, had made most of it up.

On April 23, Chief Judge Platt convened a hearing to deal with the matter and addressed each point Lee had made. It was quite contentious and lasted most of the day. Despite *TIME* magazine letting the cat out of the bag, James Shaughnessy and the other defense attorneys continued to vehemently deny having had anything to do with its publication, the timing of the release, and the content.

But Lee had an ace up his sleeve.

The *TIME* article had received extensive publicity before its appearance. When ABC's news program *Nightline* devoted the entire hour to the piece, going into the story's details, Lee made a tape of it. The anchors repeated the Aviv-Coleman-*TIME* magazine scenario of the baggage handlers in Frankfurt switching suitcases and displayed alleged polygraph sheets as supporting documentation. They also showed a letter written to Lee by an assistant of the Lord Advocate of Scotland. Lee had sent the original, among other documents to Judge Platt and copies to the defense counsels. As he watched the show, he was surprised to see the letter and wondered how *Nightline* got hold of it.

At the hearing, Lee played the tape of the show. Then, he brandished the letter and said, "Your Honor, just fifteen minutes ago, I asked your clerk to check the docket to see if it had ever been filed. He checked and it wasn't."

He decided to have some fun and continued, "I said, 'I doubt if you gave it to *Nightline*. I guarantee I didn't give it to them. Mr. Shaughnessy said it wasn't him. So, it must be Mr. Connors here."

When everybody chuckled, he added, "Of course, this is proof positive that all the nonsense on *Nightline*, including this letter, emanated from the defense lawyers."

Caught red-handed, Shaughnessy sputtered about how the court's handling thousands of documents could have been the unwitting culprit. That earned him a stern rebuke from Judge Platt. "I run a tight ship, Mr. Shaughnessy. You do not advance your cause by impugning carelessness on the part of my staff."

Chastened, Shaughnessy apologized, "I'm sorry, Your Honor. I meant no disrespect."

Ultimately, Judge Platt was reluctant to grant the plaintiffs' petition to dismiss the jurors and start over. "If I grant your motion, we won't be able to get to trial for about two years," he said. "I set aside time for this case; this is the only time I can try it." After denying the motion, he promised, "The problem of the false magazine article will be dealt with through detailed voir dire of the jury." He also deferred the motion for an evidentiary hearing and sanctions of the defendants' insurance company and its lawyers.

Lee managed to extract an important concession, however. He had noticed the defense attorneys using buzzwords from the *TIME* article, such as "rogue bag" for the allegedly switched suitcase and "rush tags" for the luggage of the airline pilot. Lee was certain they would attempt to sway the jury with them. So, he asked for an order barring the defendants from using such buzzwords in the opening statement and witness examinations. Judge Platt granted the request.

Meanwhile, the *TIME* article dominated the news for the remaining week while its outrageous claims went unchallenged.

* * *

As with a lot of disinformation and fake news, it took some time for corrections to appear. On August 31, 1992, after the trial concluded, two major magazine cover stories that were highly critical of the *TIME* article appeared. One was published in *New York Magazine* by Chris Byron, and the other in the *American Journalism*

More Disinformation

Review by Steve Emerson. Both exposed *TIME* magazine as being taken in by a bogus tale concerning CIA and DEA involvement in the Lockerbie bombing. In debunking many of the article's falsehoods, they also laid bare the dubious backgrounds of Yuval Aviv and Lester Coleman.

Byron revealed that *TIME* never mentioned a potential conflict of interest: Yuval Aviv was working with Rowan on a book project regarding Lockerbie for *TIME*'s sister company, Warner Brothers, and had received substantial "seed money."

Perhaps the most amusing misstep *TIME* magazine took was including a passport-sized photograph in the article of a "reported double agent for the U.S. and Iran." The caption identified the man as "David Lovejoy." But it turned out that the person was Michael Schaffer, who owned a cleaning company in Atlanta, Georgia. Schaeffer had worked as a cameraman with Lester Coleman for the Christian Broadcasting Network in Lebanon in 1985. He had been best man at his wedding.

Coleman gave the photo, deliberately misidentified, to Pan Am's attorneys to bolster his made-up conspiracy stories. He figured they would fall for his fabrications without checking. He never dreamed that it would appear in *TIME* magazine. Like all the other lies Coleman peddled, the magazine's editors bought the attribution lock, stock, and barrel.

When Schaffer and his attorney complained about the accusation of being a terrorist, *TIME* ran a one-paragraph "correction" four weeks after the original Pan Am story.

On September 21, 1993, *New York Magazine* published another article, even longer than the first. In it, Chris Byron pointed the finger of responsibility for the many falsehoods directly at USAU. In subsequent columns, Byron provided more details of the background of Yuval Aviv and Lester Coleman. Finally, *60 Minutes*, the leading TV news magazine, followed up on the story in its program on December 20, exposing the gullibility of the *TIME* editors.

The gist of all these reports was that Pan Am's insurance company and defense lawyers cooked up the phony tale to avoid having to pay fair damages to the victim's families.

But at the time, Lee had to contend with a tainted jury pool. He could only hope that the facts and the chain of causation he and his team had painstakingly established would persuade the jurors to bring a "Guilty" verdict on behalf of the victim's families.

23

THE TRIAL BEGINS

Late April 1992

Two weeks before the start of the trial, Lee received a phone call at his office. Pat Robinson announced the caller over the intercom, "Clinton Coddington for you, Mr. Lee."

When he got on the line, Lee recognized the voice of his old nemesis right away—high-pitched, artificially jovial, with a West Coast inflection. They had been on opposite sides of the Air India trial a decade earlier.

In 1978, shortly after takeoff from Mumbai (then still called Bombay), a jumbo jet rolled over to the right and plunged into the Arabian Sea, killing all 231 passengers and flight personnel aboard. The partially recovered wreckage included the cockpit voice recorder, in which the desperate captain shouted that the attitude indicator was "toppled," meaning stuck. Because he could not rely on accurate readings, he overcompensated in the wrong direction, causing the disaster. After the victims' families settled with Air India—$75,000 per passenger according to the Warsaw Convention limits—they decided to sue Boeing, the aircraft builder, and Rockwell International, the manufacturer of the cockpit instruments.

Four years later, as lead counsel for the plaintiffs, Lee pursued the claim based on the recovered voice recorder indicating a serious system malfunction. Clinton "Bud" Coddington represented Boeing.

They argued the case in a West Coast Federal Court non-jury trial. Even though Lee had a pilot testifying that a similar system failure occurred on one of his flights, the judge dismissed the case. Since then, Lee and Bud Coddington had had no contact, professional or otherwise.

After saying hello, Coddington cheerfully announced, "I just wanted to tell you that I'll be the First Chair for Pan Am and Alert Management in the trial." He chuckled. "Give you a chance to even the score."

Lee was not about to engage in verbal fencing and mock the seriousness of the Pan Am case. He answered, "See you in court," and hung up.

But the phone call gave him pause. Pan Am, or most likely the insurance company and John Brennan, had replaced James Shaughnessy with Coddington as lead attorney. No doubt they intended to rattle Lee. Well, it was not going to work. This was a very different case. Still, Lee knew he had to be on guard. Coddington was a showman in the courtroom and not above using devious tactics.

Meanwhile, jury selection was already in progress.

The initial questionnaire, which was 35 pages long, had been argued over, debated, and negotiated by lawyers from both sides. It eliminated people who worked for airlines and supporting companies or had lost relatives in other plane crashes. Other issues, such as family hardship for a trial lasting longer than two months, whittled the pool from 550 to about 150 jurors.

Lee's main concern was that the *TIME* article had biased the remaining prospects. He tried to persuade Judge Platt to have them fill out another questionnaire to reveal how aware they were of the Pan Am case.

Instead, the judge asked the group, "Have any of you formed opinions that would make it impossible for you to be impartial?" Some hands went up.

Then, he asked, "Have any of you read any stories in the press or magazines or elsewhere?" More hands went up.

Judge Platt excused them, 65 people altogether.

But Lee was not satisfied. He proposed dismissing everyone who had a subscription to *TIME* or frequently read the magazine, even if they claimed not to have looked at the article about Lockerbie. That led to a heated exchange among plaintiff and defense attorneys. In any event, Judge Platt rejected the motion.

The Plaintiffs Committee had hired V. Hale Starr as jury consultant. As one of the pioneers in the field, she had considerable experience in damage litigation trials. Although she always dressed in a business suit, she had the ready, open smile and outgoing personality of a Midwesterner—she had grown up in South Dakota and spent much of her career in Iowa. Lee respected her expertise and sound judgment.

At one of the pretrial strategy sessions, Starr challenged the prevailing belief that the most advantageous jury for a civil case should consist of working-class people and minorities—tradesmen like plumbers and electricians, factory workers, and homemakers—because of their anti-corporation and anti-big business bias.

"Based on my research," she said, "the best jurors for the Pan Am trial are people used to dealing with rules and regulations—decision makers who will take seriously Pan Am's responsibility to follow government directives."

Lee and the other attorneys were intrigued and soon persuaded.

Using their preemptory challenges to dismiss prospects they did not like, the Plaintiffs Committee ended up with a mix of male and female jurors, ten Caucasian and two African Americans. They included the manager of the meat department of a Pathmark supermarket, a supervisor for the New York Board of Health, a subway train operator for the City Transit Authority, a legal secretary for the Dewey Ballantine law firm, a restaurant worker in the J.P. Morgan Bank building on Wall Street, a manager in an electrical company, and an insurance company representative.

Most of them were politically conservative Republicans. That was deliberate, too. In those days, Republicans were considered more serious about following rules and laws than Democrats. There were a few dark horse jurors whose views and preferences were hard to read. But overall, Lee and his fellow attorneys were pleased.

The other partners at Kreindler & Kreindler who were watching the trial thought Lee had gotten a terrible jury. Legal observers unfamiliar with jury research thought so, too. Whenever someone tried to commiserate with Lee, he did not let on how deliberate the selection had been. He just shrugged his shoulders and kept his own counsel.

Before every trial, Lee had a ritual. He visited the courtroom to get a feeling for the space. So, during lunch on the final day of jury selection, he went to the fourth floor of the courthouse, opened the heavy, wood-carved doors to courtroom number 7, the venue designated for the trial, and stepped inside.

It was a medium-sized room with an aisle between seating for spectators that led to the tables for the plaintiffs and the defendants. The walls were light brown wood paneling, as was the judge's bench. Mounted high on the wall behind the judge's chair was the large United States District Court seal. To the left, the American flag hung on a pole topped with a golden eagle. In front of it was the witness box, close to where the jurors would sit in two rows against the wall. A door at the rear led to the jury deliberation room. To the right of the judge's bench were seats for the court stenographer, bailiff, and clerk, who would record the testimony and take exhibits into evidence. Behind them was the exit to the judge's chambers.

The plaintiffs' attorneys would sit at the table to the left of the aisle, like the prosecution in a criminal trial. The defense table was on the right side. Between them, a few feet forward, stood a wooden podium from where attorneys would make their opening and closing statements to the jury and question the witnesses.

Lee walked around the room, not unlike an actor familiarizing himself with the stage where he would perform. He cleared his throat and clapped his hands twice to gauge the acoustics. There was a hint of an echo. He imagined it would disappear once people filled the room.

The image of Eichmann prosecutor Gideon Hausner flashed though his mind, and Lee recalled their conversation about the wider ramifications of a trial, beyond the immediate legal outcome. This case wasn't just about monetary compensation but airline safety and corporate accountability. Lee took a deep breath, nodded to himself, and returned to the jury selection floor.

* * *

There was one final thing to do in anticipation of the trial in Brooklyn Federal Court. He and Ruth moved into the Union League Club near the Kreindler & Kreindler office. Spending the nights there and returning to their home in Chappaqua only on weekends eliminated a daily two-hour commute each way.

Founded in 1836, the Union League Club was the oldest private social club in New York City. The dining and meeting rooms' plush, ornate furnishings reflected its history of catering to a conservative clientele. But the accommodations were like modern hotel rooms, with contemporary furnishings—a king-sized bed, sofa, armchair, working desk, and television.

Ruth packed family photos from home and a tape player for Lee's favorite music—K.D. Lang and Luciano Pavarotti—to help him relax after his stressful days in court. Lee never slept much during a trial and on this one, he got up early to read and hear what the British and Scottish newspapers and television programs had to say. Then, he and Ruth had breakfast in the club dining room. Afterward, Lee checked in at the office in person or by phone before taking a cab to the courthouse in Brooklyn.

Ruth attended the trial as much as possible and scheduled her commitments—ballroom dancing lessons and competitions, and board meetings for her charities—so she could be there for the most critical testimony.

Having worked on his opening statement for several weeks, Lee felt confident that he was ready. He knew how crucial it was to make a good impression by outlining the case well and establishing rapport with the jurors.

On April 27, he arrived early, took out his trial book, and placed it on the table before him. Tabbed and marked up with a multitude of colored sticky notes, his "bible" was an itemized compilation of all relevant discovery material and applicable laws. It summarized every aspect of what he wanted to prove and covered court rulings in prior cases and claims, facts, witness statements, and jury instructions.

Soon, his fellow attorneys arrived: Jim, both Granitos—Frank Jr and Frank III—Mitch Baumeister, and Steve Pounian. They nodded casually to one another, hiding the tension they all felt.

The defense table also filled up, with James Shaughnessy, Steve Fearon, and several other Pan Am attorneys. The rest of the enormous defense team occupied the row directly behind them. John Brennan of the USAU sat in the back of them, like a ruler overseeing his dominion, with Thomas Plaskett, the last president of Pan Am, at his side.

As Lee looked over at the defense squad, he was surprised to see Richard Sharp and his partner Fred Shaffrick from the law firm Shea & Gardner in Washington, D.C., join the lead lawyers at the table. He knew them by reputation not as litigators but appeals specialists. Was Pan Am anticipating losing the case already or just hedging its bets?

The Trial Begins

Clinton Coddington arrived last. About fifteen years younger than Lee, with chiseled features and an expensive haircut, he looked smart and dashing in his custom-tailored $2500 suit. After putting down his briefcase, he approached the spectators behind the table. He shook hands enthusiastically with John Brennan and Thomas Plaskett as if posing for photographers and the benefit of the audience.

Lee was amused. The show had begun. When Coddington returned to the defense table, he nodded to Lee with a curt smile but made no further effort to engage him. Lee gave a slight nod back.

As more spectators filed in, Lee acknowledged the relatives of those who had perished in the bombing. Many knew each other from the Victims Committee. Some exchanged hugs and chatted in muted conversations. In the back, various news reporters congregated, talking. Lee recognized some from the local New York newspapers. The trial was a big international case, and he imagined representatives from England, Scotland, and other nations were also in attendance.

Lee recognized John Connors taking a seat near some of the Kreindler & Kreindler partners. When he looked for Ruth, he found her sitting in the last row talking to Dona Bainbridge.

Soon, the courtroom was crowded with people, and an expectant buzz filled the air. But when the jurors filed in, everyone quieted and watched them take their seats. They seemed tense, staring straight ahead or looking down, not speaking to each other.

People resumed talking in low murmurs until the bailiff announced the entry of Judge Platt. Instantly, conversations came to a halt. All the attorneys at the plaintiffs and defense tables rose.

The district judge took his seat on the bench, banged his gavel, and looked out over the courtroom. After welcoming everyone, he turned to the jury and laid out the terms of a civil trial, explaining the process and what to expect.

"Unlike a criminal case, in which the prosecution must prove guilt beyond a reasonable doubt, in a civil trial the burden of proof is by what we call a preponderance of evidence," he said. "That's 50.0001 percent to 49.9999 percent. The burden of proof rests on the plaintiffs. At the conclusion of the case, you will be called on to render a unanimous verdict one way or the other."

He continued, "The plaintiffs have to prove what is known as willful misconduct on the part of the defendants, that willful misconduct caused the accident in this case, or that it was a proximate cause. So, keep an open mind until you've heard both sides."

Then Judge Platt introduced two people sitting to the side, near the defense table: Carla Martin, an attorney from the FAA's Office of Intelligence, and David Smith, an aviation security specialist. "They represent the government to make sure none of the testimony is classified, or if it is and needs to be kept secret, that the courtroom be cleared except for the jury, lawyers, and witnesses," he explained.

Before sending the jurors to lunch, Judge Platt warned them not to discuss the case with each other. He added, "When you return, the plaintiffs will begin with their opening remarks. They go first because they have the burden of proof."

When they jurors were gone, Judge Platt and the opposing attorneys addressed some "housekeeping" issues. Frank Granito, Jr wanted it made clear again that the defense could not use any terms from the *TIME* magazine article, such as "rogue bag," in the opening statement.

Judge Platt reinforced that demand. He also wanted to know where spectators were seated since there were many more victims' families than defense supporters. Everyone agreed they could sit as much as possible behind the respective tables, although there would be inevitable spillover.

Finally, Lee said, "I have just one question: is it your desire that I stand at the lectern?"

Judge Platt smiled and said, "You can stand anyplace you want except in the jury box. If you want to move the podium, you can move it."

"I think I would like to do that if you don't mind," Lee said.

Then the attorneys went to lunch. Lee did not eat much. Even after more than 30 years of practice, he still got nervous before his opening statement. Ruth squeezed his hand under the table.

As the courtroom filled for the afternoon session, it took some time for everyone to settle in, chatting with eager anticipation. Judge Platt arrived from his chambers and struck his gavel twice, quieting the room before starting the proceedings.

He reiterated to the jury that they would now hear opening statements from the plaintiffs and the defense, "Keep in mind that the opening statements are not evidence or proof, nor are the attorneys permitted to argue to you what they think the evidence will show," he said. "They are entitled to lay out what their proof will be so you can follow their case as they present it piecemeal." Then he turned to the plaintiffs' table. "All right, Mr. Kreindler."

Lee took a deep breath, rose, and went to the podium, which he had angled to face the jury. He took no notes with him.

For the next hour and a half, Lee outlined the case against Pan Am. Speaking casually, he told the jury that he and the Plaintiffs Committee had researched the case for over three-and-a-half years and taken 180 depositions in Europe and the United States.

He painted Pan Am's senior management as driven by profit rather than safety concerns. "The conditions, as you will soon learn, in Frankfurt, Germany, and elsewhere in the Pan Am system, were abominable," he said. "They were the product of corporate greed."

Lee discussed Pan Am's special advertising campaign, promising enhanced security at all airports and imposing a five-dollar charge on its trans-Atlantic flights to pay for it. "The airline netted eighteen million dollars a year in fees but did nothing to improve security," he said. "And so, as I said before, the conditions in Frankfurt, which was where the bomb got on the airplane, were abominable, shocking."

Bud Coddington rose to object. "Excuse me, your Honor. The continued use of words like abominable and shocking."

"Yes." Judge Platt admonished Lee. "Don't argue your points. Just tell us the facts."

Lee continued without responding to the interruption. He discussed the Helsinki warning that Oliver Koch found on his supervisor's desk the day after the disaster. And that when Koch confronted Ulrich Weber, his boss told him to shut up and forget it. A few days later, anticipating an FAA visit to see what had happened in Frankfurt, Weber took a stamp and back-dated the document to give the impression that he had distributed the warning.

"Totally false," Lee said. He and his team had discovered the fraudulent actions in April of 1989, shortly after they'd begun their investigation. "The world at that point didn't know that the conditions in Frankfurt, Germany, and elsewhere were abominable from a security standpoint."

This time, Coddington jumped up. "I will object!"

"Strike out those words," Judge Platt told the court reporter. "Mr. Kreindler. This is not a summation. Words like "abominable," "shocking," and so forth are not proper. You know it. You've been trying cases before me for years."

Again, Lee did not let the interruption affect his rhythm. He continued to sketch out the assertion that a bomb disguised as a cassette player radio was packed into a suitcase and shipped from Malta to Frankfurt, Germany, where it was missed by Pan Am's security and loaded onto Flight 103 to London.

The Trial Begins

That could only have happened because Pan Am did not heed the warnings by the FAA of a bomb attack at Frankfurt. Failing to "rigorously apply" the measures required to ensure that unaccompanied baggage was identified and searched by hand, the Alert Management screeners just passed them through an X-ray machine.

Lee finished by referring to the two questions the jury would have to decide at the end of the case: Did Pan Am and Alert commit willful misconduct? And was that misconduct a substantial contribution to the cause of the passengers' and flight crew's deaths?

"I promise you that this is what we shall prove in this case," he said. "This is our contract with you. When the case is over, I believe you'll have more than sufficient evidence to conclude that it was the corporate misconduct of Pan Am and Alert that created this disaster."

He let his eyes travel along the two rows of jurors to allow his message sink in before returning to his seat. He felt satisfied that he had accomplished his primary goals: outlining the case and establishing a connection with the jury.

There was an added benefit. Coddington had helped to cement the word "abominable" in the jury's mind in connection with Pan Am's corporate behavior by making an issue of it.

Judge Platt wasted no time and gestured to the defense table. "Counsel, your turn."

Bud Coddington rose and stepped up to the podium with a serious expression. He placed a stack of note cards before him, suggesting he had a great amount of material to cover. As Lee suspected, he never referred to them. Instead, he began by talking at length about Pan Am's illustrious history—from its beginnings in 1925 carrying mail from Key West to Havana, Cuba, to becoming the flagship international American airline.

Then, he laid out the defense's contentions: the security programs of Pan Am and its subsidiary, Alert Management, were the best possible. The FAA had approved them. And yet, the terrorists somehow managed to smuggle the suitcase containing the bomb aboard the plane in Frankfurt, and in such a way that Pan Am could not have been expected to prevent it. "There is no question we made slip-ups and goofs, but they did not cause the tragedy," Coddington insisted.

He further asserted that the bomb could not have come from Malta. "We call this case, if your Honor please, 'The Case of the Thirteenth Bag,'" he commented. "If this were a Perry Mason mystery, you would probably call it 'The Case of the Phantom Bag.'"

Coddington claimed that the airline's security measures—using X-ray machines for baggage check—were more than adequate and superior to physical inspection for bomb detection. Daniel Sonesen, the assistant director of corporate security, would testify to Pan Am leading the way to search for advanced security technology to improve airport security. Coddington singled out Kurt Maier, the X-ray machine operator in Frankfurt, and insisted that his testimony would be significant.

He further promised that experts would testify on the nature of terrorists' operations and preferred methods of sabotage.

Lee took copious notes on his yellow pad. He underlined Coddington's statements and claims that he knew to be false. They would require a thorough rebuttal.

Coddington spoke for nearly another hour before he finished, "When this enterprise is concluded, you will believe in your hearts and minds and souls, as we do, that there was no willful misconduct by Pan Am or Alert. There was no causative relationship between our conduct and this tragedy. It was the sole, proximate result of the act of murderers and monsters who put this bomb aboard our airplane and killed these innocents."

Returning to his seat, he tried to catch Lee's eye. But Lee paid no attention to him. He was watching how the jurors reacted to the speech. They did not show any signs of being swayed one way or another. If anything, they seemed relieved that the lengthy opening remarks were finally over. Several stretched their arms. One massaged her neck. Another repressed a yawn.

The day concluded with Judge Platt going over scheduling conflicts and times when he would not be available. Otherwise, the trial would generally proceed from Monday to Friday unless otherwise noted.

Finally, he dismissed the jury, telling them again not to discuss the case with anyone.

As the courtroom emptied, Lee gathered his notes and workbook and put them in his briefcase. He felt guardedly optimistic. Coddington had rambled on longer than necessary but hadn't alienated the jury. Lee's opening had piqued some interest. He thought he had provided a better narrative and framing of the issues.

The battle lines were drawn.

24

THE PLAINTIFFS' CASE

May to June 1992

Lee had anticipated most of the issues Bud Coddington raised in his opening statement. Boiled down to essentials, it rehashed the *TIME* magazine article, suggesting the Lockerbie disaster was caused by an unaccounted suitcase switched somewhere in Frankfurt airport's labyrinthine baggage transfer system and loaded onto Pan Am Flight 103 to London. Although there was not a shred of evidence for such a claim, it worried Lee. If the defense could introduce an alternate theory into the proceedings—that the bomb bag on the plane had nothing to do with Pan Am's lax security—it might distract the jury from what really mattered.

More serious was the allegation that FAA officials had granted Pan Am permission to use X-ray screening instead of relying on physical search of unaccompanied luggage. That meant that the testimony of Kurt Maier would be crucial. Of course, Lee knew that already. James Brennan had mentioned it as his ace in the hole on several occasions when he refused to settle the case.

Lee and his team had held numerous planning sessions before the trial to counter these defense machinations. Mapping out a coherent strategy to best present their case to the jury, they agreed to divide the questioning of witnesses among each other, distributing the burden of preparation.

THE FIGHT FOR JUSTICE

Unlike a criminal trial, a civil one has little potential for high drama. The plaintiffs' attorneys lay out the case they have developed for the jury step by step. There are no smoking guns or surprises. That is why less than 10% of legal television shows and movies deal with civil cases—no fireworks, no unexpected revelations, or confessions on the witness stand. Nonetheless, the stakes were high.

Lee understood he and his team would have to present a tremendous amount of detailed information to prove their case. It would be a lot for the jury to digest, and he thought a great deal about how to impart all the evidence in a clear, penetrating manner. For Lee, it was always about what story to tell and how to frame the argument, and he came up with what he considered a persuasive strategy.

They would call two expert witnesses early on: Billie Vincent, the former Director of Security for the FAA, and Rodney Wallis who, at the time of the Lockerbie disaster, had served as president of the International Air Transportation Association (IATA), which included Pan Am among its members. Both men had many years of experience with airline crashes and now worked in the private sector as aviation security specialists.

Lee had known Vincent for many years as a trustworthy expert and hired him as a consultant a month after Lockerbie to help with the case. Wallis was a more recent acquaintance. Lee had met him casually at several air security conferences in Washington, London, and, most recently, Bangkok. They had seen eye to eye on many issues concerning airplane safety. When Lee laid out the case against Pan Am over a shared meal in a Thai restaurant, Wallis agreed to testify at the trial on behalf of the Lockerbie families.

Lee decided to call Vincent and Wallis to the stand twice. The first time, they would provide a fact-based overview to show that Pan Am had reduced security measures in Frankfurt and London in violation of FAA rules and had ignored the Helsinki and Toshiba warnings.

Then, follow-up witnesses would testify in greater detail to security lapses and how the bomb, in an unaccompanied suitcase, was flown from Malta and then loaded onto Pan Am Flight 103. When that process was complete, Wallis and Vincent would return, this time as experts. They would offer their analyses of the testimony and evidence introduced at the trial, draw conclusions, and give their professional opinions.

By then, Lee figured at least three weeks to a month would have passed—an eternity in a trial as complex as this one. Connecting the dots with earlier testimony, Vincent and Wallis would allow Lee and his team to consolidate all the information—almost like a summation—and cement Pan Am's culpability for the Lockerbie disaster in the jurors' minds.

Bud Coddington well understood the strategy when he received the initial witness list from the plaintiffs' attorneys, and he did not like it. He tried to quash the use of Vincent and Wallis as "split" witnesses appearing more than once, but Judge Platt allowed it.

The plaintiffs began their case with Mitch Baumeister questioning Walter Korsgaard, who had spent 20 years as an aviation explosives security manager for the FAA. They wanted to show the jury right away that other attorneys besides Lee would try the case.

Recently retired, Korsgaard had investigated every commercial flight accident where a bomb was suspected from 1971 through 1990. He was soft-spoken, matter-of-fact, and had a disarming smile that almost made listeners forget that he was talking about horrific events.

Korsgaard had been called to Lockerbie after the disaster to help determine the cause of the crash. As a factual witness, he explained the process by which the investigation in Scotland established that it was a bomb and exactly where in the aircraft it was located. The decisive factor was soot and residue on a recovered section of the airplane where the bomb had exploded in the cargo hold beneath the passenger seats.

To make that clear, Baumeister introduced blowups of photographs to set on an easel in front of the jury. Korsgaard would point out the pitting, cratering and soot on the fuselage that were the signature signs that a bomb caused the crash.

Bud Coddington rose and objected. In the ensuing sidebar, he explained, "My concern is that the witness was not denominated as an expert. I don't know how far we're going here."

Judge Platt gave him a puzzled look and said, "There is no question that this was a bomb, Mr. Coddington. This is a silly objection. Overruled."

Later, Baumeister wanted to present sector photographs showing the extent of the wreckage. "We have excluded the remains of the passengers' bodies," he said.

This time, James Shaughnessy objected, "These photographs are inflammatory, your Honor. They don't serve any purpose in this litigation at this time. Since we have agreed the airplane crash resulted from an explosion, what is the relevance?"

Lee was about to jump in and present counter-arguments, but Judge Platt spoke first, schooling Shaughnessy on the photographs' relevance, "They show the painstaking effort taken that indicates just how this all occurred and where this particular baggage was located. This is all part of the picture to show this was part of an interline transfer, and the plaintiffs are entitled to put it in. Your objection is overruled."

As Baumeister continued to take Korsgaard through the evidence step by step, Lee marveled how well his former protégé and partner consolidated the accumulation of evidence. However, the frivolous defense interruptions worried him. He figured it would become one of Bud Coddington's go-to tactics—to interrupt as often as possible

The Plaintiffs' Case

and break any rhythm and developing narrative in the testimony established by the plaintiffs' attorneys.

And he was right.

As the trial progressed, Coddington and Shaughnessy continued to object to questions as hearsay, leading and irrelevant at every possible turn. They opposed the introduction of documents, graphs, charts, and photographs, calling them unnecessary and prejudicial.

Early on, in the many sidebars before Judge Platt, out of earshot of the jury, Coddington argued with ingratiating collegiality, addressing Lee as "Brother Kreindler." Later, he switched to the formal "Mr. Kreindler." And when the exchanges became increasingly testy, he called Lee and Jim and the two Granitos "tag teams" referencing the overblown performances of professional wrestlers.

For many of these discussions, the Judge excused the jury. At various times, Carla Martin, the attorney representing the FAA, also objected, asserting that the material covered was too sensitive and needed to be shielded from the public for the sake of national interest. The spectators had to go into the hallway for half an hour or longer. With all the comings and goings, the courtroom often seemed like Grand Central Station at rush hour.

Judge Platt handled the interruptions with patience and good humor, even when they were baseless and misleading.

Meanwhile, Lee followed the plaintiffs' strategy and called Billie Vincent to the stand. The former FAA Director of Security was in his early 60s but looked like a much younger man. Unpretentious and relaxed, he had a thick mustache and thinning brown hair and seemed like everyone's favorite uncle. As Director of Security of the FAA, he had testified before Congress in Washington and been an expert witness in several aircraft disaster trials.

In clear, easy-to-understand language, he described the rules and regulations he had helped develop in the 1980s in response to international terrorist attacks on passenger planes. He mainly focused on the Airline Carrier Standard Security Program (ASSCP), which established the FAA regulations for American carriers, including Pan Am.

Lee took Vincent through the safety requirements at the extraordinary security risk airports, notably Frankfurt and London—the matching of bags to passengers, the search protocols for selectees, and the rules for unaccompanied bags that demanded physical search or a minimum of 24-hour sequestering in a pressure chamber.

In addition, Lee elicited testimony about one of the cornerstones of the plaintiffs' case, "Describe the procedure Pan Am would have had to go through to obtain permission to use different security measures from those stated in its ACSSP."

Vincent said, "They would have needed to apply to the FAA in writing, stating precisely how they wanted to change their program and request approval to do so."

"Then what would have happened?"

"After an internal review, it would have gone to the person within the FAA who was responsible for approving it. In this case, that would have been the Office of Civil Aviation Security Director, Raymond Salazar."

"Would he have had to approve it in writing?"

"Yes, sir, in writing."

With his calm, forthright manner, Vincent was a powerful witness.

For his cross-examination, Bud Coddington took nearly twice as long as Lee. He tried every trick in the book to discredit Vincent, frequently interrupting him as he answered questions. Lee rose and objected, demanding Vincent be allowed to finish, and Judge Platt admonished Coddington several times.

When Vincent indicated that, to reach his conclusions, he had read over 125 depositions more than once, plus a substantial amount of additional material, Coddington questioned his expertise. He asked

The Plaintiffs' Case

Vincent in order, "Are you a lawyer, a graduate law student, a paralegal?" After receiving a "No" to every question, he insisted that Vincent had no standing as a legal expert.

Coddington accused Vincent of being hired by the plaintiffs just a month after the Lockerbie disaster and receiving $100,000 in payment for his more than three-year service. "What you have done is read a bunch of papers that Mr. Kreindler and his friends have given you when you met with them," he attacked. "Then you have come here not as an advocate but as a teacher to deliver your opinions in his Honor's court. Isn't that true?"

Vincent kept his composure. "No, it is not."

When Coddington resumed cross-examination the following day, he sparred with Vincent over the Helsinki warning and tried to get him to admit it was a hoax, but Vincent refused to bite. Coddington also tried to imply that the U.S. government bore some responsibility for the disaster.

That earned him another strong objection from Lee.

The lengthy sidebar exchanges concluded with Judge Platt's warning the jury, "Ladies and gentlemen, I want to remind you that the lawsuit before you is between the plaintiffs, who are various representatives of the deceased people on the aircraft, and Pan Am and its wholly-owned subsidiary Alert. There are no suits pending before you against the United States government or any of its agents."

In his redirect, Lee cut through the clouds of smoke raised by Coddington and allowed Vincent to reiterate the main points of his testimony. That evening, when the Plaintiffs Committee met, everyone agreed that their witness had succeeded in laying the beginnings of a strong foundation for their case.

Next came Rodney Wallis, the former president of IATA. Of Anglo-Indian descent, he had dark brown skin and short-cropped, black hair graying at the temples. His large, rectangular, wire-rim glasses gave him a scholarly appearance, and he spoke in well-formulated, deliberate sentences.

With Wallis, Lee established the specific changes in Pan Am's security practices, starting in 1986, including the decision in March of 1988 to abandon positive luggage matching altogether.

Despite a barrage of objections from Coddington, Lee went over the "lock and load" memo that Daniel Sonesen, Pan Am's chief of security, had sent to Martin Hübner in Germany and James Berwick in London, insisting that FAA regulations of how to deal with unaccompanied bags be ignored.

"What was Mr. Sonesen in plain language telling Frankfurt and London to do?" Lee asked.

Without hesitation, Wallis replied, "Unaccompanied bags can travel without physical search."

"What was the effect of the abandonment of a positive match?"

"It left Pan American services of Frankfurt and London vulnerable to unaccompanied interline bags."

Finally, Lee drew attention to the FAA bulletins regarding the Helsinki and Toshiba warnings, which ordered that search and security regulations be "rigorously applied." As president of IATA, Wallis had received a copy, and he testified that the other ccs included Daniel Sonesen and Martin Shugrue, Pan Am's vice chairman at the time, confirming that the airline's leadership knew of the requirements.

In his cross examination, Coddington again honed in on the monetary compensation for expert witnesses. The Plaintiffs Committee had paid Wallis $25,000, and the defense attorney pointed out that this compensation for three-days' work was considerably more than any jury member earned in a month. But Wallis did not let himself get rattled and continued to answer questions calmly. He corrected Coddington when the defense attorney misquoted him or misrepresented his answers.

Then, Coddington ventured into territory Carla Martin did not consider suitable for public disclosure and invoked national interest. Judge Platt excused the public and cleared the courtroom.

Over the next hour, Coddington focused intently on the bomb's detonating substance. Because Semtex is a plastic compound, dogs can't smell it, and X-ray machines can't detect it. In the process, Coddington tried to make the case that Pan Am had no defense against terrorists determined to get a bomb on board a flight. He also tried to introduce hypothetical alternatives about how the unaccompanied bag might have made it onto the airplane.

Then he asked, "The three ways you worry about bombs getting on the airplane are checked baggage, people bringing carry-ons, and cargo coming through. Is that correct?"

"Yes," Wallis answered.

"As a matter of fact, on Pan Am 103, they were carrying cargo?"

"I expect them to."

"They carry all kinds of cargo?" Coddington asked.

"Yes."

"Sometimes, for example, they carry the cremated remains of people who have died?"

"Yes."

"Religious articles and icons and special religious things important to people."

"Maybe."

"They carry diplomatic pouches and materials that are sealed. Is that true?"

At that point, Lee had enough and interrupted, "Excuse me, we are getting off into an area far afield from the scope of direct testimony. Mr. Wallis testified to warnings and specific procedures."

In the sidebar, Judge Platt agreed with Lee and told Coddington, "There is no reason you can't cross-examine their theory to death, but I'm not going to permit you to create an inference this bomb was shipped in an icon from the Vatican or some hypothesis you might have dreamed up last night. If there is a good faith basis for these hypotheses you can show to me, I would be glad to let you cross-examine the witness."

"Judge, you are constraining me," Coddington complained.

Judge Platt looked at him with amusement. "If I'd been sitting in Mr. Kreindler's chair, you would have seen the jack in the box at work objecting,'" he said. "I would probably have lost ten pounds by this time. He's been incredibly lenient with you."

Lee could not resist getting a dig in. "Sitting here listening to this, ninety percent, in my opinion, has been objectionable," he said. "I don't like to object, so my rule is: if it doesn't hurt me, I let him go on with irrelevancies."

The sparring continued for some time before Coddington finally conceded. "The fact that I cannot join you on this issue has me almost bollixed," he told Judge Platt. "I don't accept your view, but I accept your ruling, of course."

In the remaining cross-examination, Coddington focused on the Helsinki warning again and on the process of X-ray screening as a way to detect bombs.

"X-rays are intended to search for guns, grenades, pipe bombs, those sorts of things?" he asked.

"They have been used to do that," Wallis answered. "They weren't designed for that purpose."

"The ACSSP written by the federal government has a provision for their use as test objects to see if the X-ray is working properly. Am I right there?"

"Yes."

"For example, they used nylon dowels, one-and-a-quarter inch in diameter by eight inches. Right?"

"They may have done."

"They used sticks, simulated dynamite time bombs, grenades, pistols, automatic and revolvers."

"Yes."

"And when they come around and check people's X-rays, they put these things through, separate and in suitcases, to see if the operators were picking them up?

"Right."

Lee did not know what point Coddington was trying to make—that emerged later in the trial—and decided to let him go on.

But during his redirect examination, he reviewed the Helsinki warning and Jim Berwick's response, much to Coddington's chagrin. Lee asked Wallis, "Mr. Berwick, was he the same one who, back on March 10, 1988, pointed out that, in his experience and his opinion, X-raying was inadequate?"

Coddington interrupted, "Objection, your Honor. Leading."

Judge Platt said, "I'll allow it on redirect."

Lee rephrased his question, "X-raying was inadequate because both the machinery and the personnel were inadequate, and Mr. Berwick raised a question about abandoning positive match?"

Wallis answered, "Yes."

Coddington interjected again, "Objection to the characterization."

"Overruled."

"What should Pan Am have done after the Helsinki warning?" Lee asked.

"They should have made absolutely certain that all the procedures required by the government, and perhaps even more, were applied, particularly at Frankfurt," Wallis replied. "They should have gone back to full positive passenger bag match as the cornerstone of the defense against a baggage bomb."

"And did they do that?"

"I have seen no evidence to show that they did."

When Lee and the other plaintiffs' attorneys met late that afternoon, they concluded that things were going well. Despite Coddington's frequent interruptions and vulgar efforts to derail the testimony of Vincent and Wallis, they had made the crucial points. The first part of their strategy had succeeded as well as expected.

It was Friday, and everyone was looking forward to getting some rest over the weekend while preparing for the next phase. On Monday, Lee and his team would begin building their case of willful misconduct from the ground up, like a good construction crew putting up a house, block by block.

25

THE DEFENSE PLAYS GAMES

Over the next five weeks, Lee and this team called 53 witnesses. While a few appeared in person or on videotape, most testified via transcripts of depositions taken during the past three years. The plaintiff attorneys who had conducted the examinations—Mitch Baumeister, Frank Granito Jr, Frank Granito III, Steve Pounian, Lee, and his son Jim—stood at the podium and read the questions matter-of-factly. Other lawyers and paralegals from their firms took the witness stand and read the answers in a straightforward manner. It did not make for very exciting testimony, but it was the customary way to present witness statements to the jury.

For Lee, the first few exchanges always felt odd because he remembered the actual witnesses—their appearance, tone of voice, and quirks: hesitating, looking away, clearing their throat, rubbing their forehead before answering a question. He had to remind himself that jury members would not experience that kind of disorientation but could listen to the words attentively.

As Lee and his team examined live witnesses and heard the objections from the defense, they jotted down notes and additional questions on small pieces of paper. Then, they would pass them to the interrogating attorney so he could emphasize an important point or drive home a particular argument during direct testimony or redirect.

Although having others conduct interviews gave Lee some respite, he could not relax. He had to maintain laser-sharp focus, especially when Coddington or Shaughnessy cross-examined and tried to sneak irrelevant or misleading information past the judge to influence the jury.

When he wasn't examining a witness, Lee also watched the jury to see what captured their interest, made them sit up, or seemed to bore them. He was pleased to see that they paid attention most of the time, even when the testimony dealt with the technicalities of baggage handling and computer classification. They had dedicated themselves to their task and paid attention. To Lee, it meant that the plaintiffs' presentation was working.

The legal team often met during lunch and at the end of the afternoon sessions to discuss how the day went. They strategized about the next day's testimony and determined the best order of witnesses in the weeks ahead—they had to give the defense three days' notice of who they planned to call. In addition, they had to alert paralegals and aides at their firm about the documents and exhibits to prepare for use in the courtroom.

Lee also met with the victims' families over dinner to assure them things were going well. As he started to unwind in a more relaxed atmosphere, he sometimes had to stifle a yawn.

When it happened more frequently, some of the clients became concerned. On one occasion, Jeannine Boulanger took Ruth aside and asked, "Is Lee okay? He looks exhausted." On another, Dona Bainbridge told her, "I'm worried about Lee."

Ruth assured them that he was fine. But by the time she and Lee returned to their room at the Union Club, he often felt like a punch-drunk prize fighter who had absorbed too many blows during the round and barely managed to stumble back to his corner. The wrinkles in his face became furrows. Ruth became increasingly worried herself.

She asked Lee to take it easy but knew full well that her husband never did anything halfway. Once he was in, he was in all the way.

And by the next morning, he always looked fresh and ready to go, with a reassuring smile for everyone.

* * *

The first eight written depositions established the changes in Pan Am's security measures and documented the lax practices at the Frankfurt Airport. They included Mitch Baumeister reading from his questioning of Thomas Plaskett, president of Pan Am at the time of the disaster. Plaskett was not among the spectators that day:

> *Baumeister: Were you aware in December 1988 of the fact that a security or a surcharge was being charged to many of your passengers?*
>
> *Plaskett: Yes.*
>
> *Baumeister: What was the relationship between collecting the surcharge and providing security services?*
>
> *Plaskett P: None, really.*
>
> *Baumeister: But that surcharge was labeled a security surcharge.*
>
> *Plaskett: Yes.*
>
> *Baumeister: Was that because of public relations?*
>
> *Plaskett: No.*
>
> *Baumeister: What was the reason for it?*
>
> *Plaskett: I wasn't at Pan Am when the security surcharge was put into effect, so I don't know anything about what they did at the time.*

Lee noticed looks of distaste on some of the jurors' faces. They did not like the president of Pan Am passing the buck and stole disapproving glances at the defense table where Coddington watched impassively.

Next, Alan Berwick, Pan Am's security manager in the United Kingdom, detailed the changes in security practices starting in 1987. He testified that when Pan Am's leadership had become frustrated with delays due to positive baggage matching and physical examination of unaccompanied bags, it instituted X-ray screening exclusively at all of its airports.

Martin Hübner, Herbert Leuniger, Burt Mayer, Alfred Kunz, Monika Diegmuller, and other employees from Frankfurt revealed that training security personnel, including the X-ray machine operators, was rudimentary at best. In the case of Diegmuller, she had received only three hours of training when regulations called for a minimum of 29 hours.

Then came the video deposition of Raymond Salazar, the former director of the Office of Civil Aviation Security at the FAA. Wallis had identified him as the highest decision-maker who interpreted or amended security regulations at the time of the Lockerbie disaster. Lee and his team had arranged the order of witnesses deliberately to emphasize the importance of his video testimony.

Court deputies rolled out a large viewing screen and positioned it so the jury and spectators could see the version edited by the plaintiffs' attorneys. After several days of unemotional, written depositions, it was a refreshing change, and everyone—jurors and spectators—leaned forward with eager anticipation.

The video was made on June 5, 1990, at Salazar's home. By then, he had retired to Florida, and palm trees swayed in the background during the deposition.

Expanding on Wallis' testimony, Salazar outlined the formal process for making changes in the air carrier security program (ASSPC). In the case of Pan Am, the application would have originated with Daniel Sonesen, director of systems security at the airline's New York headquarters.

The Defense Plays Games

Mitch Baumeister asking the questions zeroed in on the crucial issue:

Baumeister: From time to time in 1988 and prior to Lockerbie, did you have occasion to personally talk to Mr. Sonesen about security matters at Pan Am?

Salazar: I recall conversations generally with Mr. Sonesen.

Baumeister: Have you ever, on and prior to December 21, 1988, given any air carrier oral permission to amend or to get an exemption from provisions of the ASSPC?

Salazar: Absolutely not.

Baumeister: Did you ever grant to anyone at Pan American Airlines on and prior to December 21, 1988, permission to use X-ray as an alternative to searching passenger baggage at Frankfurt or Heathrow?

Salazar: At either Frankfurt or Heathrow? No.

Lee could tell from how the jurors and the spectators shifted in their seats that the exchange had hit home. Everybody understood that the testimony contradicted Bud Coddington's claim in his opening statement that Sonesen had received oral permission from the FAA to change its security protocol.

As far as Lee was concerned, this was the most significant testimony in the early stages of the plaintiffs' presentation.

Over the next three weeks, Lee and his team introduced further testimony documenting the lax and often sordid practices at Pan Am's and Alert Management's Frankfurt Airport offices via Stella Schneider, Sabine Fuchs, and others. They also traced the movement of the Samsonite suitcase containing the bomb from Malta to its exact location in the cargo hold of Flight 103 at Heathrow Airport.

One of the highlights was the videotape deposition of Oliver Koch, in which he described discovering the Helsinki warning the day after Lockerbie among the papers on the desk of his boss, Ulrich Weber. Lee was pleased that some jury members sat back in surprise when they heard that Weber predated the document with a stamp before an FAA inspectors' visit to back up the claim that he had disseminated it to all Pan Am security personnel at Frankfurt airport.

Lee himself read the questions for the deposition testimony of Bogomira Erac ("Mrs. Schmidt") regarding the discovery of the computer printout in her locker that identified an unaccompanied interline bomb bag from Malta in the FAG system on December 21.

Depositions by Frankfurt computer coders Yasar Koca and Mehmet Candar, their supervisor, Gunter Kasteleiner, and baggage handler Kiling Tuzcu tracked the bag from the FAG onto the Pan Am aircraft as one of 13 interline bags.

Ziogas Dimitrios and Sidhu Amarjit at Heathrow Airport testified that these bags ended up on the second level in luggage container 4041 of Pan Am Flight 103, the very spot where the bomb exploded in midair over Lockerbie.

Police constables Mick Charles and Peter Clayden and bomb expert Alan Feraday provided pinpoint confirmation of the location of the bomb suitcase in that container based on debris recovered on the ground.

The plaintiffs' attorneys read in detail from the deposition of Scottish Police Constable Harry Bell—how he traced clothing remnants from the bomb suitcase to Malta and the retail shop Mary's House, and that the shopkeeper remembered the buyer selecting the items at random.

Because Lee knew that the defense planned to make a big deal of X-ray security at the Frankfurt and London Airports, he included a short section from the deposition of Daniel Sonesen, Pan Am's assistant director of security. Frank Granito Jr read the questions.

The Defense Plays Games

The exchange demonstrated Pan Am's involvement at the highest corporate level:

> *Granito Jr: A decision was made sometime prior to the Lockerbie disaster to implement X-ray screening at Frankfurt.*
>
> *Sonesen: Yes.*
>
> *Granito Jr: Was that a decision made by Pan Am at a particular corporate level?*
>
> *Sonesen: Yes.*
>
> *Granito Jr: What was the highest level that the decision was made?*
>
> *Sonesen: I believe it would have been Mr. Shugrue.*
>
> *Granito Jr: What was his title?*
>
> *Sonesen: Vice Chairman.*

Bud Coddington kept disrupting the orderly presentations by the plaintiffs' attorneys in every way he could. The frequent disturbances—lengthy sidebars during which the jurors were sent to their meeting room, and testimony considered sensitive for national security when the spectators had to clear the courtroom—added time to the proceedings.

As a result, the trial went on longer than Judge Platt had anticipated. He had hoped that the plaintiffs' attorneys would wrap up their case by the end of May but had to keep extending the timeline into the second week of June.

During discovery and pre-trial motions, Judge Platt had been leaning toward the defense contention that an airline could not protect itself against terrorist attacks. But as the trial progressed, he became increasingly dismissive of Bud Coddington's attempts to muddy the waters. He refused to allow defense attorneys to introduce alternative theories of how the "bomb bag" got onto the airplane during cross-examinations. "Unless you can provide some supporting evidence, overruled!" became a common refrain.

Coddington also tried to elicit or introduce testimony regarding security measures taken by Pan Am after the Lockerbie disaster to show the airline in a more positive light. But Judge Platt rejected those attempts, allowing only discussions for the period leading up to and including December 21, 1988.

He continued to preside with patience and humor, never losing his composure. However, his comments made clear what he thought of the distractions. When Coddington flew to California to look after other legal commitments, he left James Shaughnessy in charge, who was not as polished or smooth, and whose arguments were far less convincing. At some point, Judge Platt commented during a sidebar, "Mr. Shaughnessy has gone from one unreality to another."

When the time came to recall Billie Vincent and Rodney Wallis to the stand five weeks after they first appeared, Lee was confident that he and his team had presented a compelling case.

Coddington must have thought so, too. He not only renewed his assault on the expert witnesses but unveiled new strategies of deliberate distraction.

When Lee began with Wallis, he asked him to provide a thumbnail sketch of his credentials to remind the jurors. Then he said, "What I want to do with your testimony now, your expert testimony, is focus on airline security. Within that area, I will be asking you two general questions, and then we'll get into detail. The first relates to the adequacy of Pan Am's performance with respect to security, and the second is the question of causation—how the bomb got onto Pan Am 103."

Bud Coddington rose quickly and objected. During the ensuing sidebar, he elaborated, "I object to opinion testimony by this witness, your Honor, to the extent that it involves any conclusions of law and to the extent it involves his dual role as summarizer of testimony, as an expert witness, who in addition, has also read an enormous

The Defense Plays Games

amount of material which is outside the evidence of this trial. On all these bases, I object to his opinion."

Judge Platt looked at him perplexed. "Where have you been for the past eighteen years?"

Taken aback, Coddington said, "I've been practicing in state and federal courts throughout this country, Judge."

"Are you familiar with a set of rules that begins with 700 of the Federal Rules?"

"Yes."

"Federal Rules of Evidence?"

"Intimately familiar with them."

Tilting his head and raising his eyebrows in mock surprise, Judge Platt said, "You don't sound like it from your objection. Every expert who elicits testimony based on evidence introduced at trial is entitled to tell a jury the basis, which is opinion and conclusion. That has been true for forty years. Your objection is overruled."

In summarizing his findings, Wallis drove the point home, "By violating the mandated requirements of the FAA, Pan American had left its passengers and crews vulnerable to attacks by terrorists. Given the dangerous environment that existed in December of 1988, the tragedy which overtook Pan Am 103 was a disaster simply waiting to happen."

Many newspapers and television reports quoted the last part of his answer the next day verbatim.

Regarding the second question—how the bomb made it onto Flight 103—Wallis was just as concise and forceful. "The bomb was contained in a suitcase which was carried unaccompanied from Malta to Frankfurt, where it was placed on board Pan Am 103, which was ferrying passengers from Frankfurt to London. There, it was transferred onto the 747, which subsequently was destroyed over Lockerbie."

During cross-examination, Coddington again interrupted Wallis' attempts to answer. Lee was compelled to object three times, with Judge Platt admonishing him before he stopped. Then, he attacked the testimony as biased, again calling Wallis "a paid reader" and trying to trip him up in inconsistencies.

After ranging far afield from what the direct examination had covered, he asked, "X-ray technology is a more modern way when coupled with physical inspection than hand searching of bags or physical match that you previously talked about; isn't that true?"

Wallis replied decisively, "No, it is not true."

"X-rays, if properly accomplished by people who know what they're doing, can discover the kinds of devices just as well as people who physically go through bags. Isn't that true?"

"That is not true either."

Coddington tried another tack. "How is the security in here?"

Puzzled, Wallis said, "The security against what, terrorists?"

"A lot of things can get through that X-ray machine and metal detector downstairs?"

Wallis agreed. "They can."

Coddington held up his hand, signaling Judge Platt. "May I have just a moment, your Honor? I've lost my toy."

As he went to the defense table and rummaged in his briefcase., Lee stood up and complained. "Your Honor, I don't know what in the world this has to do with our case. I object on the grounds of relevance."

Straightening, Coddington said, "A bomb, Judge, and –"

"You are the bomb. We might stipulate to that," Lee interrupted, letting his irritation get the better of him.

Returning to the podium and wearing a small metal square, about a quarter inch in size, on a black cord like a pendant, Coddington said, "I want to ask Mr. Wallis a couple of security questions."

The Defense Plays Games

Judge Platt wrinkled his brows. "What do you need that device for that you have around your neck?"

Coddington turned to Wallis and said, "Well, if this were primer cord or C-4, and I had walked through a metal detector at an airport or his Honor's courthouse, would the alarm have gone off?"

Wallis answered, "If you're using a plastic explosive, an alarm would not go off."

"So if I walked through the courthouse today with this primer cord around my neck –"

At that point, Lee interrupted again, "Your Honor, I object. There is no evidence that it has anything to do with the kind of security involved in our case. I think draping a cord around one's neck in sideshow fashion is inappropriate. We object to it. It appears to be an effort to create a circus atmosphere."

But Judge Platt let the questioning go on. Ultimately, Coddington took four times as long as Lee but made no dent in Wallis' testimony. After Judge Platt quickly dismissed another attempt to implicate the U.S. government in the disaster, Coddington finally rested.

Lee's last witness was Billie Vincent. Once again, Coddington objected to him as an expert witness, but Judge Platt made short shrift of the interruption and overruled the lawyer.

This time, Lee asked Vincent to give an opinion on whether Pan Am violated any statutory, regulatory, and ACSSP provisions.

Vincent testified in his easy-going, straightforward manner, as before, "Evaluating all of the testimony that is available to me in this trial transcript, as well as other data I have seen, has led me to the conclusion that Pan did indeed violate the ACSSP, which requires having a positive passenger bag check."

After taking Vincent through documents that backed up his conclusion, Lee said, "In summary, how would you characterize Pan Am's security operations at the time of Lockerbie?"

Vincent did not mince words. "Taken in its totality, I can only characterize Pan Am's system and their behavior as absolutely outrageous. They did these things consciously and deliberately." He paused and looked toward the jury. "Pan Am played Russian roulette with the lives of the passengers on those airplanes, and the number came up, the bullet came up in the cylinder on Pan Am 103 on December 21, 1988.

Lee said, "Thank you," and turned to Coddington. "Your witness."

Coddington started his cross-examination with a sarcastic dig, "I guess they got their money's worth from you, Billy Vincent."

He spent the next hour and a half hammering away again at Vincent for having been hired by the plaintiffs just three weeks after the disaster and the "excessively high" compensation rate he was being paid—$900 a day!

At some point, Mitch Baumeister let out a groan.

Flushing red with anger, Coddington turned on him. "Excuse me!"

Baumeister replied wryly, "I have a back problem."

Coddington pivoted toward Judge Platt and said, "I take exception to counsel groaning in opposition!"

Baumeister said to Judge Platt, "I explained that I pulled a muscle in my back this morning, and he's making something of this."

But Coddington was not satisfied. "I object to counsel's exhalations –"

Interrupting, the Judge told him, "Proceed and stop playing. Mr. Vincent is a valuable witness. You pointed out that his time is valuable."

Unchastened, Coddington continued to attack Vincent's earnings before turning to X-ray detection and training in light of the Helsinki and Toshiba warnings. "According to FAA regulations, what would have been an appropriate mandate for the screeners?" he asked.

The Defense Plays Games

Vincent answered, "The X-ray operator, properly trained, should have been instructed both at Frankfurt and London to be looking for electronic devices, not just radios."

"Electric shavers?"

"Yes, shavers as well."

"Hearing aids?"

"Perhaps, but it does not in any way relieve them of the responsibility to conduct a full passenger baggage match –"

"Watches? Calculators?"

Coddington went to the defense table and removed an object from a box. Keeping it behind his back, out of sight of the jury but in Vincent's view, he asked, "What about this?"

Seeing it was a small radio, Lee leaped to his feet and objected.

Judge Platt called the attorneys to his bench and excused the jurors.

When they had left the room, Lee said heatedly, "Mr. Coddington just showed the witness a radio cassette player. He has not shown it to us before. We have seen it now. No authentication we know of relates this machine to the one in the bomb bag. This procedure is improper."

Coddington argued, "I had it behind my back and kept my front to the jury so they couldn't see it. I made sure of that until I had your approval. I have a whole variety of cassette radio models I want to show the witness."

Judge Platt stared at him, incredulous. "There isn't any way I will permit it in evidence."

But he allowed Coddington to ask his questions out of earshot of the jury to preserve them for the record in case an appeals court held that the evidence had been improperly excluded.

Pleased, Coddington asked, "Mr. Vincent, I show you now this object in the absence of the jury. I ask you if you recognize it."

Vincent replied drily, "It seems to be a radio. A radio cassette player."

"And it is, if you look at it, a Toshiba radio cassette player. Right? Does that look like the radio that was aboard the Lockerbie aircraft?"

"I haven't the foggiest notion."

"I have others to show you. With one or two speakers," Coddington said.

Once again, Lee objected. "Mr. Vincent said he hasn't the foggiest notion. I'm sure the answer will be the same for the rest. We don't know what the radio on the plane looks like. Nobody does. Except for the Scottish police."

Judge Platt agreed. He looked hard at Coddington and said, "I think you should make sure that those boxes and those radios are not displayed to the jury."

Coddington took the radio to the defense table and stashed it. Then he said loudly, "I've put all the boxes back in the bag—I mean all the radios back in the bag."

But he was not done. He took another box and put it on the plaintiffs' table, saying, "If you give me a second, I'll pass this box out."

After glancing inside, Lee said, "Your Honor, we now have been presented with a host of new circus toys by Mr. Coddington. I think it is an effort to turn this trial into a sideshow. I think it's demeaning. I object to it."

Digging through the box, Frank Granito III said, "Wait until you see these, Judge."

He, Steve Pounian, and Jim Kreindler started to hold up various items—a clock radio, a small dictating machine with two little batteries, a calculator, a gun, and a hand grenade.

At the sight of the weapons, Judge Platt recoiled. "I hope those things are not real."

James Shaughnessy interjected, "It's a replica of a gun and grenade. They're FAA-approved test objects."

Mitch Baumeister asked, "Did this come out of Frankfurt?"

Bud Coddington cleared his throat to get everyone's attention. "Now that the fellows who object to the circus have finished their circus, with Your Honor's indulgence, I will represent to the court that these are official test objects prescribed by the FAA in December of 1988 to be sent through X-ray stations to test operators whether they are doing a proper job," he said. "I propose to show them to this witness."

Once again, Judge Platt allowed Coddington to question Vincent to preserve the testimony for the record. But he refused to let him show the test objects to the jury.

The remaining cross and redirect went over points already made. When both sides were done, the plaintiffs rested their case. Lee felt that they'd managed to contain Coddington's most flagrant excesses. His grandstanding had not diluted the final two witness testimonies because he had to conduct his irrelevant discussion of X-ray machines and their usage out of earshot of the jury.

Coddington's antics did not sway the reporters attending the trial either. The following day, Lee was delighted to see the newspaper accounts of the trial. They all featured Billie Vincent's assertion that "Pan Am played Russian roulette with the lives of the passengers."

26

THE DEFENSE CIRCUS

On the afternoon of the plaintiffs' final witness testimony, after he sent the jury home, Judge Platt met with the attorneys to review upcoming scheduling issues and the defense timeline. During this "housekeeping" session, Bud Coddington announced that he intended to call 33 witnesses instead of the 25 he had previously submitted.

Lee immediately objected on the grounds it gave him and his team too little notice to prepare for cross-examination. He accused his opponent of holding back this information deliberately. Judge Platt was not happy about it either—it would extend the trial by at least a week—but he granted Pan Am's lawyers their request for an expanded witness list.

Similar to the plaintiffs' presentation, early defense testimony came in the form of written depositions. James Shaughnessy read most of the questions while other Pan Am defense attorneys read the answers from the witness box. Meanwhile, Bud Coddington stepped out to interview witnesses who'd flown in from other states and countries to testify.

Right from the outset, Shaughnessy tried to mislead the jury. He wanted to include testimony about the FAA verbally authorizing Pan Am's security director, Daniel Sonesen, to use X-ray screening instead of positive passenger baggage matching.

Sonesen was on the witness list, but Lee was not concerned about him. He had testified under oath several times, claiming that his "understanding" of the FAA verbal dispensation from the certain provisions of the ACSSP dated from a meeting in Miami in October of 1987. But Sonesen also admitted that the discussions never dealt with "extraordinary security airports" such as London and Frankfurt. Later, he claimed that the authorization stemmed from senior FAA personnel in 1986. But he could not provide the content of the conversations or the dates and venues when they supposedly occurred.

Lee was actually looking forward to cross-examining Sonesen and tying him up in knots, using his contradictory testimony against him.

Still, he and his team objected to Shaughnessy's attempt. They also caught the defense attorney referencing changes in FAA regulations post-Lockerbie despite Judge Platt's earlier ruling that such information was not admissible.

When he finally returned to the courtroom, Bud Coddington unveiled another obfuscation strategy by calling two security experts from Scotland Yard's bomb squad as witnesses. Peter Gurney and John Horne would offer anecdotal histories of pipe and car bombs, booby traps, mortars, and other improvised explosive devices (IEDs) encountered throughout their careers.

Lee knew what their testimony would cover from the depositions taken in London and objected. He and the other attorneys on the plaintiffs' team argued that their contributions were irrelevant to the issues of the trial.

Coddington countered that their testimony was essential and that they would "educate the jury on the make-up and use of IEDs and other types of bombs."

Judge Platt agreed with the plaintiffs' attorneys but allowed Coddington to take the testimony absent the jury to preserve it for the appeals court. Because Carla Martin raised national security concerns, he also excluded the public.

John Horne talked about metal fatigue, barometric switches, and other details of bomb manufacture, as well as explosives like Semtex and C-4. His testimony dragged on for hours.

In contrast, on cross-examination, Mitch Baumeister asked only one question, "The IED device that destroyed Pan Am 103—do you have any knowledge what the components were or what constituted the IED?"

"No," Horne admitted.

During Peter Gurney's testimony, Bud Coddington resumed his circus sideshow tactics. As Gurney discussed the limitations of black and white X-ray screening in detecting bomb initiators concealed in objects such as electric razors, Coddington brought out a small device and asked, "Can you identify this for us?"

The bomb expert explained, "It's a firing switch, a timing switch based on an electronic component known as a capacitor. The timing delay is built in during manufacture. This one should run for about four-and-a-half minutes if it has not been damaged. Then the light on the end will flash."

Looking at the wall clock in the back of the spectator seating, Coddington said, "Then let's wait until sixteen-and-a-half minutes past. It's very hard to tell with these clocks here."

Taken aback, Judge Platt interrupted, "You're going to have a little explosion here?"

"Yes, Judge," Coddington said.

Giving him a stern look, Judge Platt said, "Anybody that does that in this courtroom goes to jail for the night. That's what I have told the marshals."

"How about if it's a light bulb?"

"If it's an explosion, you're going."

"It's an awfully small bomb," Coddington wheedled.

"Should I send for the marshals?" Judge Platt warned.

Coddington refrained from demonstrating his little bomb.

During cross-examination, Frank Granito Jr read from the Gurney deposition that he had conducted in London:

> *Granito Jr: Do you plan to offer any opinion in this case that the bomb couldn't have been loaded onto the aircraft in Frankfurt?*
>
> *Gurney: I do not. I do not intend to voice an opinion on what brought down the plane or where it was loaded. Simple as that.*

After verifying that Gurney still held those views, Frank had him admit that he had nothing to say about the plaintiffs' contention that Pan Am had been negligent in its security measures.

Yet, following redirect, Coddington offered the Horne and Gurney testimonies in evidence, along with a slew of exhibits, slides, blowups, charts, and posters.

Judge Platt wouldn't have it. "In view of the answers about their knowledge on the Lockerbie incident itself and the facts concerning what went into the Lockerbie incident, I'm going to have to exclude all that testimony, at least for now," he said

Coddington did not hide his disappointment. "Just for the sake of the completeness of my record, I think the prejudice by the preclusion of this testimony is irredeemable."

Judge Platt responded, "You're entitled to your view."

"We are in great disagreement about this case."

"I know."

Coddington put on a pouting expression. "I am mindful of the fact that I am being eviscerated from time to time in your Honors' rulings. It is enormously painful to be so wrong so often in your court."

The Defense Circus

But Coddington turned petulant and played the victim only during sidebars and when the jury was absent. The rest of the time, he was all smiles and projected unwavering confidence.

Lee kept worrying about the effect of the many interruptions on the jurors. Would they feel the plaintiffs' attorneys were trying to hide something from them by excluding certain defense witnesses?

He and his team were also troubled by Judge Platt's increasing indignation at the conduct of Pan Am's lawyers and the strong anti-defendant position he took on some issues. They were concerned that he might go too far, which would lead to reversible errors on appeal.

In the meantime, Coddington tried his next ploy. He called Charles Stallings, the director of manufacturing and engineering for Samsonite, to identify the make of the suitcase that contained the Lockerbie bomb. At first, Lee did not realize why Coddington took that tack, but his intentions soon became clear.

The next witness, Derek Kemp, was the managing director at a subsidiary of Astrophysics, the company that manufactured X-ray machines. It had built and delivered the X-ray scanner to Alert at the Frankfurt airport used to examine the interline bags loaded onto Flight 103.

After establishing Kemp's background, Coddington sprung his surprise. "Have you had a chance to look at the X-ray machine you installed in the basement?" he asked his witness.

"Yes, I have," Kemp said. "It is an I-scan system seven, the largest, most powerful machine we make for baggage screening."

"How does it compare to the machine located in Frankfurt on December 21, 1988?"

"It is identical."

Coddington then turned to Judge Platt and proposed to pack a Samsonite suitcase with a Toshiba radio cassette and clothing articles and run it through the machine. "The purpose of the demonstration is to illustrate our theory of causation for the jury," he explained. "We're trying to prove the bomb didn't go through this X-ray. It found its way aboard the plane in some other fashion."

Lee objected strenuously. "There is no way to accurately reproduce the suitcase and its contents because the make and type of Toshiba radio are unknown," he said. "Furthermore, there is no way to recreate the conditions in Frankfurt at the time of Lockerbie."

To prove his point, he asked permission to question Kemp. When Judge Platt agreed, Lee began, "Mr. Kemp, do you know how the X-ray operator in Frankfurt on December 21, 1988, adjusted the contrast control on the machine he was using?"

"No," Kemp answered.

"Do you know how he adjusted the brilliance control?"

"No, I do not."

"And do you know how he adjusted the brightness control?"

"No."

"Do you personally know how long he spent examining the image of a single suitcase?

"I do not personally know."

"Did you speak to anyone who used the machine in Frankfurt on December 21, 1988?"

"No."

Addressing Judge Platt, Lee said, "Since there is no way to determine how the X-ray machine in Frankfurt was calibrated, the time spent examining the screen, the state of the operator, and more, it is impossible to reproduce the conditions accurately. Any testimony or conclusions would be speculative at best."

He turned back to Kemp and asked one more question, "Am I correct that a black-and-white X-ray machine is not designed to detect explosive devices in checkout bags?"

Kemp nodded. "Not designed to check explosives, no."

The Defense Circus

Still, Coddington continued to lobby for conducting the demonstration. "Your Honor, we would like to offer all of this testimony to the jury. We would like to have them go look at our machine."

Judge Platt disagreed, "I don't see any basis for that or the relevance."

Lee interjected, "There's no issue in this case as to whether the radio cassette player is detectable on this machine. It is. Okay? I don't know what can be clearer than that. But a bomb in a radio cassette is not visible on X-ray."

Coddington refused to give up. "I still want to go downstairs and show your Honor, and put on this whole demonstration for my record."

Lee still objected. "Judge, I would just ask Mr. Coddington what his ultimate offer of proof is on the machine. What is the purpose?"

"He hasn't made that clear yet," Judge Platt said. "Maybe he can't do it until Kurt Maier testifies."

Ultimately, he agreed to allow testimony to be taken at the machine, but by the attorneys only. However, he declined to put it into the trial record and refused to attend the demonstration despite Coddington's repeated requests.

Then, Judge Platt brought the jurors back and dismissed them for the rest of the day with the usual order not to discuss the case with anyone.

But before letting the attorneys head to the basement, he raised the issue of damage trials. Everyone knew it was a foregone conclusion that the case would be appealed regardless of the outcome. But if the jury held for the plaintiffs, the applicable law required monetary damages to be determined before an appeal could be launched.

"I've been thinking we can put the damage trials on right afterward, one after another," Judge Platt said. "We have ninety-three cases that we can try in a couple of days. Use the same jury. Dispose of them very rapidly, perhaps in two to three weeks. Save me and a lot of other people a lot of headaches. Save the government a lot of money."

The attorneys on both sides looked at each other in surprise.

Judge Platt continued, "I don't want to go through the jury selection process again. The last time, out of five-hundred-fifty prospects, we found only forty who didn't have extensive knowledge of the case through the media. It will take several months to get another." He looked at Lee and added, "I think you should start lining up your plaintiffs."

Lee considered the proposal. It would mean double work for the Plaintiffs Committee—participating in the current trial while simultaneously preparing for more to come. But he could see the benefits of not prolonging the litigation any more than necessary.

After receiving nods from everyone on his team, Lee agreed. "We will get ready, Your Honor."

* * *

The following day, Coddington called to the stand Richard Cozzi, Pan Am's systems director for airport services until shortly after Lockerbie. In 1987, he was co-chair of the Security Task Force created to respond to increased terrorist threats against airlines. Coddington took Cozzi through advisories and procedures, the installations of black and white X-ray machines in London and Frankfurt in 1987, the creation of Alert Management in 1988 to run airport security for Pan Am, and the training of operators. In the process, he painted a picture of an airline going out of its way to ensure the safety of its passengers.

Lee noticed that John Brennan was back in the courtroom, occupying his perch behind the defense table. He followed Cozzi's testimony closely.

Exploring how the task force wrote the Pan Am security manual, Coddington elicited from Cozzi that he thought the language of the ACSSP section dealing with screening and unaccompanied bags was "ambiguous." He also, finally, managed to introduce the idea that Daniel Sonesen had gotten oral permission from the FAA to replace positive passenger baggage matching by getting Cozzi to say that he used that understanding in his work with the task force.

"We met with Sonesen and subsequently did receive approval from the FAA that I don't believe was ever in writing. The procedures were taking place until I left Pan Am," Cozzi said.

Over Lee's objection that this was hearsay, Judge Platt allowed Cozzi to continue to testify in explanation of how the task force operated—that the committee was told the procedures were approved and wrote the Pan Am manual regulations accordingly.

In his cross-examination, Steve Pounian showed how little Cozzi knew about Alert's security employees' training at international airports. He began by asking, "Now, you agree, sir, that it was critical for the X-ray screener you were using to be properly trained, am I right?"

"Correct," Cozzi agreed.

"And that included a video course and demonstration models of explosive devices?"

"Yes."

"Would it surprise you to learn that the screener in Frankfurt, Mr. Maier, never received that course?"

"That would surprise me. Yes."

Pounian then got Cozzi to admit that the ACSSP language was "not in any way ambiguous" and made clear it required matching and did not allow X-ray as a substitute. "Am I correct that the section requires a positive passenger checked baggage match?" he asked.

"Yes, it does," Cozzi said.

"Do you have any doubt about that, sir, that it requires a match?"

THE FIGHT FOR JUSTICE

"It did require, for unaccompanied or interline baggage, that there be a match accomplished or the bag be properly security screened."

Glancing at the defense table, Lee was pleased to see Coddington tighten his fists in frustration. Brennan's self-satisfied smile had transformed into his familiar scowl.

Toward the end of the cross-examination, Pounian had Cozzi confirm that Pan Am, contrary to FAA regulations, relied on X-rays as the first and last line of defense to prevent a bomb from getting on the plane. He had all but turned Cozzi into a witness for the plaintiffs.

Coddington may have lost that battle, but he continued to fight the war. Next, he called three witnesses from Malta to demonstrate that security procedures were so tight that the bomb bag could not have originated there. Emmanuel Aigus was an official of Malta Airlines; Major Joseph Saliba, a government employee, served as a security officer at Loqua Airport in Malta; and Wilfred Borg was a ground manager for Malta Airlines.

But contrary to the defendant's claim that there was no unaccompanied luggage on KM 180, the feeder flight to Frankfurt, Frank Granito Jr, during cross-examination, pointed out that Air Malta's records indicated a discrepancy in the number of bags. The handwritten documents indicated 14, but a film crew that checked the actual load showed 16. Besides, half of Air Malta's baggage records were lost. And neither Major Saliba nor Wilfred Borg was directly involved in loading the luggage. Borg was not even at the airport when the Malta flight left for Frankfurt.

Surprisingly, the Malta witnesses also shed light on the involvement of Lamin Khalifa Fhimah, one of the two Libyans indicted for the Lockerbie bombing but ultimately not convicted. Fhimah was the Libyan Airlines station manager at Locqua Airport. Lee elicited testimony that Libyan Airlines used the same baggage tickets as Air

The Defense Circus

Malta and that a flight to Tripoli and KM 80 to Frankfurt were being processed simultaneously at the same counter. Therefore, Fhimah had unlimited access to the area where the bags for the flight to Frankfurt were put aboard.

For his next effort to distract the jury, Coddington proposed that the bomb bag had been switched with the "rush bag" of Captain John Hubbard, a Pan Am employee stationed in Berlin. Hubbard was about to pilot a flight to Karachi, Pakistan, before heading home to Washington State for Christmas. Because he did not want to carry all his luggage, Hubbard checked two brown Samsonite suitcases through to Frankfurt, destined for Seattle. They were X-rayed by Kurt Maier and put on Flight 103. But only one bag was found on the ground at Lockerbie after the disaster. The other arrived unharmed in Seattle.

According to Coddington, the suitcase that survived had been switched in Frankfurt with the notorious, 13th "rogue bag," which contained the bomb that was loaded onto the Pan Am aircraft. But the defense attorney presented no direct supporting evidence of how the switch might have occurred. Instead, he questioned Hubbard and, subsequently, ground crew witnesses from Frankfurt airport about how many access points there were to the tarmac, relying on innuendo rather than proof.

That afternoon, with witnesses' testimony concluded and out of earshot of the jury, Judge Platt asked what progress the plaintiffs' attorneys were making in preparing for damage trials.

Lee reported that they had made good progress but that the trials would take longer than expected. Because several corporate executives were among the victims, assessing damages would require testimony from economists, HR representatives from the companies for which some of the victims worked, and family members about their earning potential had they lived a full life. "These are pretty big cases," he said.

THE FIGHT FOR JUSTICE

Judge Platt sighed unhappily and said, "You have ninety-three people. You ought to be able to streamline things. Given the horrendous status of our calendar and courtroom space, I don't know if I can do anything other than hold on to this jury and try them."

Before Lee could respond, defense attorney Richard Sharp spoke up, "If I may address that, Your Honor. I think the orthodox and most expeditious manner is to try sample cases. There is precedent for this in other liability trials."

After considering his suggestion, Judge Platt said, "As far as I'm concerned, we might as well get the cases all disposed of. But if you want to do it on a sample basis, I will be glad to do it that way."

Lee said, "I don't see why we can't go ahead with five."

Judge Platt looked at Sharp and Coddington and said, "I'm amenable if you can get your client to agree."

Coddington said, "I will speak to John Brennan about it."

When Lee met with the Plaintiffs Committee and discussed options, they divided the five damage cases. Mitch Baumeister and Frank Granito Jr would prepare one each, and Lee's law firm got ready for three.

27

KURT MAIER

As his star witness, Coddington called Kurt Maier. Knowing the defense considered him the linchpin to its case, Lee expected to see John Brennan return after a few days' absence and was not disappointed. The USAU chairman sat two rows in the back of the defense table, watching the proceedings like a hawk.

When Maier took the stand, Lee noticed that he had visibly aged since his last deposition two years earlier. His skin was sallow, and his hair had thinned further. The ill-fitting gray suit and dark blue tie he wore looked as if he'd bought them in a thrift shop just for his appearance at the trial. He seemed uncomfortable and sat in the witness box with his shoulders hunched up.

Because of his limited ability in English, Maier required an interpreter. Just like during the depositions in Frankfurt, questions and answers had to be translated from English to German and back. That made for halting and tedious testimony, especially because Maier tended to ramble. Still, the delay allowed people to closely observe his reactions when Lee asked him penetrating questions.

But first, Bud Coddington began by having Maier outline his career. He had worked nearly 40 years as supervisor, inspector, and sales manager for a company that installed large-scale, institutional bakeries. When the German economy suffered a recession, business dried up, and the company downsized. Maier lost his job and was forced to look for work elsewhere. He moved to South Africa, but his efforts to start a new career there failed. Returning to Germany, he got a job with Pan Am in Frankfurt in March 1988. At first, Maier cleaned cabins and airplanes, but when the opportunity arose, he joined Alert Management as an X-ray operator to screen baggage. He started on November 10 and continued to work in that capacity until his retirement in 1991.

Next, Coddington touched on Maier's on-the-job training, conducted by an experienced operator, and his workload of 20 days a month. By the time he asked about various warnings regarding potential terrorist attacks prior to December 21, including the Helsinki warning, Maier had relaxed somewhat.

Coddington drew his attention to a chance lunchtime encounter with his supervisor, Oliver Koch, before Lockerbie, during which they discussed radios. "What was it that Mr. Koch told you on this subject?" the lawyer asked.

Maier looked up at the ceiling to gather his thoughts and said, "He asked me to come into his office, and he showed me a file that contained special instructions and illustrations regarding Toshiba radio cassette recorders and other devices, explaining how these could be used to hide explosives. He went on to say that when I see these pictures on my monitor, I will not be able to detect whether they contain an explosive charge or not."

"Did this gentleman give you any directives on what to do if you found an item of this type?"

"Yes. He instructed me that if I were to see such a picture on the monitor, to call the supervisor of Pan Am, who alone had the discretion to decide whether to let the piece of luggage pass through or to call the passenger and open it for inspection."

Zeroing in on December 21, 1988, Coddington handed the witness the worksheets he had signed to report on the screenings he performed that day. Maier took out reading glasses to look them over.

That led to an interjection by Lee and a lengthy discussion about Maier's use of glasses. It culminating in Coddington asking Maier, "Did you wear glasses to watch the monitor on your X-ray machine?"

Maier answered, "No, I did not. I have very good optical capability and use these glasses only when I read something with a fairly small print."

Satisfied, Coddington returned to dealing with Maier's worksheets, starting with his routine at 9 a.m. "What did you do at that time?"

"I signed my name, and then I wrote, 'Equipment is being plugged in for operation use,'" Maier explained. "After making sure it was under power, I sat in my cabin, turned the switch, and checked the zoom, the luminosity, and the conveyor belt. Then I ran a test object through the equipment, checking on the screen to what extent I had to change the luminosity and contrast of the picture to have an optimum image of the bags running through."

Following some questions and clarifications regarding the exact translation of specific German terms, Coddington introduced worksheets for the earlier flights on December 21. X-raying their bags, Maier found no radios in any of them.

Lee had to acknowledge that Coddington was doing a good job building the narrative step by step to create a sense of expectation in the courtroom. He knew he had his work cut out for him on cross-examination.

Maier continued to testify that after his lunch break, he returned and restarted the equipment at 3:30 p.m. He rechecked the settings and prepared to X-ray the next flight, Pan Am 103, for luggage screening at 4:25.

Coddington handed him a worksheet and said, "Please read the entry on item ten just one line at a time, or however it is convenient so that our translator can translate."

Explaining his notes, Maier said, "I identified Pan American, which would not have been necessary since we only handled Pan American, and then I wrote, 'In the through-run, a control was made of ten suitcases, two flight bags, and one carton, having been transported through the equipment.' I saw no special markings in any of them, so I wrote 'NE,' which meant 'nothing exceptional.' The whole operation ended at 16:30 hours, meaning 4:30 p.m."

Pausing for emphasis, Coddington pointed to the worksheet and asked, "In the thirteen items that you examined on December 21, 1988, Herr Maier, were there any Toshiba radios?"

Immediately, Lee jumped up from his chair. "Objection. Leading."

Judge Platt asked, "Wait a minute. Why can't he ask that question?"

Lee explained, "I think he should ask what he saw and didn't see."

A humorous smile played at the corners of the Judge's mouth. "Well, Mr. Kreindler," he said, "it's going to be virtually impossible to get this witness to answer the questions like that. I'm going to have to let him lead and let you lead. Otherwise, we'll be here until August with this witness. Go ahead, Mr. Coddington."

Nodding with satisfaction, Coddington asked again, "Were there any radios in those items you X-rayed?"

"No," Maier said.

Lee expected the defense attorney to wind up and got ready to cross-examine the witness. But Coddington turned to Judge Platt and said, "Before I finish, we have that other matter that I should bring up to you briefly at the sidebar."

After the plaintiff and defense attorneys gathered at the judge's bench, he said, "In the bowels of your court, as if from a Stephen King novel, is located an Astrophysics Linescan machine, and I would like to take Maier and your Honor and these twelve good people on the jury down there and show them how it works, if you please."

Judge Platt was not amused. "I have ruled on this," he said, irritated. "The answer is No."

As if he expected that response, Coddington said almost teasingly, "You break my heart. Aren't you curious what it looks like, Judge?"

"No."

"Just a little?"

"No."

Lee interjected, "Your Honor, I object to this. This is once again a kind of a sideshow."

Judge Platt said, "I sustain the objection. I don't see the relevance of this. Are you finished, Mr. Coddington?"

"Yes, your Honor."

"Please proceed, Mr. Kreindler."

Lee began his cross-examination by establishing that Maier had misread the numbers on some of the worksheets, apparently needing stronger reading glasses. Over Coddington's vehement objections, he tried to raise the possibility that perhaps Maier needed them to screen luggage after all. Although he did not win that argument, he was pleased to have needled Coddington and establish that Maier was not the most reliable witness.

Then, he addressed Maier's earlier testimony about his meeting with Oliver Koch. "Did Mr. Koch, during the brief, five-minute chance conversation that you told us about, limit himself to radio cassette players or radios, or did he discuss with you all electronic equipment?"

Maier answered confidently, "He referred principally to the radio recorder of the make Toshiba and insisted that any such device cannot be passed without calling the supervisor."

"Did he mention bombs inside the radios?"

"Specifically? No."

"How about calculators?"

"No. We did not have any occasion to discuss the possibility of hiding bombs in objects prior to December 21, 1988."

Without missing a beat, Lee switched topics. "You've given your deposition twice in this case, have you not?"

Maier nodded. "Yes."

"Once in 1989 in Frankfurt and again in New York in April 1990?"

"Yes."

"And on both occasions, you testified under oath?"

"Yes."

Lee turned to Judge Platt and said, "I would like to play excerpts from the 1990 deposition."

At a signal from the judge, a clerk rolled out the large video screen and positioned it next to the witness box, angled so that the jury and most of the audience could see it. Maier had to turn and look over his shoulder to watch.

When Lee finished playing the excerpt from the earlier deposition, he asked Maier pointedly, "Was your memory, your recollection of your conversation with Mr. Koch, better at that time than today?"

Looking at his hands, Maier said, "Yes. Two years ago, it must have been fresher. But even then, one should remember that I was asked about an event that took place almost two years earlier."

Lee pressed him, "And having watched this and heard it, isn't it a fact that Koch never mentioned Toshiba? Yes or no."

Maier visibly squirmed. "I cannot remember whether he actually referred –"

Lee refused to let him off the hook. "In your statement in the deposition, you never said anything about Toshiba, did you?"

Coddington tried to run interference, jumping to his feet and shouting, "Objection."

But Judge Platt said, "Overruled," and directed Maier, "Answer the question."

With resignation, Maier admitted, "No, I did not."

Lee drove the point home, "Isn't it a fact that in none of your earlier testimony, first in the deposition in Frankfurt and then here in New York, did you ever mention Toshiba?"

"That is quite possible."

By then, it was late afternoon, and Judge Platt stopped the testimony until the next day.

The following morning, as he took the stand again, Maier looked like he hadn't gotten much sleep. The bags under his eyes had darkened. As questioning resumed, the video screen was still standing next to the witness box.

Lee took a different tack. "Did you know anything about a warning to Pan Am that a flight to the United States would be bombed within weeks?"

Maier answered, "No."

"If you had been told that, would you have acted differently in using the X-ray machine and handling the baggage?"

Maier answered more confidently, "No, I would not have acted differently, except that, as always, I would have watched for suspicious objects."

Lee said, "In your 1990 deposition, were you asked this question"—he read from a notepad: "'On December 21, 1988, you did not know that there had been a bomb threat addressed to Pan American for flights within two weeks?'" He waited for the translator to finish and continued, "And did you give this answer to the question: 'No, because then we would certainly have taken different measures because it is a very important piece of information.'?"

Maier attempted to explain, "There are various domains of security. What I meant was that other units in our system might have taken other and stronger measures. But in my area, all I could do was inspect the luggage carefully with the X-ray equipment at my disposal."

Lee honed in, "Mr. Maier, isn't it a fact that you were not stopping radio cassette recorders and other electronic devices when you saw them in luggage unless they appeared to you to be suspicious?"

After listening to the translation, Maier said, "That's a hypothetical question."

Lee refused to be sidetracked. "Let me put it this way, Mr. Maier. Are you testifying that you were stopping every electronic device you saw in that luggage? Is that your testimony?"

"Certainly not."

"And isn't it true that you would let a radio cassette recorder go through, and you would not call the supervisor unless it looked suspicious to you?"

"I would not have let any radio cassette recorder pass through."

Addressing Judge Platt, Lee said, "Your Honor, at this time, we want to play more of Mr. Maier's prior testimony on video. But I would like to ask him another question before playing the tape."

The Judge said, "Go ahead."

"Isn't it a fact, Mr. Maier, that you don't remember if there were any radio cassette recorders in the luggage that you X-rayed for Flight 103?" Lee said.

"I remember that in those pieces of luggage for Flight 103, there were no radio or electronic devices of any kind." Maier insisted.

The courtroom was dimmed, and the videotape captured several exchanges. Watching Maier in the witness box was riveting, side by side with his image on the video screen larger than life, contradicting what he had just said. Everyone could see him testify in the deposition that for each flight leading up to Pan Am 103, he could not remember if there was a radio cassette in any of the luggage bags.

When the lights came up again, Lee asked, "Do you wish now to correct your testimony that you were not routinely stopping radio cassette players unless they looked suspicious?"

Maier looked toward the defense table for help, but none was forthcoming.

Lee continued to corner him, "That was true, wasn't it, Mr. Maier? What you just said in that tape?"

"Yes."

"When you testified under oath in April of 1990, didn't you say that for every single flight that day, including and particularly Flight 103, you had no recollection whatsoever whether a radio was there or not? Didn't you say that?"

Again, Coddington tried to run interference, "I would object because it's compound and –"

Judge Platt cut him off, "Overruled."

Coddington continued, "– and because Mr. Kreindler is leaping in his face and shouting."

"Overruled!"

"And answer that yes or no," Lee demanded.

The interpreter interjected, "He wants to have the question repeated."

Lee immediately said, "Isn't it a fact, Mr. Maier, that with respect to Pan Am 103, you don't remember now, and you didn't remember on April 4, 1990, when you gave your deposition, when your memory was better, whether there were or were not radio cassette players in the bags for Pan Am 103? That testimony was true, was it not, Mr. Maier?

Defeated, Maier said, "Yes."

"And your recollection, your memory was better in April of 1990 than it is today. Isn't that right?"

"Certainly not worse."

"No further questions."

Lee returned to the Plaintiffs' table without looking at Coddington, but he saw Brennan sitting among the spectators at the back of the defense table. The USAU chairman gave him a murderous look. Lee had just neutralized his star witness by catching Maier lying throughout his testimony.

The jury knew it, too, and they did not like it. As Maier left the witness stand, he avoided looking at them, and several jurors scowled at him in disgust.

28

CLOSING ARGUMENTS

July 6—7, 1992

When Bud Coddington did not call Daniel Sonesen to testify, as promised during his opening statement, Lee knew his opponent had given up trying to prove that Pan Am received oral permission to replace positive baggage matching with X-ray screening. While not abandoning his efforts entirely, the cunning defense attorney certainly put them on the back burner.

But Coddington thought he had two more irons in the fire. Immediately after Kurt Maier exited the courtroom, he called to the stand Ariel Merari, an Israeli expert on terrorism, who had flown in from Tel Aviv two days earlier. And he had Noah Koch, another terrorism specialist, waiting in the wings. Coddington wanted to conclude with expert witnesses as Lee had with Wallis and Vincent, but he had a different purpose. Unable to counter the plaintiffs' case of how the bomb got on Flight 103 or how careless Pan Am had been about security, he wanted to leave the jury with the impression, as he had claimed in his opening statement, that it was impossible to protect an airline against terrorists determined to wreak havoc.

Lee and his team were ready. They knew from the depositions of Merari and Koch that they would offer background on extremist groups, explain how terrorists are "formidable," how terrorism is like "other forms of warfare," and how it is "virtually unstoppable." They would further contend that governments did not aid and protect airlines sufficiently against threats.

Objecting to the witnesses on the grounds of relevance, Lee said to Judge Platt, "I'd like to know what their defense is. We've been waiting three and a half years."

Stung, Coddington responded, "Then you can wait a little longer!"

Lee ignored him. "I think they should tell the court and us what they're trying to prove," he said. "They haven't explained what the testimony has to do with this case. The witnesses know nothing about Lockerbie. They know nothing about the circumstances. They just want to talk about terrorism and war."

Arguing for Merari's and Koch's inclusion, Coddington introduced different rationales, but Judge Platt would have none of them. "You're expecting me to let an expert testify to a hypothetical, that the most common way for a bomb to get on a plane is via the unwitting passenger when there is no such proof in this case," he said. "There is no excuse for what you're trying to do here. It is an attempt to get speculations before the jury about how this might have occurred without anything to back it up." He continued, "What seems to be the defense here is that, even if all feasible counter-terrorism measures are implemented, not all terrorist attacks will be thwarted."

Richard Sharp tried to come to Coddington's aid. "Your Honor, they have the burden of proof. To come forward with another theory, we don't have to have another theory of causation."

"That's right," Judge Platt agreed. "But you want to produce this other theory out of thin air."

"We want to show that their theory is weak, if not unlikely," Sharp answered. "And to do that, we lay out a number of circumstances, probabilities, and possibilities."

Judge Platt scoffed, "Mr. Sharp, the fact that the Chase Manhattan Bank was robbed with a particular MO the first ten times, and I go in and use essentially the same operation the eleventh time, doesn't mean that I committed the other ten robberies. This is the kind of evidence that you're trying to get me to buy here. You have to have something more to hang it on."

Ultimately, Judge Platt allowed the witnesses to testify out of the jury's presence. Lee and his team did not bother to cross-examine.

After Merari and Koch finished Monday morning, Judge Platt announced that closing arguments would begin when everyone returned after lunch.

Because several law firms represented the victims' families, the Plaintiffs Committee had decided that Lee, as lead attorney, would go first to set the tone and present the evidence. Frank Granito Jr would follow him. After Bud Coddington and Jim Shaughnessy had their say for the defense, Mitch Baumeister would conclude with a rebuttal.

Lee was not happy to receive so little advance notice and said so, but Judge Platt insisted on moving things along. The trial had gone on much longer than anticipated, and he was impatient to finish it. Lee objected that proceedings would continue in their courtroom rather than in the larger venue he had requested to accommodate the many family members who wanted to attend in person. He knew how much it mattered to them to be there and witness the finish. The press and television reporters constituted a bigger presence as well. But Judge Platt remained adamant that he wanted no further delay.

Of course, Lee had spent much of the Fourth of July weekend at his home in Chappaqua, preparing his summation. He knew from first-hand experience that closing arguments could be more important than the rest of a trial.

Some years earlier he sued Delta Airlines on behalf of the three daughters of an IBM executive and his wife for wrongful death in a plane crash in Dallas. The defense had better witnesses, and Lee thought he had lost the case, but his summation made the difference. One juror later said that the closing arguments of IBM's attorneys were thorough, detailed, and too slick. In contrast, Lee did his best with what little he had available. Without trying to be "folksy," he had talked to the jurors like they were regular people. Ultimately, they believed him rather than his opponents because he was honest and more real, and they held in his favor.

Holed up in his study, Lee did not even take time to enjoy the fireworks but kept refining his final arguments because so much was hanging on the Pan Am case. Kreindler & Kreindler was still hovering on the edge of financial ruin, as did the law firms of Frank Granito and Mitch Baumeister. Even if the verdict were favorable, they would have to figure out how to survive during the appeals and settlement process afterward. If they lost, they would have to declare bankruptcy.

After lunch, when everyone had settled in the courtroom and the jury came in, Lee looked for Ruth. She sat in the rear, as always, to avoid attention. She gave him a reassuring smile, although she was as tense and nervous as he was.

When Judge Platt gave him the floor, Lee did not glance at his notes. He took off his glasses, rose from his chair, and went to the podium. He briefly made eye contact with each jury member. Then, he laid out what was at stake and outlined the two areas he would cover in his closing statement—summarizing the evidence and explaining why the jurors should hold for the plaintiffs.

> I can say to you today that I believe we have fulfilled our contract, that everything the plaintiffs said they would prove to you has, in fact, been proven. I firmly believe that we have established the elements of our case arising from tragic, tragic circumstances.

For the first time, he uttered the words "willful misconduct." Judge Platt had not permitted him, or any other plaintiff or defense attorney, to say them during the factual portion of the trial.

Closing Arguments

> When you retire to deliberate, to reach your verdict, you will essentially be answering two questions. The first is whether there was willful misconduct, and the second is whether the willful misconduct—if you answer yes to the first question—caused or was a substantial factor in causing the deaths of all the decedents.

He then spent the next hour discussing eight points of willful misconduct and three of causation in easy-to-follow language.

Starting with the applicable law, he went over the requirement of airlines to follow the ACSSP regulations to the letter.

Next, he addressed deceit: how Pan Am had lied to the public about its state of security in its advertisements.

Then, he discussed Pan Am committing fraud: collecting a surcharge for extra security measures but not implementing them as promised.

Fourth, he covered neglect: failing to inform the pilots of the Frankfurt and London flights that there were unaccompanied bags aboard.

Fifth, he explored Alert Management's deliberately deceiving the FAA during inspections.

With point six, he cut to the heart of the plaintiffs' case: Pan Am intentionally abandoning the positive match requirement to cut costs and time.

For point seven, he dealt with the ground operators not receiving the warnings of a planned terrorist attack on Pan Am; possibly with radio cassette recorders containing bombs.

Finally, he spoke to the willful misconduct of intentionally failing to train, supervise and warn the ground security operators and screeners, as required by the ACSSP.

In addressing causation, Lee delved into the bomb traveling in the unaccompanied interline bag on Air Malta. Then, he examined the ground operations in Frankfurt and concluded that they were "so mindless, so permeated with fault, that however that bag got on the airplane, Pan Am was responsible." And he reviewed the expert testimony of Wallis and Vincent, their opinions and conclusions.

Lee also singled out Kurt Maier. "I never expected to see an important witness with testimony at the core of the case show up in court and change his testimony that he had given on two earlier occasions," he said. "Utterly, utterly shameful."

He concluded on a personal note and raised the larger implications of the trial.

> My father told me a couple of things when I started as an attorney. He said never underestimate the intelligence of a juror and always have faith in the jury.
>
> I believe the jury is the community in microcosm. But I submit to you that you are not only the local community but the world community. Your verdict, ladies and gentlemen, can determine in large part whether, in the future, other mothers and fathers, wives and husbands, will have to suffer the same kind of agony that the Lockerbie families have suffered. I believe, truly, that you can make it impossible for another Lockerbie to happen.
>
> Therefore, I earnestly suggest to you that your message to this and other airlines should be, "You cannot do it. This must never happen." And I don't think it's an exaggeration to say that the whole world is listening and waiting.

Lee took a moment to let his final words sink in and returned to his seat at the plaintiffs' table. He felt surprisingly calm and barely registered the encouraging nods from Jim, Steve Pounian, Frank Granito Jr, and Mitch Baumeister. Although the emotional appeal at the end may have seemed calculated, Lee believed what he said with all his heart. That made him so compelling—he never lied to the people he tried to persuade.

Closing Arguments

When Frank Granito Jr asked for a short break before commencing his summation, Judge Platt said, "I think it will just prolong this matter. Let's continue."

So, Frank buttoned his jacket, cleared his throat, and began. He concentrated on the two witnesses Bud Coddington had mentioned in his opening statement as important to the defense: Daniel Sonesen and Kurt Maier. He demonstrated their unreliability and appalling lack of knowledge about airport security. Focusing on Sonesen, the "absent witness" and number two man in security at Pan Am's headquarters, he read a section of his deposition testimony.

> *Granito Jr: Is my understanding correct that unless the FAA says otherwise, the ACSSP represents the minimum acceptable standard for air safety in the area of security?*
>
> *Sonesen: Yes.*
>
> *Granito Jr: Unless the FAA says differently, it is the duty of the air carrier to comply with the provisions of the ACSSP.*
>
> *Sonesen: Yes.*
>
> *Granito Jr: And unless the FAA says differently, there must be strict compliance with the provisions. Is that correct?*
>
> *Sonesen: Yes.*

Lee was impressed. They had discussed the strategy of using Pan Am's executive to make the case for the plaintiffs, but these admissions made for powerful closing testimony.

After going over Maier's selective memory, the betrayal of the pilot, and the clothes in the bomb bag being traced back to the same shop in Malta, Frank built on Lee's closing and concluded by referencing Rodney Wallis.

> I want to join Mr. Kreindler in expressing the thought that you are probably being asked to deliberate on the most significant aviation case in the 20th century.

> I believe that a yes answer to the questions that you will be asked to decide—yes, there was a causal relation between the conduct and the tragedy—will send a message to the entire aviation world that we will not tolerate the air carrier playing Russian Roulette with their passengers.

After Frank sat down, Judge Platt dismissed the jury with his usual admonition, "Don't talk to anyone about the case."

Reading the courtroom—the jurors' body language leaving, the spectators' muted conversations, and the guarded acknowledgments of some of the victims' family members—Lee concluded that he and Frank had presented convincing arguments.

As he met up with Ruth, she hugged him and said, "You did great, darling."

The next day, the spectator seats behind the defense table were filled with Pan Am and USAU personnel, notably Tom Plaskett, James Brennan, and Russell Mirabile. Except for the insurance company president, the others had avoided most of the trial.

When Judge Platt called on him, Bud Coddington adjusted his tie, rose, and approached the podium with a melancholy, hang-dog expression. After acknowledging the judge, the defense VIPs, and the jury, he professed his deep concern for his client.

> I am saddened to see what was once the world's greatest airline having to pass through one of the most awful ordeals ever visited upon an air carrier; ever visited upon men and women in the transportation business. That airline, of course, itself was a victim of the disaster.

Then, he tarred the plaintiffs' attorneys with the brush of prejudice and emotional blackmail.

> Most of all, I think I regret the hateful attack launched by the plaintiffs' attorneys. They have tried to arouse you against us because the terrorists who did this deed and

the states who sponsor them are beyond their reach. We are the only ones they can reach. For that reason, they ask you to wreak private vengeance against us.

He singled out Lee specifically.

From the beginning of this case, Mr. Kreindler has played to your sympathies, your passion, and your prejudice. He tried to whip you up to make you lose sight of the real issues. He started right off in his opening statement using the word "abominable." Do you know what this word means? That's a sixty-four-dollar word, which means worthy of hatred, loathing and disgust.

Do you think we are worthy of hatred, loathing, and disgust? I mean, abominable is about as mean a word as you can put on somebody.

Of course, he came up with a lot more—amazing, utterly shameful, flagrant, awful, fraud, deceit, and money-grubbing.

Listening to the litany of grievances, Lee suppressed a smile. Coddington had reminded the jury of a word he had not used since his opening. The man could not have done him a better favor, bringing his accusations of Pan Am full circle.

Meanwhile, Coddington broadened his personal attacks to include various plaintiff witnesses. He called Detective Henderson "a low-ranking police constable" and referred to Rodney Wallis once more as a "paid reader." He argued at length that the terrorist bombing was a deliberate act of murder and retaliation for the accidental shooting down of an Iranian passenger aircraft by the U.S.S. *Vincennes* six months before Lockerbie. "It is a case about terrorism, political vengeance, violence, retribution, hatred, bombs, state sponsors, low-intensity warfare and sophistication, and of course, evasion of security," he said.

After attacking the Malta bomb bag theory using selective testimony from his two Malta Airport witnesses, he asked his "friend Jim Shaughnessy" to refute the plaintiffs' witness testimony of what happened in Frankfurt.

For the next hour, Shaughnessy inundated the jury with details from various records and computer printouts, using large charts and exhibits, to show that FAG was too complex to determine a single bag's location in the transportation system. He read out the numbers of the transfer stations, bag tags, and flight baggage containers and concluded, "Therefore, there is no way, looking at the FAG record, that you can really tell whether any particular bag came from any particular flight. The records are a shambles."

Watching the jurors when Shaughnessy finished, Lee noticed them shifting in their seats, taking deep breaths, loosening stiff muscles, and hiding yawns. It seemed that they had endured the presentation rather than absorbed it. The defense lawyer had done his cause little good.

When Coddington returned, he tried to debunk the notion that Pan Am decided to switch to X-ray screening deliberately. He spent a considerable amount of time attacking the testimony of Billie Vincent and quibbled about the meaning of "inspection" vs. "search," claiming they can mean the same thing when it comes to unaccompanied bags.

Unlike Lee, Coddington packed his summation with hyper-emotional appeals. He told a story by the 19th-century Russian novelist Fyodor Dostoyevsky about an old horse, a little sorrel mare, being flogged to death by its cruel owner when it did not do his bidding. "Man's cruelty to man. It is a terrible thing," he said with a sorrowful expression. "And you know, sometimes I think we at Pan Am feel like the little sorrel mare. They beat us and beat us, and we didn't do it."

He finished with a warning, raising his hand like a minister testifying:

Closing Arguments

> I say before God I believe Pan Am did no wrong here. If you can look at one another and at me, with the light that God gives you, to see a fair and just result, I think you will bring it back in favor of Pan Am. If you return your verdict against Pan Am, it is my fear that you will hear in your dreams for the rest of your life the whispered laughter of the terrorists who did this deed.

As Coddington returned to the defense table, he nodded to Plaskett and Brennan and sat with his head down as if overcome by emotion.

Lee glanced at the jurors to gauge the impact of his closing statement. Several looked at each other in dismay. He felt a moment of dread. Had they been taken in by Coddington's showmanship? Would his emotional appeals sway them in Pan Am's favor?

After a short recess, Mitch Baumeister wasted no time in his rebuttal to inject a dose of reason into the proceedings.

> One thing missing in this case is a defense. We have heard Mr. Coddington and Mr. Shaughnessy talk to you for two-and-a-half hours. They haven't presented one shred of evidence to you. Lawyers' arguments, lawyers' tactics to create a smoke screen, a red herring, but no evidence. If you take enough mud and throw it against the wall, maybe some of it will stick.
>
> How many aviation security experts have they produced in this courtroom to tell you that Pan Am did everything properly? Not one. Not a single one. Only smoke. Smoke and mirrors.

He summarized the core issue of Pan Am's failure to provide the required security and argued that the case is about corporate responsibility. He echoed Vincent's words, "This was a disaster waiting to happen," and appealed to the jury's common sense before concluding:

> The families have waited three and half years to have their story told. You will now have a chance to render

your verdict on behalf of the families and the victims.
Let your verdict speak the truth about Pan Am's conduct.

Lee thought Baumeister did a superb job countering Coddington's emotional bravado with clear reality checks. He could only hope that it was enough.

After the lunch recess, Judge Platt gave his instructions to the jury. He reiterated what Lee had said at the beginning of his summation, that the jury was to decide two questions: Had the defendants engaged in one or more acts of willful misconduct? And, was any willful misconduct a proximate cause of the destruction of Flight 103 and the deaths of its passengers? Then, he elaborated:

> Willful misconduct does not mean that the defendants or any of their employees had a deliberate intention to kill any of the passengers or wreck the airplane. Willful misconduct is the intentional performance of an act with the knowledge that it will probably result in injury or damage, or it may be the intentional performance of an act in such a manner as to imply disregard of the probable consequences.

He discussed the jury's mandate and responsibilities and reminded them that the plaintiffs must prove their case by a "preponderance of evidence." He also discussed the law as it applies to FAA directives, such as the ACSSP, and explained the difference between factual and opinion-based evidence. Altogether, he spoke for nearly an hour. Then, he sent the jurors to their room to begin deliberations. It was 3:10 p.m.

Lee watched them exit the side door of the courtroom slowly, as if they carried a heavy burden on their shoulders. None of them looked back. He would have preferred Judge Platt's instructions to be more tilted toward the plaintiffs' side, but he had to admit they were fair, and he could live with them.

29

THE VERDICT

Jury deliberations in complex trials do not offer the courtroom participants much of a breather. The lawyers for both sides had to wait in the courtroom or hallways in case jurors asked for clarifications or wanted to hear the testimony of certain witnesses again. Judge Platt would confer with the attorneys for both sides to decide how to present the material. If it was a legal question, he would provide the answer with input from the plaintiffs and defense counsels. If it was a document or chart, clerks would take copies or a blown-up version to the jury room. If it was live or deposition statements, the jury returned to the courtroom and listened to one of the judge's law clerks read the relevant passages or, in some cases, the entire testimony.

Shortly after the jurors began their deliberations, they sent a note to Judge Platt asking for maps of the Malta, Frankfurt, and Heathrow Airports, and the opinion testimonies of Rodney Wallis and Billie Vincent.

As the jurors filed into the courtroom for the reading of testimony, Jim whispered to Lee, "It's a good sign that they want to go over our expert testimony right away, don't you think?"

Lee was less confident. "I have learned never to second-guess what jurors mean when they ask for clarification or ways to refresh their memories," he said. "Once you start playing that game, you're on an emotional roller coaster ride to nowhere."

As expected, everyone went home that evening with nothing settled.

Early on July 8, the jurors asked Judge Platt to clarify the definition of willful misconduct, and he reiterated his earlier explanation:

> Willful misconduct does not mean the defendants had a deliberate intention to kill the passengers or wreck the airplane. It is the intentional performance of an act with the knowledge that it will probably result in injury or damage. Or it could be the intentional performance of an act in such a manner as to imply disregard of the probable consequences. Likewise, the intentional omission to act with knowledge that it will probably result in damage or injury would also be willful misconduct.

The jurors also asked to hear again the testimony of the two Malta Airport employees. Then, they wanted the blow-ups of the ACSSP regulations for online/interline passenger baggage searching brought to their deliberation room.

At the end of a long day, Judge Platt brought the jurors back into the courtroom. They looked tired and dejected. When they had settled in their seats, the judge singled out the heavy-set, middle-aged woman sitting closest to the witness box. Wearing a dark gray dress, she looked ready to go to a funeral.

"Juror Number One, are you acting as foreperson?" he asked.

She nodded hesitantly.

"I'm not trying to pressure you," the judge continued. "I'm trying to find out whether you are close to a unanimous verdict on each of these two questions, or whether it would be wise to send you home to get a good night's sleep and bring you back tomorrow."

The woman sighed and said, "We are not close at all."

So, Judge Platt excused the jury with the usual admonition not to discuss the case with anyone.

The Verdict

Lee and Ruth went to dinner with several victims' families, doing their best to buoy everyone's spirits. They kept the conversation light, asking about children, travel plans, and favorite summer movies. Neither had seen *My Cousin Vinnie* and *Batman Returns*, but they had heard about them and considered them "safe" topics.

Later, in their room at the Union Club, Lee called John Merritt in England. He knew the reporter was an early riser. Since helping break open the Lockerbie case for the plaintiffs, John had contracted leukemia and had been in and out of the hospital several times. Although his doctors told him to take it easy, he never stopped writing. Lee considered him a friend and had updated him throughout the trial. That night, John had good news: his wife Lindsay was pregnant with their second child.

Lee was delighted. He put Ruth on the phone so that she could congratulate him. They signed off, wishing John all the best, and slept better that night than in weeks.

Soon after the trial resumed the following morning, one of the clerks handed Judge Platt a note signed by Jurors Number 1 and 9. They were unhappy with spending another day deliberating and did not want to sit beyond today.

In discussing the matter with the attorneys, the judge voiced his concern, "It's quite clear that by the end of the day, I will have two rebellious jurors here. Perhaps it is time to give an Allen charge to the jury."

When jurors cannot agree on a verdict and report it to the judge, he can issue further instructions to encourage those in the minority to reconsider their position. The name dates from an 1896 Supreme Court case, Allen v. United States, which first approved offering such instructions to prevent a hung jury.

Lee suggested giving the jurors more time and was surprised that Bud Coddington backed him up. It was a rare moment of agreement.

As an alternative, James Shaughnessy offered an earlier motion he had made asking for a summary judgment to dismiss the case.

Judge Platt looked at him with irritation. "I thought I'd made myself clear. I am not going to take the case away from the jury."

Instead, he called the jurors into the courtroom. When they were seated, he said, "We all know you are attempting to discharge your duties conscientiously. However, I want to charge you additionally at this time because this is an important case. Your failure to agree upon a verdict will necessitate another trial. Nothing indicates that it can be better tried or presented any more exhaustively than it has been by both sides. Also, there is no reason to believe that the case will be submitted to a jury more intelligent, impartial, or more competent to decide."

The judge waited as several jurors looked at one another in surprise and continued, "Now, it is your duty to decide the case if you can conscientiously do so. In order to bring twelve minds together to a unanimous result, you must consider the matters submitted to you with candor and with proper regard and deference to the opinions of others. You should not, any of you, adopt a stubborn, close-minded attitude here."

He took a moment to let the impact of his words sink in before he concluded, "I am going to ask you to return again and carefully consider all of the evidence. I know it's hard. I know it's difficult. I know it's exasperating at times. Do the best you can. Thank you."

Throughout the rest of the day, the jurors asked for additional material and clarifications.

In the hallway, several attorneys took to pacing like prospective fathers in the waiting room of a hospital during a prolonged and complicated labor.

That evening, Judge Platt queried the jury again, "Is there any possibility in the near future that you will be able to reach a verdict?"

Lee looked at the tired faces. Three of the men and one of the women looked sullen and resentful.

So, it was no surprise when the foreperson pursed her lips and said, "I don't think so."

Once again, the judge excused the jurors with his usual admonition. After two-and-a-half days of deliberation, it was clear that they were deadlocked.

On Friday morning, after the jury resumed, Judge Platt expressed his frustration to the attorneys, "We have had ten weeks of trial and a week of deliberations in this case, and it's just too much. To go through another jury selection process will take 1,000 jurors the next time."

Again, Lee suggested waiting longer before putting more pressure to bear. "I don't think this is the kind of case that ought to be decided by a distressed juror," he said. "We might get more mileage telling them, 'Give it another try today, but we are not going to ask you beyond today.' I don't want those people in there trying to decide the case while they are seething."

Judge Platt disagreed. "If we reach the end of the day and they haven't reached a verdict, I have no alternative but to go tomorrow. However, if you all agree to excuse the two unhappy jurors, we can get by with ten. We can also resolve it if you agree to stipulate a nine to three verdict."

Coddington said, "I would be amenable to that."

But Lee dissented, speaking for everyone on his team, "I would like to keep it at twelve, without intimidating or threatening them, and to see what will happen."

After the morning recess, the jurors asked for the testimony of Ulrich Weber, Stella Schneider, and Oliver Koch regarding the deceptive practices during the FAA visits following the Lockerbie disaster. A clerk read the testimony to them, and the court took another recess while the jurors continued their deliberations.

THE FIGHT FOR JUSTICE

In the hallway, Lee, Ruth, and the other plaintiff attorneys mingled with partners from their respective firms who had come to offer support. Lee noted Bud Coddington and James Shaughnessy engaged in a tense conversation with Thomas Plaskett and John Brennan in a side niche. He talked to Dona Bainbridge, the Boulangers, and other victims' families, whose faces were etched with worry and exhaustion.

When he decided to return to the courtroom early, Ruth remained with the families, doing her best to reassure them and keep up everyone's spirits.

Suddenly, the heavy wooden courtroom doors opened, and a bailiff stuck his head out through the crack. "They have reached a verdict!" he called out, his words echoing in the marble hallway.

For a moment, the scene turned into a frozen tableau. Then, everyone surged toward the courtroom. Because of the bottleneck at the door, it took some time for all the spectators and attorneys to get inside.

By the time Ruth took her seat in the back, the attorneys had settled at their tables. She glanced at Lee. He was sitting in a position she recognized from many of his trials—slumped in his chair, left hand on his chin, head bent, eyes forward. Next to him, Jim sat upright, with his broad shoulders pulled back, playing with his mustache. The other attorneys kept to themselves as well.

As the spectators kept filling the long wooden benches, the victims' families huddled anxiously in a tight-knit group. Some held hands. Others had their eyes closed in silent prayer. Reporters whispered among themselves in the back.

Lee tried to empty his mind, but his ears were ringing. He adjusted his hearing aid, but it did no good.

When Judge Platt took his place on the bench, all conversations ceased. In the silence, his banging gavel sounded like a thunderclap. He glared at the gallery and admonished everyone, "Now, ladies and gentlemen in the courtroom, I don't want any display of emotion one way or the other after this verdict. If you want to expel your emotions, I suggest you go outside the building. If there is any demonstration in the courtroom, I will have to take appropriate action. This is a courtroom, not a town meeting."

Then he asked his clerk to bring in the jury.

Lee watched the jurors as they came through the side door. In every case he had won, at least one juror made eye contact with him. But none of them looked at him. They were all stoic and stern-faced as they filed into the jury box, where they remained standing, staring straight ahead.

Lee felt a clenching fist in the pit of his stomach. "The curse of Lockerbie," flashed through his mind.

Judge Platt turned to the heavy-set woman closest to him and said, "Now, Mrs. Foreperson, if you will remain standing."

The other jurors sat down. When they had settled, the judge asked, "Have you agreed upon a unanimous verdict with respect to both questions?"

She answered firmly, "Yes."

The silence in the courtroom deepened.

Judge Platt said, "I'm going to ask you the first question. Did Pan Am, including Alert, engage in willful misconduct?"

She did not hesitate. "Yes."

There were gasps from the audience.

After a stern glance toward the spectators, Judge Platt asked, "Secondly, was it a substantial factor in causing the disaster?"

Again, with no hesitation. "Yes," she said.

The tension drained from the courtroom like water from a dam whose floodgates have opened, and a wave of relief washed over Lee. He felt light as air and barely heard Judge Platt asking each juror, "Is this your verdict?"

One at a time, they responded, "Yes." None of them cracked a smile.

Judge Platt concluded, "So say you all."

Murmurs and sighs of relief erupted throughout the courtroom. Suddenly, there was a commotion in the back as reporters rushed to the door, trying to get out.

Lee looked at his colleagues, their eyes glistening with barely contained excitement. Jim pumped a clenched fist. Even the usually stone-faced Steve Pounian grinned broadly.

A glance at the defense table showed Bud Coddington staring daggers at Judge Platt. Lee had never seen an attorney glare at a judge with such undisguised hatred. James Shaughnessy was frozen like a statue. John Brennan, sitting behind him, had his eyes shut tight, his lips clenched, and the muscles in his jaws working hard.

Lee saw the victim's families embracing, clasping hands, and weeping openly.

It took some time and repeated gaveling for Judge Platt to get the courtroom under control. When everyone finally settled down, he addressed the jury, "Now, ladies and gentlemen, I will have to ask you to go back into the jury room because there has been a subsidiary question. I don't think dealing with that will take too long."

After the jury left, Judge Platt called the plaintiffs and defense attorneys to the bench. To everyone's surprise, Bud Coddington got up, gathered his notes into his briefcase, and left the courtroom without looking back.

The bewildered expressions of the remaining attorneys soon cleared up as Judge Platt explained what had happened. Coddington had submitted an affidavit in anticipation of the outcome, claiming extreme prejudice on the part of Judge Platt. He accused him of being a racist, recognizing black jurors only late in the proceedings, and that he had tried to "stick it to Brennan." In his most passive-aggressive mode, the victim he liked to play had suddenly become the spiteful attacker.

Lee was taken aback. He had witnessed plenty of flagrant behavior by Coddington. But he could not have imagined that he would to go to such lengths, attacking the judge and then exiting the courtroom like an angry child leaving the schoolyard with his marbles when he didn't get his way. This was thoroughly unprofessional behavior.

"I am outraged by it," Judge Platt said. "I will have nothing to do with Mr. Coddington unless he apologizes about that affidavit. Because that hurt, and it isn't true."

Then, he returned to the matter at hand—the damage trials. The jurors, unhappy about the lengths of deliberations, would be even more upset when they heard they had to stay on. "Federal regulations permit me to let the two disgruntled jurors go and proceed with the ten remaining," he pointed out. "The minimum required is six."

Everyone agreed to proceed.

When the jury returned to the courtroom, Judge Platt explained that they would have to sit for damage trials—as many cases as necessary to get a clear indication of the compensation that should be awarded to the victims' families.

"The problem we currently face is this: getting another jury such as you would take at least six months to a year," he said. "So, the obvious thing to do is to proceed to the damage cases with as many of you as possible in August and after Labor Day, if needed. They would probably run one, two, or three days apiece. You'd have some weeks off, and there would be breaks."

He did not give them time to react before continuing, "What I really want to know—since I can order you all to serve—if it will involve real hardship for any of you. I want to talk to those who feel that way in person in another room, away from the public, before possibly excusing you."

When Judge Platt asked them to raise their hands accordingly, six jurors did. The clerk recorded their numbers. Then, the judge, plaintiffs' counsel, and defense lawyers went to an empty courtroom nearby to interview them.

After hearing about all the conflicts, including a trip to Disney World and scheduled surgery, Judge Platt excused two jurors. One cared for her 86-year-old father and held two jobs to make ends meet. The other had two young children, ages three and five. He had missed the birthday of his older son in the course of the trial.

All other jurors agreed they would serve after the two-week break when Judge Platt took his vacation.

After the judge dismissed everyone, there was still plenty to do for Lee. Spectators had stayed, milling about, not ready to go home, needing to unburden themselves, letting go of feelings they'd carried for so long. He talked to as many families as possible, thanked his colleagues, and accepted the congratulations of his firm's partners who had come to witness the outcome.

As he and Ruth made their way down the courthouse steps, they saw Thomas Plaskett, the former CEO of Pan Am, carrying a picket sign, "Unfair Trial!" His assistants were handing out public relations pamphlets, claiming the verdict was unjust and caused by the judge's errors in excluding Pan Am's evidence of terrorist operations and the rogue bag theory. Plaskett had orchestrated an immediate public response in anticipation of verdict against Pan Am.

Lee was appalled by their audacity but not surprised. After so many blatant lies in and out of court by Pan Am and USAU officials and attempts to use the media to sway the jurors, this was just the most recent example of business as usual for a crooked gang of greedy people.

He and Ruth checked out of the Union Club—they'd left their clothes and a few possessions in anticipation of having to attend another day of jury deliberations.

The Verdict

On the way home to Chappaqua, Lee thought about what he and his team had accomplished. They had traveled more than 100,000 miles in pursuit of the truth. They had overcome false leads, lies planted by the defense in the news media, and Brennan's effort to bankrupt the firm, which had almost succeeded. In the face of overwhelming odds, they had prevailed. But Lee knew it was just a milestone—albeit a big one—more would come before they were done.

It was well after midnight when they reached their house. A lamp by the entrance cast light on the walkway and the surrounding shrubbery. The rest of the house was shrouded in darkness.

Lee was still energized from the day and called John Merritt in England. Although he sounded weak, John already knew about the verdict and wanted to hear about everything that happened. Lee gave him a blow-by-blow account with details he knew a reporter would appreciate. He thanked him for all his help and promised to call again soon, sensing that John's leukemia was in its final stages.

After hanging up, Lee asked himself, as he had many times before, "What is there about Lockerbie that touches and ruins everything?"

* * *

John Merritt died six weeks later, in late August, during the last damage trial. Several months later, his wife Lindsay gave birth to their second daughter and named her "Hope."

30

THE DAMAGES TRIALS

July—August 1992

In the end, Judge Platt and the attorneys agreed to hold three trials for damages with the clients represented by Kreindler & Kreindler. Because the victims of the bombing of Flight 103 included business executives, entrepreneurs, airline and government employees, and blue-collar workers, the cases needed to cover a range of "samples" and set the standards for future damage awards. The 35 Syracuse University students were excluded from the pool because, as dependents, their cases would not command the same kind of compensation as family breadwinners.

To determine the damages in each case, the plaintiffs would offer evidence regarding the victim's potential earning power had their life not been cut short. In addition, the jury could award compensatory damages to the decedent's spouse and children based on the loss of services, loss of society, companionship, and parental care.

As lead counsel of the Plaintiffs Committee, Lee went first. Judge Platt's courtroom on the fourth floor served again as the trial venue. It felt like a homecoming since it was the same jury panel, minus the two members who had been excused. Lee welcomed the familiar environment and thought that it gave him an advantage. He did not have to convince the jurors of Pan Am's guilt and responsibility. He looked forward to the proceedings being less tense and contentious. That did not mean Lee came less prepared or took things lightly. This was, after all, what the case was ultimately about—getting the victims' families some compensation for their loss.

On July 20, Lee tried the first sample damages case with Judith Pagnucco as plaintiff. The courtroom was not as crowded as during the initial liability trial, with fewer reporters and Pan Am personnel in attendance. However, many families and members of the Victims of Pan Am Flight 103 group came to watch and offer their support.

Judith Pagnucco's husband, Robert, had been assistant general counsel to PepsiCo, Inc., the food and drink giant headquartered near White Plains, New York. He was 51 years old at the time of the Lockerbie disaster and left behind a wife and four children. Two were already in college. The youngest was 12. They all sat behind their mom at the plaintiff's table.

Lee began by calling the head of the PepsiCo HR department to determine Bob Pagnucco's earning power. She was dressed in a light brown business suit and testified that when he died in the bombing, Pagnucco's salary was $160,000 a year. He also received nearly the same amount in annual bonuses and had millions of dollars in stock options.

Then, Lee called an expert economist to the stand. The man looked like a college professor from central casting, attired in a dark gray herringbone jacket with leather elbow patches, and a bow tie, and his delivery was thorough and precise. He testified that assuming retirement at 65, with regular salary increases, retirement benefits, and stocks, and an average lifespan for American males in 1988 of 74.77 years, Bob Pagnucco would have left a legacy of more than $15 million.

Next, Lee called several character witnesses—friends and colleagues who attested to Bob Pagnucco's outgoing personality, work ethic, and social involvement. What emerged was a portrait of a model citizen.

The Damages Trials

Bob contributed to non-profit organizations, coached his sons' little league baseball teams, and attended church regularly. In short, he was a pillar of his community.

Finally, Judith Pagnucco took the stand. An attractive woman in her mid-forties, she looked composed but haggard, her face pale and worn out. Grief and the burden of taking care of her family by herself had taken its toll, and she had lost weight. As Lee questioned her gently, she talked about her husband's 24-year career with PepsiCo and how he helped raise their four children. Holding back tears, she described how difficult her life had been since his death. Although PepsiCo had been generous with financial support, she worried about the cost of college for all her children. She said, "Bob was an excellent husband, a wonderful father, dedicated to his family, to his God, and his business."

The defense team, led by James Shaughnessy, did not cross-examine her and the others, and offered only one counter-witness, their own economist. He did not look as academic but kept referring to Lee's witness as "his esteemed colleague" while disputing his findings. He had calculated the dollar amount of Pagnucco's lifetime earnings prospects differently and quoted a figure of $5 million, two-thirds less than the proposed amount.

During his summation, Lee built on the victim's portrait as an exemplary, upstanding citizen and said, "There aren't too many people in our society who have achieved what Bob Pagnucco has achieved." He pointed out that his lucrative stock options could have netted him millions through the years and asked for $25.25 million in damages.

Although the trial lasted three days, it took the jurors only two hours to decide. They awarded the Pagnucco family $9.25 million, of which $6 million was for economic loss, and the rest for loss of services Mrs. Pagnucco and her children had to endure by losing a husband and father. At the announcement of the verdict, Judith burst into tears. She embraced Lee and then hugged her children.

Watching them, Lee felt satisfied with the outcome. While the settlement would not return Bob Pagnucco to his family, it would go a long way toward his family's financial security.

When he met Ruth in the hallway afterward, she greeted him with a wistful smile. She understood the bitter-sweet nature of Lee's success. However, Jim came up to him and, in a brief moment of levity, said, "Good job, Dad. But I'm going to beat you."

The following Monday, the next trial commenced, with Jim representing Dona Bainbridge. Her husband Harry, an attorney in PepsiCo's legal department, had attended a corporate law conference in London with his boss, Bob Pagnucco. They were returning on Flight 103 together. Harry was 34 when he was killed in the crash. He never saw his son, Harry Jr, who was born 11 weeks after his death and was now three years old.

Lee thought back to when he first met Dona at the Kreindler & Kreindler office three years earlier. Since then, they had talked on the telephone many times, and he had seen her at victims' family gatherings and during the Pan Am trial.

Because several witnesses had testified during Lee's trial, Jim did not have to establish their credentials. As a result, it took only two days to reach a verdict. Lee enjoyed sitting behind the plaintiffs' table and watching Jim perform as if in his element. After Jim asked his last question of the first witness, he sat down, never referring to his notes. Although they had never discussed the lesson after the deposition in Germany, Jim had heeded Lee's advice. As a father, Lee could not have been prouder.

For Dona Bainbridge's testimony, her mother brought three-year-old Harry Jr into the courtroom and sat behind the plaintiff's table with him on her lap. He seemed intimidated by the goings-on and kept quiet throughout the proceedings. When Dona took the stand, Harry waved shyly to her, eliciting sympathetic murmurs from some spectators. Dona was a generation younger than Judith Pagnucco but had the same haunted, forlorn appearance and looked ten years older than her 28 years. She and Harry had been high school sweethearts in West Virginia.

"He was good-natured, humorous, and adventurous and was so looking forward to being a dad," she said tearfully toward the end of her testimony. "I miss him every day."

The jury awarded Dona and her son $9 million in damages.

Although $250,000 less than Lee's verdict, Jim claimed victory because Harry Bainbridge occupied a lower tier in the corporate earnings structure than his boss. And he had only one child requiring support.

Lee was amused. He understood his son's competitive nature and secretly applauded it. "Why don't we call it a draw," he offered.

Jim accepted good-naturedly.

But he was deeply moved when Dona Bainbridge told him, "You know, Jim, Harry Jr obviously can't understand what went on here today. But on his 18th birthday, I'm going to show him the transcript of this trial, and he will know his father in a way no one else can."

The third damage trial commenced in mid-August after a two-week break. Steve Pounian represented Molina Porter, the wife of Walter Porter, an electrician and part-time musician—he had played saxophone in a jazz trio. They lived in Queens in an African-American neighborhood and had two young children. Walter was returning from Europe, where he had toured with his band. Eager to get back to his family, he booked the earliest flight home possible. The other musicians had stayed behind an extra day.

Molina Porter testified to the hardship she had experienced for the past three-and-a-half years because of the unwillingness of Pan

Am's insurance company to settle the case. She had been working three jobs to make ends meet, and there were months when even that was not enough. She would not have known how to cope if she did not have her mother taking care of her children and helping out financially.

After two days of testimony, the jury awarded Walter Porter's family $1,735,000.

Lee felt that they had established an excellent baseline, including the highest damage amounts awarded until that time in wrongful death cases. Providing for the victims' families had been at the forefront of his mind throughout the trial, motivating him when he was exhausted and worried about the outcome.

Yet, despite the clear indication that juries were willing to award significant monetary damages, John Brennan continued to refuse to settle any case for more than $100,000 until after the appeal.

Because the chairman of USAU had set aside a mere $60 million of reserves for damages at the outset of the case, Lee and the victim's families worried that the insurance company might declare bankruptcy to avoid paying the more significant damage verdicts. To prevent that from happening, Lee and the Plaintiffs Committee filed a motion requiring USAU to post a surety bond for $750 million.

Meanwhile, John Connors made good on the promise he made in December 1990, when the U.S. government had to join Pan Am and Alert Management as a third-party defendant. He brought a motion for massive sanctions against the airline, its defense attorneys, and its insurers. The State Department, FBI, CIA, and other agencies had gone to great trouble and expense combing their records and preparing affidavits to counter Pan Am's accusations that they had had a hand in the Lockerbie disaster.

The motion contained a detailed narrative of the defendants' false assertions, including their false claims of CIA and DEA agents' involvement in the bombing. It asked for $20 million in compensation, damages at private sector rates for the more than 18,000 hours the government's attorneys and employees had spent fighting off Pan Am's and USAU's bogus claims.

The Plaintiffs Committee attorneys and their firms had suffered monetary hardship because of the defense machinations, too, and decided to file for sanctions as well. They joined the government motion but added an application for discovery. They wanted to take depositions of the defense lawyers and USAU's insurance claims officials to determine if they had engaged in any conspiracy.

But Judge Platt showed little interest in ordering sanctions when the government's motion came up for oral arguments in early October. "Without passing on the merits, the government's motion is premature," he said. "Suppose the court of appeals holds that I was wrong in denying Pan Am the opportunity to do its discovery against the United States, and I have already ordered sanctions. Then where are you?"

He refused to issue a ruling and told the government lawyers they could renew their motion after the appeal was decided.

However, the USAU and defense lawyers became worried. In discussions about potential settlements with victims' family members, the insurers insisted that they sign release forms absolving USAU of any claims of bad faith.

James Shaughnessy, Pan Am's lawyer from the beginning of the case, submitted a lengthy affidavit, attempting to justify his conduct by indicating where the information supporting his claims against the U.S. government came from. While he did not directly identify any of his sources by name, he supplied enough information that Lee and his team could figure out who they were.

What emerged was a roundabout admission that Shaughnessy had met with several of the authors of the alternative scenarios,

THE FIGHT FOR JUSTICE

even though he had denied having any contact with them in the past. He acknowledged that he had paid Lester Coleman's expenses in London. Besides Coleman, the rogue gallery of phony tipsters included Yuval Aviv, Scott Malone, the Lebanese Intelligence Forces, and others. They were all involved in creating and leaking false narratives to the news media and floating outright lies worldwide.

Lee had dealt with these stories already ad nauseam. There was one new revelation, however—Pan Am records that showed the four CIA agents aboard Flight 103 changed their reservations from December 22 to the day the airplane exploded over Lockerbie. Those records had never been part of the discovery required by law in the pre-trial stages. Now, Shaughnessy argued that they "corroborated" what he was told by Aviv and Coleman when he seemed to be the source of the story.

Lee expressed his shock and outrage at Shaughnessy's duplicity. He had expected Coddington to use underhanded tactics. But now it was clear that Pan Am's principal lawyer had engaged in deceptive schemes from the start.

Incensed, Lee prepared a "Reply Affidavit" to Shaughnessy's, using Kreindler & Kreindler's research and some of the articles that began to appear in *New York Magazine* after the willful misconduct verdict in July. He outlined all incidents of deliberate spread of misinformation, from the *Barron's* article to *TIME* magazine appearing on the eve of the trial, and concluded:

> There is no doubt that a bogus story was launched and perpetuated despite the development of clear evidence in the case that it was phony. There is no doubt that it vastly multiplied the proceedings and cost the plaintiffs a fortune in time and money. There is considerable evidence that the defendants (i.e., Pan Am, its insurers, and its lawyers) were responsible for it.

The Damages Trials

> All of this points to a fraud of monumental proportions on the Lockerbie families, the court, and the government, and it warrants a renewed discovery process of the defendants.

As with the government motion, Judge Platt decided against ruling, although he held out the possibility of revisiting it after the appellate verdict.

In the end, the Plaintiffs' attorneys never renewed their motions for sanctions. But they kept the underlying threat of doing so as a weapon during subsequent negotiations. And documentation remained in the public record of the highly questionable activities of Pan Am's insurers and defense attorneys.

Meanwhile, on November 2, 1992, nearly four years after the Lockerbie bombing, Pan Am and its attorneys appealed the damage verdict of Pagnucco, Bainbridge, and Porter and the finding of willful misconduct to the U.S. Court of Appeals for the Second Circuit in lower Manhattan.

The trial entered a new phase.

31

THE APPEAL

November 1992—September 1994

Located in Foley Square in Southern Manhattan, the Second District Court of Appeals in New York was established in 1891, with jurisdiction over Connecticut, New York, and Vermont district courts. As one of the largest and most influential American federal courts, many notable judges served there. Some, like John Marshall Harlan II, Thurgood Marshall, and Sonia Sotomayor, were later appointed to the U.S. Supreme Court.

Walking up the massive steps to the main entrance of the classical revival building, Lee glanced up at the four-story columns that formed an impressive portico, with the 31-story tower above. He felt momentarily awed by the significance of the occasion and the responsibility he carried. Stepping into the grand main hall with its marble floors and walls reinforced the feeling of being in a special place.

Because the case was so important, the hearing took place in the building's largest courtroom. Everything in the décor suggested solemnity and consequence, from the arches with woodcarvings above the windows to the wooden benches for the spectators, which looked like elegant church pews.

Looking around him, Lee took a deep breath. He was not easily cowed, but he knew he had his work cut out for him.

His opponents, Richard Sharp and Frederick Shaffrick from Shea & Gardner in Washington, were prominent appeals attorneys. It had become clear that Pan Am had retained them two months before the willful misconduct court case started to advise the defense team on legal issues. They assisted in the hearing on the *TIME* magazine article, participated in jury selection, and made suggestions to Coddington and Shaughnessy along the way. Sharp was there for the entire trial. And, while Lee and the Plaintiffs Committee attorneys tried the case, he and his partner were planning the appeal.

Their brief to the Second Circuit Court was well-prepared and characterized the civil trial as grossly unfair to their clients. Sharp and Shaffrick ignored the fact that Lee and his colleagues had proved an overwhelming case of willful misconduct. They also failed to mention the many efforts of Pan Am's attorneys to spread confusion and inject a circus atmosphere into the proceedings. They accomplished this sleight of hand by distorting the evidence, misrepresenting the positions taken at the trial by defendants and plaintiffs, and faulting Judge Platt for refusing to allow certain testimony in the jury's presence.

Sharp and Shaffrick contested the Malta origins of the bomb bag, lamented that the X-ray machine Coddington had put up in the basement mainly sat idle, and attacked the claim that the FAA had never given Alert and Pan Am permission to replace positive matching of baggage with X-ray screening.

They skillfully wove the distortions through virtually every sentence of their initial 85-page brief, which presented Lee and his team with enormous problems.

During several strategy sessions, the Plaintiffs Committee hashed out how to best respond.

At the initial meeting in the Kreindler & Kreindler conference room, Frank Granito Jr voiced everyone's concern. Looking up

The Appeal

from the document spread out on the table, he said, "There isn't enough room in the hundred pages we're allowed to expose all of their falsehoods."

"Yes," Mitch Baumeister agreed. "Answering just one distorted sentence will take at least a paragraph."

Steve Pounian rubbed his forehead. "What if we pick the most egregious and refute those?" he said.

"There is no way to know which ones the judges will single out," Jim countered.

Lee steepled his hands at his lips, thinking. Then he said, "If we focus on the slew of distortions, we will come off as negative and defensive rather than positive and assertive."

In the end, they decided to emphasize the overwhelming evidence of Pan Am and Alert's misconduct. They dealt with the misrepresentations at the end of the brief, addressing only the major ones, and hoped for the best.

As Lee prepared for oral arguments, he realized he faced an even greater challenge. The Second Circuit was an extremely busy court, and attorney's presentations were limited to 15 minutes for each side.

There was always the possibility that one or more of the three judges would be taken in by the defendants' distortions and come to the hearing biased, believing that Pan Am had not received a fair trial. Lee would have to address the multitude of lies and misrepresentations quickly and demonstrate that the truth was on the plaintiffs' side.

Lee obsessed for many days about how to deal with that challenge. He finally decided that it came down to a matter of credibility. There was no way of knowing which of the hundreds of distortions would come up at oral argument. Whatever the issue, he had to be ready to direct the court to the appropriate page of the record and, if possible, read to the judges the precise testimony that demonstrated that the defendants were not telling the truth. The problem was that the trial record was huge. The transcript alone ran over 7,000 pages. The Joint Appendix comprised 14 thick volumes containing charts, graphs, and other exhibits. Stacked on top of one another, they were three feet high! How could he possibly have the correct page at his fingertips at a moment's notice?

After much deliberation, Lee hit upon a workable method. First, he read through the entire record and marked every section that could come up during oral argument. Then he went through it again, extracting "kernels"—the best, most revealing testimony on every point. He planned to make a reference book of the kernels.

By the time Lee finished, the book had grown to five volumes, far too big and unwieldy to be useful. Somehow, he had to shrink them to one and then figure out how to get hold of the information he needed in seconds.

It took several weeks, but he managed to gather all the relevant points in one book. Each page had excerpts of testimony and exhibits to read to the court, with the page numbers of the full trial transcript as references. So far, so good. But how to locate any one of them quickly?

First, Lee tried putting tabs on every page, but there were so many it took too long to get to the pertinent testimony. Then he hit upon the solution. He boiled down the issues into eight main categories and gave each a different color. "Administrative Match," one of the defendants' principal distortions, was blue. Another, "Oral permission" to deviate from the FAA requirements, was orange.

When Lee opened the book, all he could see were the eight colored tabs. Turning to any of them, he would see subdivisions on slightly smaller pages, also tabbed in that color. Opening the subdivision tabs would take him to still smaller sections, directing him to the specific page he needed. Altogether, there were over 200 tabs.

The Appeal

Lee figured he needed to practice until he could find anything in the book in his sleep. He had Pat Robinson take a stack of index cards, each listing one discrete issue, and rehearse with him. Pat quizzed him with card after card until Lee's retrieval speed was two seconds. Only then did he feel ready to go before the three appellate judges. He had no idea how many tabs and pages he would need.

As the day of the oral argument of the Lockerbie appeal approached, Lee felt jittery, due to worry, sleeplessness, and anticipatory excitement.

Ruth tried to cheer him up by kidding, "All you have to do to win the case is show the panel of judges the book and all the tabs. They'll figure, with that much work invested, you must be right."

Lee smiled gratefully but kept fretting. He was confident that he was as prepared as could be. But would it be enough? Would he be able to persuade the judges?

The day before the hearing, the court calendar clerk called the firm to confirm that the Lockerbie case would be first on the calendar, and that each side would have 15 minutes for oral arguments. Around lunchtime, he called again. The hearing had been moved to the afternoon and the last slot on the calendar.

To Lee, it was a tip-off that the judges were not in agreement and would want more time for argument. Although it was too early to tell what it meant for the case, it added to the nerve-racking suspense.

On the day of the hearing, May 13, 1993, the courtroom was as packed as Judge Platt's court was for the original verdict. All the important Pan Am and insurance company officials were there. John Brennan sat next to Thomas Plaskett. Many of the Lockerbie families squeezed together on the dark wooden benches. All the lawyers who had worked with Lee on the case sat at the back of his table.

The three judges entered from the robing room and took their seats on the raised bench. Richard Cardamone, a Reagan appointee, was the presiding judge. He looked placidly out over the spectators in the courtroom. On his left sat Judge Frank Altimari, white-haired with bushy black eyebrows and penetrating gray eyes. Flanking him on his right was Judge Ellsworth Van Graafeiland, wearing black-rimmed glasses. None of them smiled.

After the clerk announced the case, Judge Cardamone asked the defense to begin its presentation, telling Richard Sharp, "You may take more than your allotted fifteen minutes. However much extra time you use, up to thirty minutes, I will also give to the plaintiffs."

"Thank you, Your Honor," Sharp replied.

That was the last congenial exchange of the proceedings.

The Washington attorney barely had time to introduce himself and begin his argument before Judge Altimari started firing questions at him about the Helsinki warning. It was a severe assault, leading to further queries about Pan Am's security failures. Sharp, a very accomplished appellate lawyer, was startled. It took him several moments to catch his bearings and respond. But the rapid-fire questions never let up. In the end, Sharp acquitted himself well. Lee had to admit that he did an effective job. He even managed to introduce some of his distortions and made the exclusion of the testimony of the terrorism experts of the defense sound reprehensible.

Lee knew he needed to be on his toes when it was his turn, but nothing prepared him for what was to come.

When Judge Cardamone called on him, he stepped up to the podium and said, "Good afternoon, my name is Lee Kreindler, and I'm chairman of –"

Before he could get out "Plaintiffs Committee," Judge Van Graafeiland started to shout at him.

His voice was so loud and so unexpected Lee could not understand what he was saying. Taken aback, he asked the judge to repeat his words. Afterward, the court reporter showed him that the sound system speakers were all pointed at the podium so that, even when he spoke, his own voice came booming back at him. And Judge Van Graafeiland was yelling!

Lee never got to give the arguments he had prepared for weeks: laying out the overwhelming evidence of Pan Am's gross misconduct due to the corrupt attitude of its officials and offering solid proof of causation—how the bomb got on the airplane.

Instead, he spent nearly 45 minutes responding to the barrage of questions, particularly those shouted at him by Judge Van Graafeiland. The judge interrupted him frequently, rarely letting him finish a sentence. He even tried to trip up Lee by arguing hypothetically about the exclusion of Richard Sonesen's hearsay testimony that the FAA had given oral permission to replace positive bag matching with X-ray screening.

> Judge Van Graafeiland: Let me ask you this, Mr. Kreindler. If I read the record, and I decide that Judge Platt said, 'I'm not going to hear from Mr. Sonesen no matter what,' would you concede that is a very prejudicial error?
>
> Lee: But that's not what happened. That's –
>
> Graafeiland: I'm not asking you that. I'm asking you if I read this record and I decide that Judge Platt just simply said, 'I'm not going to hear Mr. Sonesen,' that would be prejudicial error, wouldn't it?
>
> Lee: Your Honor, even –
>
> Graafeiland: Counsel, wouldn't it be prejudicial error?
>
> Lee: Of course, if the judge were hearing –
>
> Graafeiland: Of course it would. Then we have got the issue: did he refuse to hear him, or didn't he?
>
> Lee: No.
>
> Graafeiland: All right, that's the issue. I'll read the record very carefully, Mr. Kreindler.

Although Lee stood his ground against the relentless onslaught, he felt frustrated that he could not follow his plan or point out Richard Sharpe's misrepresentations. Thanks to his tabbing system, however, he responded readily to the judges' questions and directed them to the sections of the record where they could find the evidence. He ended up using only six of the 200 kernels. But in each instance, he felt the court would have to admit he was telling the truth about what was in the record. When it was over, he thought that he had established the credibility of the plaintiffs' case. On balance, he was pleased with his performance.

Leaving the courthouse that afternoon, Lee thought that Judges Cardamone and Altimari had been even-handed, perhaps even leaning slightly in the direction of the plaintiffs. However, Judge Graafeiland was clearly in Pan Am's camp. The decision would be a close call.

The Second Circuit had the best record of any appeals court in the United States for expeditiously deciding its cases, averaging two months to reach a decision. But after the bitter arguments and apparent differences among the judges, Lee figured it would take longer. He advised the victims' families to expect a six-month wait, probably until mid-November.

In October, there were rumors that the decision was imminent, but weeks passed and nothing happened. November and December came and went as well, and still no decision.

Finally, on January 31, 1994, the Second Circuit Court handed down its decision late afternoon. It was two judges to one in favor of the plaintiffs. Judge Cardamone wrote the opinion joined by Judge Altimari. The court's order stated that a dissent by Judge Van Graafeiland would follow.

Lee was amazed. He had never heard of a decision of the court being filed without the dissent. One potential hint of what had happened was an introductory remark in Judge Cardamone's opinion. He stated that the disaster had occurred "over four years ago." Yet, the court did not publish its findings until the fifth year!

Apparently, Judge Cardamone had written his opinion before December 31, 1993, quite possibly in October, when rumors first surfaced that a decision was forthcoming. Lee could only speculate that Judge Graafeiland had been dragging his heels. The filing of the majority opinion and the entry order, with the dissent to come later, seemed to be the act of two judges who had waited long enough.

Judge Cardamone's opinion was straightforward and, in some respects, masterful. It meticulously and methodically dealt with all the defendants' arguments that, by Judge Platt's exclusions of essential testimony, he had unfairly denied them the opportunity to present their case.

Affirming the unambiguous nature of the ACSSP regulations regarding the positive matching of passenger luggage and the required physical search of unaccompanied bags, he upheld Judge Platt's actions, disallowing the Sonesen testimony.

Discussing the botched response to the Helsinki warning, Judge Cardamone commented, "This and other evidence overwhelmingly supported the jury's conclusion that, but for Pan Am's wholly inadequate terrorist prevention techniques and its deliberate indifference and overt acts of willfulness, the bombing and the senseless loss of life would not have occurred."

He briefly confirmed the plaintiff attorneys' causation theory and Pan Am's inability to mount a credible defense, noting that the applicants, in their brief, "did not undertake to prove how the terrorists managed to bomb the aircraft, but contended that the method of bombing has not yet been established." Thus, Judge Platt was correct in his decision to exclude all testimony regarding terrorist behavior in general, unrelated to the specifics of this case.

Ultimately, Judge Cardamone concluded that there was no judicial error except in two minor areas. Judge Platt should have allowed statement testimony on the difference between British and FAA security regulations at London's Heathrow Airport. And Billie Vincent's opining "that Pan Am did indeed violate the ACSSP" embodied a legal conclusion that he should not have been permitted to make. Still, in the face of the airline's massive security lapses, neither constituted a reversible error for the jury verdict.

The decision also addressed an important question of damages. Based on the application of the plaintiffs' attorneys, Judge Platt charged the jury that it was possible to recover for loss of society and companionship. The majority of the Second Circuit panel concurred. That was good news for the victim's families, particularly in the non-dependency cases—the college students that had died in the crash. It would allow for greater than usual compensation.

In one respect, however, the appellate opinion was weak, namely in its treatment of the proof of causation. The hard evidence in the record was abundant, but Judge Cardamone hardly discussed it.

Judge Van Graafeiland seized upon that gap in his dissent, filed two and a half weeks later. He began by claiming in capital letters, "NO ONE KNOWS WHEN, WHERE OR HOW THE BOMB GOT ON THE PAN AM PLANE EXCEPT THE PERSON WHO PUT IT THERE." Then, he continued sarcastically, "The jury had to content itself with 'expert testimony,' more properly described as educated guesses."

How Judge Van Graafeiland, who had professed to have read the entire record dispassionately, could say that was beyond Lee. There was strong factual evidence, supported by expert testimony, regarding when, where, or how the bomb was placed on Pan Am Flight 103.

Van Graafeiland also did his best to rescue Pan Am's claim that it had received verbal permission to use X-ray screening. He argued that Sonesen had never sought a waiver of ACSSP regulations, merely an interpretation, something that FAA personnel could legitimately make. Thus, Pan Am employees acting in the belief that X-ray inspection complied with the regulation indicated that they acted in good faith.

Regarding the X-ray machine that Bud Coddington had brought to the court building, he lamented that "at the district court's direction, it sat in the basement of the courthouse, alone and unobserved." In a remarkable twist, worthy of a verbal contortionist, he cited the plaintiffs' attorney objecting to a jury inspection as evidence that the district court erred in not permitting it.

Judge Van Graafeiland essentially argued the case for Pan Am, giving credence to the notion that the jury should have heard all unsubstantiated theories of how the bomb bag wound up on the plane. Concluding, "Plaintiffs' attorneys were permitted to range far and wide with prejudicial, irrelevant testimony, while Pan Am's counsel was precluded time and again from presenting relative and probative proof," he called for the case to be retried.

Lee found the dissenting opinion zealous and vitriolic. He wondered why the judge responded as if he had been personally insulted. There was no way to determine the answer, and it didn't matter in the end because the victims' families had prevailed. Everyone on the plaintiffs' team was pleased. It felt good to be vindicated.

That was not the end of the appeals process, however.

Soon after the verdict, the defense submitted another brief and a Petition for a Rehearing en banc, meaning that the full court—the panel of all 13 judges—reconsider the case. Lee felt it was a nuisance filing, designed to draw out the process further. A revised opinion handed down on April 6, 1994, again held in favor of the plaintiffs. Yet another defense brief and second Petition for Rehearing en banc followed. It took until September 12, 1994, for the court to reject that petition. The appeals verdict finally stood once and for all for the plaintiffs.

As expected, the defense appealed the verdict to the United States Supreme Court.

The victims' families who had been waiting nearly five years, many suffering severe financial hardships, continued to be denied justice.

32

FINAL JUDGMENT

1994 to 1997

There was nothing Lee could do to prevent Pan Am's lawyers from filing a Writ of Certiorari with the U.S. Supreme Court, seeking a judicial review of the Appeals Court's decision. He was not worried about arguing the case before the nation's highest court. He had done so successfully more than 30 years before on behalf of Peter Brown, a veteran whose leg had been permanently damaged by negligent treatment during a knee operation at a Veterans Administration hospital.

Lee was confident that three appearances before the Appeals Court with his "kernel" book had prepared him to make a persuasive case for willful misconduct and refute any further false flags Pan Am's lawyers could raise. But waiting for a SCOTUS hearing and decision could drag out the case for another year. And there was always the possibility that too many of the justices shared Judge Graafeiland's bias.

John Brennan continued to wage his disinformation campaign, now aimed at influencing the Supreme Court. He had previously boasted of his closeness with Justice Antonin Scalia, whose conservative, pro-business stance was well-known. Seemingly out of nowhere, a Scottish newspaper ran an article about an "Airforce Intelligence Report" that claimed Iran had paid a terrorist $10 million to blow up

Pan Am 103 in retaliation for downing one of its passenger planes by the U.S. Navy. The piece was a rehash of the rumors and lies spread by Coleman and Aviv, designed to deflect from the real culprit—Libya—and cast doubt on the plaintiffs' case. When Lee managed to obtain a copy of the fax that was the article's source, it was clear that it had come from Bud Coddington. That meant Brennan was the hidden hand pulling the strings behind the scenes.

On January 19, 1995, Lee attended a seminar on aviation and aerospace programs at Embry Riddle Aeronautical University in Daytona Beach, Florida. Ruth accompanied him. The weather was sunny and warm, a welcome change from the bleak New York winter.

Late that afternoon, Pat Robinson called from New York and reported, "Word is that the Supreme Court will announce its decision tomorrow whether or not to take the case."

The following day, Lee and Ruth flew to a federal bar conference in Charlestown, capital of Nevis and Saint Kitts, a two-island nation in the Caribbean about 220 miles southeast of Puerto Rico and 50 miles west of Aruba.

The weather was balmy there too when they arrived, and Lee was hoping for good news. But when they got to their hotel, they learned that the Supreme Court announcement would not happen until Monday. Usually, they would have used the time before the conference to enjoy the beach and sunshine, but it was hard to relax with the decision looming ahead.

As it happened, Justice Clarence Thomas and his wife Virginia were attending the conference—he was one of the speakers. Lee introduced himself at dinner, hoping to get a hint of which way the decision would fall, but the associate supreme court justice volunteered no information.

On Monday morning, after breakfast, as Lee was freshening up in the bathroom of their suite to get ready for the first session of the day, the telephone rang. It had that shrill, ear-piercing hotel sound designed to wake the dead, and he winced in surprise. When he picked up the receiver, he heard the voice of his son Jim, bubbling with excitement. "Great news, Dad! The Supreme Court has denied certiorari!"

For a moment, Lee felt as if the world had stopped. Then, a rush of energy surged through him that almost lifted him off his feet, followed by an overwhelming sense of relief. It was over! It was finally over!

"Dad, did you hear me?" Jim asked at the other end.

"Yes. That is great news! Let everyone know," Lee managed to say. "Can't wait to get back to New York to celebrate."

When he got off the phone, he did a little cha-cha step. Coming out of the bathroom, Ruth saw him dance and realized what was happening. She rushed to him, and Lee embraced her and lifted her off her feet. "We've won, Ruthie!" he cried out, laughing. "We've finally won!"

"That's wonderful, darling," she said happily and kissed him.

Lee set her down and collapsed on the sofa, overcome with emotion. He shuddered as layer after layer of tension he had carried for so long drained from his body. "I almost can't believe it!" he said in a subdued, weary voice.

Ruth joined him, taking his hand. "Yes, darling. You won. We all won."

After he regained his self-possession, Lee headed downstairs to the meeting room. He hardly paid attention to the speakers. Thoughts about the case and the implications of their victory kept tumbling through his mind. They could finally take care of the victims' families. The firm would be financially sound again. They could pay bonuses to all the employees and partners who had stuck by them for six long years.

The feelings of almost otherworldly joy accompanied him throughout the day.

That evening, at the end-of-the-conference cocktail party, Ruth saw Clarence Thomas. Impulsively, she wrapped her arms around him and kissed him, all memories of the Anita Hill hearings momentarily banished. Thomas was taken aback but kept his composure. "What was that for?" he asked.

Lee came up to him. "My wife is happy that the court denied certiorari in the Pan Am case," he volunteered. "I'm ecstatic myself. Thank you."

Thomas looked at him, puzzled. "I don't recall the case being discussed," he said. "I know of it, of course, but I don't have oversight responsibilities for the Second Circuit, so the decision was reached without me. Congratulations!"

The following morning, Lee and Ruth flew back to New York. They took a limousine from Kennedy Airport to Manhattan. It was early afternoon when Lee made it to the office. Someone must have been on the lookout because, as he got off the elevator, partners, paralegals, secretaries, and other aides greeted him with a rousing round of applause. Jim gave him a big hug. So did Steve Pounian.

When Lee called their clients, most had heard the news already. Judith Pagnucco told him she had screamed so loud for joy her neighbors knocked on the door and asked if she was all right. Dona Bainbridge had kept laughing through a flood of tears. Everyone said how grateful they were. Some thanked Lee over and over.

That evening Lee, Jim, some of the firm's partners and paralegals went to dinner to celebrate. Frank and Frankie Granito, and Mitch Baumeister joined them. The atmosphere around the large round table was festive and triumphant.

"Finally, we can get to back to work and see some real money," Frank Granito Jr said jovially.

"Bet John Brennan is kicking himself that he didn't settle," Mitch Baumeister said gleefully.

"Yeah, he's going bananas," Frankie Granito agreed.

Everyone chortled.

Lee was not a vindictive man, but the thought of the head of the USAU ranting and raving warmed his heart, and he joined in the laughter whole-heartily.

* * *

With the case finally over, Pan Am's insurance company stopped its stone-walling. In early February, the Plaintiffs Committee heard from Russell Mirabile, chief of claims for USAU. "We are now ready to settle the cases," he said.

At the first meeting in Kreindler & Kreindler's conference room, they reviewed the three cases already tried for damages in Judge Platt's court. As a show of good faith, Mirabile agreed to round up the award figures of the verdicts. He offered $2 million to Melinda Porter and $10 million each to Judith Pagnucco and Dona Bainbridge. Lee, his fellow attorneys, and their clients were happy to accept.

The settlements for the two PepsiCo lawyers represented the largest awards ever in an injury case until that time. They exceeded by nearly $3 million the 1986 jury verdict, in which the widow and five children of the singer Harry Chapin received $7.2 million after he died in a fiery car crash on the Long Island Expressway.

When Lee and his team informed Judge Platt of the positive outcome of the negotiations, he was pleased and suggested appointing mediators to expedite the settlement process. Both sides submitted a list of suitable candidates. Ultimately, they chose Ed Wesley to handle the cases involving spouses and children. Saul Schreiber of Milberg Weiss took on the non-dependency cases, mostly Syracuse University students who were killed on the flight.

Meetings for the latter took place at the Milberg Weiss office above Penn Station. After they settled the first case for $575,000, the others followed quickly, the largest monetary damage awards until then for children survived by their parents. Under New York law, the highest compensation had been $100,000.

The dependency cases took longer. The mediator would meet with Lee, Jim, or Steve Pounian and their clients at the Kreindler & Kreindler office. For the other cases, Ed Wesley also went to Speiser Kraus, Frank Granito's firm, and to Baumeister & Samuels.

The settlement meetings occurred one or two days a week and resolved two cases, one in the morning and the other in the afternoon. The mediator would speak with both sides and ask, "What are you offering? What are you looking for?" Then, he tried to bring them together. As with the court damage cases, sessions often included testimony by economists and the surviving spouses before everyone reached an agreement.

By the end of 1995, the attorneys for the plaintiffs had settled 99% of the cases.

The amounts ranged from five to nearly 10 times what they would have been in 1989 and 1990 when Lee first met with John Brennan, going as high as $13 million. Altogether, the cost to USAU, not counting the money spent on the litigation, exceeded $500 million. By then, Brennan was no longer president and CEO of the insurance company. He had retired.

During the early stages of mediation, when the dollar amounts for damages started to climb, Lee often wondered why Brennan refused to settle. He could not understand why a man of his experience had been so short-sighted.

The truth emerged over the next year and a half.

On May 5, 1995, the U.S. Attorney for the Southern District of New York brought an indictment against John Brennan and USAU for alleged wire and mail fraud arising from their handling of insurance claims for the crash of a Pacific Southwest Airlines (PSA). Forty-three passengers and crew died on December 7, 1987, when a disgruntled former employee of the company shot his supervisor and the pilot and co-pilot aboard the plane. The indictment stated that Brennan had manipulated the claims from the crash and defrauded the airlines and other insurance companies to evade paying as much as $7.5 million in claims.

It turned out that Brennan had a personal stake in USAU. After he became an underwriter there, he and his partner, Frank Lynch, worked their way up to control the company, making a lot of money for themselves. In 1986, they sold USAU for $100 million to General Reinsurance (Gen Re), a large reinsurance company based in Stamford, Connecticut (reinsurance is the system whereby insurers cover their liability). Brennan took his $40 million payout in Gen Re stock, making him the largest stockholder in that company. As his holdings appreciated, he was getting rich. By the time Lockerbie happened, his stock was worth about $100 million.

After Robert Alpert, chief of claims, resigned in 1989, he became increasingly critical of Brennan's handling of the PSA and Lockerbie claims. In a speech to the Beaumont Insurance Conference in 1994, he charged that while USAU had complete reinsurance protection on all claims against PSA, there was a significant gap in its reinsurance for the airline's security company. So, Brennan attributed the total loss to PSA to the airline's detriment, which would incur higher insurance premiums in the future. And PSA's co-insurers were stuck paying an inordinate part of the loss.

Concerning Lockerbie, Alpert revealed a gap in USAU's "war risk" reinsurance program. The company was wholly reinsured on passenger liability payments up to $100,000, reflecting insurance reserves of $60 million. Increasing the reserves to $300 million would have cost USAU $5 million. That would have negatively affected its bottom line and Brennan's stock earnings.

Alpert attributed Brennan's failure to settle to pure greed. Despite knowing the plaintiffs had a strong case, he did not want to accept the financial consequences to himself and his company.

The Brennan and USAU trial at the District Court in Brooklyn took less time than the Pan Am case. A jury found them guilty of 41 charges of mail fraud. On July 7, 1995, Judge Sifton imposed a sentence of 57 months in prison and a fine of $100,000 for the former president and CEO of USAU. The insurance company was also convicted, sentenced to five years probation, and fined $20.5 million to pay to the victims of the mail fraud.

Lee followed the case at a distance and took grim satisfaction in Brennan's woes. No trial lawyer wishes to see a fellow attorney in a defendant's shoes. The embarrassment, stress, and harm to one's reputation, even if acquitted, were considerable. But after seeing what his callous lies and machinations did to the families of the Pan Am victims, Lee felt that Brennan deserved everything he got. He was disappointed when the case was overturned on appeal because of a technicality.

The same grand jury that indicted John Brennan also recommended bringing charges against Yuval Aviv for defrauding General Electric. The company had hired Aviv and sent him to St. Thomas in the U.S. Virgin Islands in 1991 to determine if there was any danger from terrorists to the junket planned by GE Capital Corp officials. The federal indictment alleged that he falsely misrepresented in his report that he had interviewed several government and security officials on St. Thomas.

His defense attorney argued that Aviv had gone to St. Thomas in good faith, had interviewed the officials in question, and had provided GE with a valuable report. "The FBI and DOJ trumped up the whole case in retaliation for Mr. Aviv's role in investigating the 1988 bombing of Pan Am 103 over Scotland," she said.

Although the jury in the trial acquitted Aviv, the blow to his reputation was severe, and his security business suffered.

* * *

In October of 1996, Lester Coleman was arrested when he entered the United States from abroad. He had been indicted for lying on an affidavit three years earlier and fled to Sweden, seeking asylum from prosecution. Upon arrival, he claimed he was returning to "set the record straight."

After taking him into custody, the U.S. government brought charges against Coleman for perjury and illegally applying for a passport under an assumed name. The main accusations concerned making false statements in an affidavit supporting Pan Am's claims against the federal government in the Pan Am Flight 103 civil suit. The arraignment occurred on November 1, 1996, before U.S. District Court Judge Thomas Platt. Coleman did not enter a plea and was held without bail.

Nearly a year later, at the conclusion of the trial, Coleman admitted to the court that he lied when he claimed that a secret drug sting enabled terrorists to evade airport security in the Flight 103 bombing. He had wanted to bolster his image as an international security and terrorism consultant, get money, and exact revenge against the DEA for firing him. Pleading guilty to five counts of perjury, he signed a public apology.

Judge Platt accepted the plea agreement and imposed a sentence of time served plus five months in prison and six months of home confinement with electronic monitoring. He also fined Coleman $30,000 and insisted he spend three years on supervised release. Coleman later claimed that he signed the statement under duress.

Conspiracy theories circulated on the internet alleging that the federal convictions of Lester Coleman were an effort to silence him and to hide the truth about Pan Am Flight 103. As far as Lee was concerned, the conspiracies were as phony as all the lies that had poured from his mouth.

33

LIBYA

1996 to 1999

When the initial investigation of Lockerbie found evidence of a bomb exploding on Flight 103, the Scottish authorities assumed that Iran and Syria were behind the attack in retaliation for the U.S.S. *Vincennes* downing of an Iranian airbus. But the discovery of the Samsonite suitcase and articles of clothing traced to Malta were strong evidence that it was a Libyan plot carried out by intelligence operatives of Muammar Gaddafi's secret service.

Many of the victim's families wanted to hold the Libyan perpetrators accountable who had ordered the bombing and were directly responsible for the murders. As early as 1990, Captain Bruce Smith, a Pan Am pilot whose wife Ingrid was a flight attendant killed in the Lockerbie disaster, brought suit in New York against the Libyan government and Gaddifi, its leader.

At the time, Lee and the Plaintiffs Committee opposed that approach. Focusing on the terrorists responsible for the crash undermined the case of willful misconduct against Pan Am. Everyone involved in that litigation felt relieved when Smith's suit was dismissed before it went to trial because Libya had sovereign immunity in U.S. courts. At that time, ordinary American citizens had no legal standing to sue another country.

Families of the Victims of Pan Am Flight 103 took note and set their sights on changing the law granting other nations immunity from private suits. They lobbied Congress to amend the Foreign Sovereign Immunities Act to allow them to sue Libya, and Captain Bruce Smith joined their efforts.

When the Scottish and U.S. governments indicted two Libyan intelligence agents, Abdelbaset al-Megrahi and Lamen Khalifa Fhimah, in November of 1991, Gaddafi resisted all calls to have them extradited to Scotland or the United States to stand trial.

In response, the United Nations and the U.S. government imposed sanctions on Libya. The Victims of Pan Am Flight 103 added their strong vocal support and sent repeated messages to Libya that there would be no relief until it owned up to its role in the Lockerbie bombing.

The U.N. resolution contained four demands that Libya had to meet before sanctions would be lifted:

1. Provide compensation to the families of the victims.
2. Accept responsibility for the bombing.
3. Cooperate with the trial against the two intelligence agents implicated in the Lockerbie tragedy.
4. Formally denounce terrorism.

As Lee and the Plaintiffs Committee completed the trial against Pan Am in 1992, Libya continued to deny any involvement in the bombing and refused to give up Megrahi and Fhimah.

The Victims of Pan Am Flight 103 lobbied then-President Clinton, the State Department, and the U.S. Congress to keep up the pressure on Gaddafi. In 1995, the Clinton administration announced it would ask the U.N. to impose a worldwide oil boycott against Libya in retaliation for its refusal to turn over the accused suspects. By the time the Pan Am lawsuit was finally settled and damages were awarded, the sanctions were taking their toll on Libya. Unable to sell its primary export—oil—and denied access to most world markets, the country suffered significant economic losses.

A year later, on April 24, 1996, President Clinton signed the Effective Death Penalty and Anti-Terrorism Act, which created new exceptions to the Foreign Sovereign Immunity Act. Until then, foreign countries could only be sued if they engaged in alleged illegal commercial activities, acting like a company or corporation. Now, they could be taken to court for murder and terrorist acts, provided they were designated state sponsors of terror. There were seven such nations on the U.S. State Department's list at the time—Iran, Iraq, Sudan, North Korea, Syria, Cuba, and Libya.

An amendment made the act retroactive so it could apply to the Lockerbie bombing.

Still, Lee was cautious when he and the Plaintiffs Committee attorneys met with the Victims of Pan Am Flight 103 to discuss bringing suit against Libya. He knew it would be a long shot at best, a slow, drawn-out process that could drag on for years. "I'm not sure the Libyan government will show up in court," he said. "They can simply ignore our suit, and there is nothing we can do to force them to come to the table."

The family representatives looked around the conference room, nodding to one another. George Williams, the president of the group, spoke for everyone, "We want you to go ahead anyway."

During his career, Lee had taken on many cases others considered a lost cause, starting with the National Airline's plane crash in Elizabeth, New Jersey. By now he was 72 years old but still excited about tilting against windmills, so long as there was a chance of success. Therefore, there was no hesitation when he said, "Okay then, let's do it!"

In June of 1996, he and Kreindler & Kreindler filed an action against Libya and its terrorists in the Federal District Court of

New York. It was another first in Lee's long career in aviation law—bringing suit against a foreign country for mass murder.

The case landed once again before Judge Thomas Platt. Because he had presided over the suit against Pan Am, all subsequent civil litigation regarding Lockerbie came under his jurisdiction. As the first order of business, he appointed a new Plaintiffs Committee. Headed again by Lee, it included many names from the Pan Am trial—Jim Kreindler, Steve Pounian, Frank and Frankie Granito, and Mitch Baumeister.

There were two newcomers. Read McCaffrey, a partner of Patton Boggs in Washington, D.C., represented the families of the crew members of Flight 103. The other, Jerry Skinner, a Michigan lawyer, was the only attorney not from an East Coast law firm.

Skinner had 12 victims' families as clients. The parents of Khaid Jafaar, a 20-year-old student and the only Arab American on Flight 103, were one of them. Ten days after Skinner signed the representation agreement with Nazir Jafaar, his father, a Detroit newspaper ran a story that Khaid smuggled the bomb aboard the plane. After the shock waves settled, the claim was debunked as one of the lies fabricated by Lester Coleman on behalf of Pan Am. Coleman supposedly contacted the airline after recognizing Khaid as one of his drug runners when he worked for the DOE. In fact, Coleman had made up the whole story. His lies were exposed when he asserted that Khaid's terrorist indoctrination took place in the Middle East, at a time when the young man actually worked at a service station in Detroit, pumping gas.

While developing a close relationship with the Jafaar family, Jerry Skinner became familiar with Arab customs. More than any other member of the Plaintiffs Committee, he understood aspects of Islam and Arab culture, and his awareness and expertise would become invaluable later on.

To everyone's surprise, Libya showed up in court when the proceedings began, represented by Robert Mirone, an American lawyer. A pleasant, likable man in his 50s, Mirone came upon his assignment by accident. A year earlier, at an international bar association conference, he had had a friendly conversation with Abdelhay Sefrioui, a Moroccan attorney working in France. Because Libya was on the terrorist nation list, it could not send its lawyers to the United States—they would not be granted visas—and had to go through intermediaries. So, the government's legal committee hired the Sefrioui law firm to find an American attorney, and Mirone was the only one Abdelhay knew.

With expertise in Admiralty and Maritime Law, as well as International Law, Mirone was an excellent candidate. But when he tried to assemble a team of high-powered legal eagles, all the major law firms he called refused to touch the case, fearing it would sully their reputation. That did not dissuade him, however. He found other lawyers working independently willing to join him.

Mirone called the revisions in the Foreign Sovereignty Liability Act "the Get-Libya Act." He filed a motion to dismiss, insisting that it was unconstitutional because Clinton was conducting foreign policy through the courts and Congress. Lee and his team disputed that contention and argued that frozen Libyan assets could be used to pay award damages.

Before long, the Plaintiffs Committee received an invitation from Vice President Al Gore to come to a meeting in Washington to discuss the lawsuit. Lee had a good idea of what was at stake and alerted his team and the Victims of Pan Am Flight 103 families. In the past, whenever there was a dispute between nations, the State or Justice Department handled compensation. After the U.S.S. *Vincennes* mistakenly shot down Iran 555 in 1988, killing 298 people, the United States agreed to pay $250,000 per death. Lee was familiar with Supreme

Court cases that allowed the American president to shut down civil litigation for national security reasons and was worried that the government would take the Libya compensation case away from them.

About 100 people crowded into a large conference room at the Naval Observatory in Washington, most of them State and Justice Department officials. A few came from the FBI and CIA, and all members of the Plaintiffs Committee participated. After introductions, the discussion turned to the complexity of the criminal case and civil trial overlapping and the danger of inadvertently revealing secrets that should not see the light of day. On that last point, Lee assured everyone he and his team were aware of the issue and sensitive to the government's concerns. He mentioned their excellent working relationship with FAA and State Department lawyers during the Pan Am trial.

The Justice Department deputy who chaired the meeting asked, "Why should we let you conduct the civil case?"

Lee, speaking for the Committee, was blunt. "It's simple," he said. "Because you are going to screw it up. You are not going to know how to get to the right settlement." Before the assembled officials could react indignantly, he elaborated, "The families don't trust you, and they won't trust you. We have represented them for nine years, and there is a level of trust. We can act quickly, decisively, and with their support."

That led to more back-and-forth discussion, which, as far as Lee could tell, was more about bureaucrats saving face and marking their territory than dealing with any substantial matters. However, in the end, the Statement Department and DOJ gave the Plaintiffs Committee a commitment that they could go ahead.

Lee breathed a sigh of relief. He was glad to have the political clout of the Lockerbie families in his corner. He did not think Washington would have agreed without the public threat they posed.

As he had predicted, the litigation was slow-going. Libya ignored any requests for documents for nearly a year.

* * *

One day in the summer of 1997, Jeannine Boulanger went to her mailbox. To her surprise, she found an official-looking envelope addressed to her and stamped with the seal of the Permanent Mission of the Republic of Libya. The letter inside was typewritten in English. Without admitting responsibility for the disaster, its author urged her to accept financial settlements and to support lifting U.N. and American sanctions against Libya. She did not recognize the signature.

Jeannine immediately called other Victims of Pan Am Flight 103 family members. They had received the letter as well. Some were angry and upset. Others took it in stride. All were outraged at Libya's insistence that it had played no role in the disaster. By now well-versed in the power of the news media, a few went on television to plead with Libya to stop sending these letters to their home because they found them offensive.

Lee understood how distressing the episode was for the victims' families. On December 12, he filed a cease-and-desist restraining order against the government of Libya in the U.S. District Court on Long Island. When questioned by reporters on the courthouse steps, he explained, "These letters come from a country that the recipients think killed their loved ones. We think it's harassment. We think it's objectionable. We think it should be stopped."

But the letters kept coming.

Robert Mirone insisted that a restraining order would violate the First Amendment right to free speech. "Libya has the right to enunciate its position to the interested parties: both Libya and the victim's families, and the world as a whole," he said.

But he lost the argument, and a restraining order was imposed. Libya never again tried to communicate directly with any of the Lockerbie families.

Although the letters were essentially a sideshow, a bothersome nuisance in a complex case, Lee considered them a hopeful sign. Discussing it with the Plaintiffs Committee and the victims' families, he noted that the mention of a financial settlement suggested that Libya and its leader were perhaps willing to come to the table to negotiate.

"It's a matter of how much international pressure Gaddafi feels," he told the families.

The Victims of Pan Pam Flight 103 responded by continuing to lobby in Congress and the U.N. to keep the sanctions in place.

On February 26, 1998, Judge Platt denied Libya's motion for dismissal and ruled that the families of the victims of the Pan Am 103 bombing had judicial standing in their suit. Mirone promptly appealed the decision. But in December, the Second Circuit Court of Appeals affirmed Judge Platt's ruling, allowing the case against Libya to go forward with discovery.

Then, a significant development occurred in the criminal case brought by the Scottish and U.S. governments against the two Libyan intelligence agents. In a deal brokered by Nelson Mandela and a Saudi prince, Gaddafi agreed to have the suspects tried in the Netherlands. Initially, he insisted the trial take place at the International Court in The Hague. Ultimately, he approved the court being convened at Camp Zeist, a former U.S. military Air Force base near the town of Utrecht, and treating it as Scottish territory.

The solution allowed both sides to save face. The Libyan despot and the Arab press claimed that he stood up to the United States and succeeded in having the trial take place in a neutral country. The American and British governments were satisfied that the defendants would be tried with Scottish judges under Scottish law. They even agreed to present only evidence against the two defendants, not against any members of the Libyan government.

Thus, a special courtroom with bulletproof glass and Scottish guards was built at the camp. On April 5, 1999, the two Pan Am 103 bombing suspects, Abdelbaset al-Megrahi and Lamen Khalifa Fhimah, were flown from Libya to The Hague and transported to Camp Zeist for trial. In return, U.N. Secretary-General Kofi Annan announced that U.N. sanctions against Libya would be lifted. However, the U.S. State Department reiterated that unilateral American sanctions would remain in force until Libya had met all four demands of the U.N. resolution.

Lee, the Plaintiffs Committee, and the Victims of Pan Am Flight 103 discussed these developments at length and visited the courtroom at Camp Zeist. Based on their conversations with staff there and State Department officials, they agreed to suspend their efforts in the civil case until after the criminal trial concluded.

The hiatus in the litigation proceedings allowed Lee and his firm to focus on two other important air disaster cases they had taken on.

34

FRAZZLED

1996 to 2002

A few weeks after Lee initiated the suit against Libya on behalf of the Pan Am families, another air disaster occurred, this time in the United States. On July 17, 1996, TWA Flight 800 took off from Kennedy Airport en route to Paris and Rome. Twelve minutes later, there was an enormous explosion and the Boeing 747 crashed into the Atlantic Ocean on the southern coast of Long Island. All 230 people on board were killed, including 18 crew members.

Because of the huge fireball burst seen by several eyewitnesses, there was wide speculation that a terrorist attack—either a bomb or a missile—destroyed the aircraft. Many witnesses said they'd seen a streak of light moving toward where the giant ball of fire appeared.

Parallel investigations by the National Transportation Safety Board (NTSB) and the FBI began with assistance from the CIA. A host of conspiracy theories circulated when traces of explosive chemicals were found among the debris recovered from the crash. Although the internet was still in its infancy, rumors spread widely, including the speculation that the bomb attack was meant to kill Henry Kissinger, the former U.S. Secretary of State, although he was not on board the plane.

THE FIGHT FOR JUSTICE

In August, *American Online*, a news website, posted a story asserting the aircraft was "shot down accidentally by a U.S. Navy guided-missile ship."

Pierre Salinger, who had circulated a false news story about the Lockerbie disaster, was at work again, claiming he had a document proving the U.S. Navy was the "friendly fire" culprit. He later retracted, saying he was merely repeating what was on the internet. It was another low point for the former press secretary of President John F. Kennedy, who kept sinking deeper into the fake news mire in his attempts to remain cutting-edge and relevant.

Lee could only shake his head. In the face of such far-fetched speculation, he quickly decided that, unlike Lockerbie, this was not a terrorist attack. He hired his own investigators and sent them to comb through the wreckage.

Meanwhile, Lee announced his theory in a press conference. He explained that he reached his conclusions based on weather conditions and the aircraft's altitude. "What made Lockerbie happen was that at 32,000 feet, the bomb punched a small hole in the fuselage, and the high winds tore the airplane apart," he said. "Flight 800 exploded among light winds at an altitude of 13,700 feet. If a bomb had been aboard the flight, it would have had to be a huge bomb. How would you get such a large device on an airplane? From a probability standpoint, it would be next to impossible."

Lee anticipated that his conclusions would meet with considerable skepticism. Structural failure did not sound as dramatic as a terrorist bomb or military mistake.

Meticulous as always, Lee cemented his conclusions by monitoring the investigation of a former Boeing engineer who helped design the 747. For six weeks, Peter Jorgenson examined a grounded jumbo jet like Flight 800 in the Mohave Desert. He concluded that gasoline vapors from a center wing fuel tank exploded during the flight causing burning fuel to flow through the vent lines of the right wing. That resulted in a chain reaction of fires and structural failures and led to the plane bursting into flames and breaking apart.

Based on Jorgensen's findings, Lee brought a lawsuit against TWA and Boeing on behalf of 86 of the victim's families. Other attorneys represented the rest. Because Flight 800 was on an international route, TWA, per the Warsaw Convention, was responsible for only $75,000 per passenger. When the Plaintiffs Committee for the suit was formed, Lee became its co-counsel. At the time, the NTSB had not reached a conclusive determination, other than that the disaster was not a terrorist attack—the explosive chemicals turned out to be a negligible amount.

A spokesman for TWA dismissed Lee's theory as hogwash. "It is analogous to determining the cause of an automobile crash by looking at a Chevrolet at a dealership across the country," he scoffed. "The most technically astute and most directly involved federal and company investigators, who have been reviewing this accident since the day it happened, have not been able to reach any conclusion by looking at the evidence."

Lee responded unperturbed, "I've won cases on theories that the NTSB rejected. It doesn't make any difference in the litigation."

As the case progressed, it became increasingly clear that Lee's early conclusions were correct, and TWA and Boeing indicated that they were willing to settle. The only remaining bone of contention was what kind of damages to award. The attorneys for the defendants contested the Plaintiffs Committee's view that they should be able to sue for loss of solatium, meaning damages for emotional pain and suffering, which would run in the millions of dollars. In March 2000, the judge in the case ruled they had standing to bring such a suit, and Boeing and TWA agreed to pay the families full compensation.

THE FIGHT FOR JUSTICE

By July 2002, the insurers for the airline, which had gone bankrupt a year earlier, and Boeing settled all the cases. The damage payout amounts remained under seal, although rumors suggested that the estimated total topped $500 million.

For Lee, the outcome was especially gratifying. Not only did the victims' families receive fair compensation. The final NSTA report confirmed in detail the conclusions to which he had come to before starting the litigation.

* * *

The other case involved Swissair Flight 111 which crashed off the Canadian coast on September 8, 1988, near Peggy's Cove, Novia Scotia. There were 229 people aboard the McDonnell Douglas MD-11 jetliner bound for Geneva from JFK. The route was known as the "U.N. shuttle" because it frequently carried officials from the United Nations.

The flight recorder revealed that the crew in the cockpit smelled smoke, indicating a fire in the instrument panel, and tried to reach Halifax Airport for an emergency landing. They never made it, and the plane plunged into the ocean. The impact tore the aircraft apart and killed everyone aboard. Rescue operations recovered about a quarter of the wreckage, an estimated two million pieces of debris.

The Transportation Board of Canada (TSB) investigated the crash and later determined that the fire spread and intensified, which led to electrical power failures and rendered cockpit instruments inoperable. As a result, the crew could no longer control the aircraft.

Most passengers, including the 14 crew members, were American, Swiss, and French. The rest came from a number of countries around the world, including China, India, Russia, and Saudi Arabia. Joseph La Motta, the son of the famous boxer Jake LaMotta, was among them. Also destroyed were two paintings by Pablo Picasso on their way to a Swiss museum exhibition.

Kreindler & Kreindler accounted for close to half of the 167 cases. Lee became lead counsel of the Plaintiffs Committee.

Once again, Mitch Baumeister was one of the other plaintiff attorneys. Representing Jake La Motta, he slapped a $50 million lawsuit on Swissair, which caused a brief stir in the newspapers and television media. The reason behind his bold approach was that, a few years earlier, Swiss Air rejected the Warsaw Convention monetary limitations to settle airliner crash cases. That boded well for all the plaintiffs.

Over the next few years, Lee juggled three cases—Lockerbie, TWA 800, and Swissair 111. That meant daily meetings with families of one of the three disasters. Often distressing and gut-wrenching, they required him to be attentive, empathetic, and reassuring. There were strategy sessions with the different Plaintiffs Committees, motions to draft and file, and discovery materials to evaluate. For courtroom appearances in the Swissair trial, he had to shuttle from New York to Philadelphia.

At a time when most people have hung up their spurs, thoughts of retirement were far from Lee's mind. He was busier than ever. As he told a reporter from *New York Magazine* in October of 1998, "I'm frazzled. I've been working my ass off lately."

On August 5, 1999, Swissair and Boeing, which had acquired McDonnell Douglass two years earlier, agreed to assume financial responsibility together for any monetary damages. While their joint statement did not admit to guilt in the crash, it indicated they wanted to speed up settling damages. They offered each family an advance of $137,000, nearly double what the Warsaw Convention allowed for international airplane accidents.

Lee commented to the press, "It was a complete shock and a reversal of what their lawyers said in previous court proceedings. I praise them for it. It's what they should have done much earlier."

But he understood that the offer came with strings attached and for a darker purpose. The defense attorneys filed a motion to transfer about 120 cases to France or Switzerland for the families of victims who were not U.S. citizens. European courts awarded much lower damages in airline cases. In addition, settling quickly could be a legal maneuver to short-circuit the lengthy disaster investigation and prevent a trial to determine greater liability and monetary damages.

So, Lee and the other attorneys for the families rejected the offer as insufficient and threatened to bring suit against Swissair and DuPont, the supplier of the insulation sheathings of wires in the cockpit instrument panels.

To their surprise, the gambit worked. Swissair and Boeing agreed to compensation negotiations in earnest, and by the summer of 2000, Kreindler & Kreindler had settled nearly 20 claims to their clients' satisfaction. Lee expected the rest to follow suit.

But the relentless work schedule and pressure took their toll on him. In November of that year, at a conference for the TWA case in a Manhattan courtroom, with his son by his side, Lee suddenly felt faint and put his head down on the table.

The judge stopped the proceedings and asked, "Is he all right?"

When Lee did not respond, everyone grew concerned.

Finally, Lee looked up uncomprehendingly. When Jim asked, "What's going on?" he seemed confused. Lee tried to speak, but he had difficulty forming words. "Feel weak," he slurred and rubbed the side of his face. "Numb," he said.

Jim called for an ambulance to take Lee to New York Hospital. He also telephoned Ruth, who was practicing for an upcoming dance competition at a studio in upper Manhattan. "Dad is in the hospital," he said. "Come now!"

Ruth rushed outside, not bothering to change out of her sequined ballgown, and caught a taxi to the hospital. She arrived, frantic with worry. Jim met her in the hospital lobby. He reassured her that Lee was all right.

When Ruth burst into his room, out of breath, Lee was sitting up in bed in good spirits, joking with a nurse.

Ruth hurried to his side. "Don't scare me like that again!" she exclaimed, slapping his arm because she was so upset.

Lee acted surprised. "I don't understand what all the fuss is about." But when he saw his wife looking dismayed, he embraced her and whispered, "I really am okay, Ruthie."

Tests revealed that Lee had suffered a TIA—a mini-stroke. The doctors insisted he stay overnight at the hospital, warning that, if untreated, TIAs were often precursors to a more severe stroke. After some additional tests, they put Lee on a regimen of blood-thinning drugs.

Ruth stayed with Lee in a chair by his bedside, nodding on and off throughout the night. The following morning, he checked out fine, and the doctors sent him home, telling him to rest.

Lee followed their orders over the weekend in Chappaqua because Ruth insisted. She pampered him preparing his favorite foods and pleaded that he reduce his workload.

But by Monday, Lee said he felt fine and headed back to New York to return to the legal fray.

35

LIBYA AGAIN

2001 - 2002

On January 23, 2001, in a unanimous ruling, three Scottish judges found Abdelbaset al-Megrahi guilty of mass murder. They sentenced him to life in prison with a minimum term of 20 years. However, they acquitted Lamin Khalifa Fhimah. Lawyers for Megrahi immediately appealed his conviction.

Many victims' families, who had observed the trial from afar and as spectators in the courtroom, were deeply disappointed and dissatisfied. Not only did one of the defendants walk free, but there had been no attempt to hold the Libyan government responsible.

During the welcoming home celebrations for Fhimah in Tripoli, Muammar Gaddafi announced that Libya would not compensate the victims' families or take official responsibility for the bombing. A few days later, he insisted that the Lockerbie verdict was "politically tainted" and repeated that Libya would pay no compensation. It was the trademark bluster of the Libyan strongman who had a well-earned reputation for diplomatic grandstanding.

Meanwhile, international pressure on Gaddafi and his country continued unabated. The U.S. government announced that the verdict in Scotland alone was insufficient to lift American sanctions. First, Libya had to meet the other requirements in the U.N. Security

Council resolution—paying damage compensation to the victims' families, accepting responsibility for the bombing, and renouncing terrorism. Great Britain supported the U.S. position.

Lee and the Plaintiffs Committee reopened their lawsuit against Libya. They made discovery requests and noticed depositions of Libyan government officials. When their demands went unheeded, they filed a motion in the Federal District Court asking for a default judgment, arguing that Libyan officials had failed to provide any of the documents. If Judge Platt agreed, the families could seek recompense from frozen Libyan assets in the United States.

In June, Robert Mirone called Lee and informed him that Libya reached out through its French attorneys and was willing to have one of its government officials deposed. Lee was surprised and pleased, but the logistics caused some difficulties. Because of the country's status as a terrorist nation, the witness could not travel to the United States. Several European nations banned Libyan citizens as well. Only France allowed them entry.

So, the entire Plaintiffs Committee flew to Paris. They were eager to find out who they would meet and headed straight from the airport to the Sefrioui law firm, before checking into their hotel. But when they arrived at the offices on the Boulevard de Courelles, it turned out that the witness was not a high-ranking member of the government but a mid-level official of Libyan Arab Airlines.

Tired from traveling, Mitch Baumeister took offense and vented his frustration out loud, "This guy knows nothing about Flight 103. It's a complete waste of time!"

The members of the Libyan delegation who spoke English got offended in turn. "How can he say our man knows nothing?!" they complained. "He is a very erudite man."

While Bob Mirone and Jerry Skinner attempted to calm the irate Libyans, Lee tried to make the best of the situation. He took

Abdelhay Sefrioui aside and said, "We want to do the deposition and make a video recording. Do you have the equipment here to do that?" When Sefrioui nodded, he turned to both indignant groups and said, "Why don't we all go to our hotel, get settled, and reconvene here for the deposition tomorrow morning? Is that agreeable to everyone?"

After further glowering and scowling, there were reluctant nods from both delegations.

The next day, everyone sat down at the large table in the Sefroui conference room. Jim Kreindler did the questioning. The executive from the Libyan Arab Airline spoke English well, eliminating the need for a translator.

The deposition went smoothly, although nothing significant emerged regarding the Lockerbie case. Afterward, Mitch Baumeister reiterated his objection. "A complete waste of time," he grumbled.

Later that day, Lee received a phone call from Mirone. During lunch, the airline executive was as happy as can be, gushing about how well it had gone. He had kept asking about his "performance" and beamed with pride when Mirone assured him he'd done an excellent job.

When Lee shared the news with his team, Skinner joked, "He got to be on camera. He thought he was a TV star!"

Everyone had a good laugh after a discouraging day.

But Lee pointed out that the proceeding provided a glimmer of hope, "It's the first time we've seen Libya wanting to rejoin the world. This may be the opening we've been looking for."

He was pleased when his prediction came true, although he was as surprised as everyone else on the team how much the Libyans' attitude changed. Before they had insisted, "We'll litigate this to the end." After the deposition, through their French representative, they floated the idea that there should be more conversations about a possible settlement. Gaddafi might be willing to entertain an offer.

Lee and the Plaintiffs Committee immediately informed their clients, Judge Platt, and the State Department. He got the go-ahead from the latter to pursue negotiations so long as they were conducted quietly. The American government wanted to keep its distance if the discussions turned sour. It was still too early to be overly hopeful, and everyone prepared to dig in for the long haul.

In a meeting with the Victims of Pan Am Flight 103, Lee talked about the new development, explaining the delicate nature of such negotiations and asserting the need for utter secrecy. "It's promising," he told the families. "But we may have to do this for two years without telling you anything."

"I wouldn't trust any of those bastards farther than I could throw them," said Susan Cohn, whose only daughter, Theodora, had died in the crash.

"I don't care about the money," said the father of another victim. "You find me a chance to kill one of the bastards that ordered my daughter's death. I'd die a thousand deaths for that opportunity."

As Lee looked at the grim faces around the conference room, he saw how tired and furious they were. Having expected push-back and anger, he said, "I understand how you feel. This is only the first step, one of four demands in the U.N. resolution. Let's start with that."

After conferring for several minutes, the group agreed. Various members said, "Go ahead, Lee." "We trust you." "We know you have our best interests at heart."

Lee was deeply moved by their confidence in him. He nodded and said, "Thank you. I won't let you down."

* * *

The first meeting between the Plaintiffs Committee and representatives of the Libyan government occurred on July 10, in a conference room at the St. George Hotel in London. Because of unrest in Tripoli, the makeup of the Libyan delegation remained unclear until the last minute. Lee and his team had no chance to find out about them. Eventually, the founder of the Sefrioui law firm, Mirone, and four Libyan officials from Tripoli showed up. They said that they were authorized to speak for Muammar Gaddafi.

The tension in the room was palpable as everyone went around the table making introductions, eyeing one another with hostility and distrust. Because the participants were French, Libyan, and American, conversations required translation to and from several languages.

The Libyans made clear from the outset that their country refused to admit any responsibility for the bombing. Requiring them to do so would be a deal breaker. "We didn't do this," they announced. "But we are willing to negotiate because of issues important to us."

The atmosphere became even more charged when Jim Kreindler, speaking for the plaintiffs, demanded compensation of $20 million per crash victim. The Libyans immediately rejected the offer, their eyes flashing with anger. Mirone and Sefrioui argued more calmly, referencing damage awards in more recent aircraft disasters. Libya had paid less than $200,000 for each of the 170 people killed in the 1989 bombing of a French UTA airliner. After the U.S.S. *Vincennes* downed an Iranian airbus, the U.S. government paid $250,000 per passenger and crew member killed. The highest damage award had come when an American Marine jet sliced through a gondola cable near Cavalese, Italy, in 1998. The U.S. and Italian governments paid $1.9 million for each of the 20 people who had died.

There seemed to be no way to breach an insurmountable gap.

Afterward, Lee discussed what had happened with his fellow Committee members. "If there is to be a settlement, there has to be some linkage to what Libya wants to achieve," he said. "Perhaps we should discuss the case more generally, from each side's point of view."

At the next meeting, the Libyans came back with an offer of $250,000. They refused to pay any punitive damages, reiterating that their country bore no responsibility for the bombing. They also wanted the compensatory damages offset by amounts previously paid by USAU, Pan Am's insurer. The Plaintiffs Committee rejected that demand, frustrated that there was so little agreement.

However, after several days, Lee and Jim Kreindler, who took the lead in the negotiations, felt they had made some progress. They flew back to the Unites States, looking forward to the next meeting, scheduled to take place in France.

Two weeks later, an entirely different Libyan delegation showed up in Paris. They insisted that the earlier group had not been authorized to speak for Gaddafi, but that they were. As a result, negotiations started from scratch.

Over the following months, that happened several times, with each new Libyan delegation seeking more concessions. Lee and his team felt that they were on a merry-go-round and going nowhere.

Learning that there were legitimate reasons for what was happening did not make it any easier. Libya did not have a state department or department of justice. Instead, there was a legal committee of more than 1,000 members, with a Lockerbie subcommittee whose makeup and chair rotated. As a result, negotiators changed frequently as well.

Whenever a new group of Libyans arrived, Lee and the Committee checked with the State Department to confirm they were legitimate before commencing talks. Some of the negotiators who showed up were experts in Sharia Law. Others knew about the French and British legal systems. None were familiar with American legal practices, making efforts to reach common ground even more difficult.

The Libyan representatives were all fluent in English, which gave them an advantage. They could listen to what Lee and his team said and confer in Arabic among themselves without being overheard since none of the American delegation spoke their language.

Sometimes, after everyone reached an agreement on a point in English and it was translated into Arabic, the Libyans would say, "No, no, no. We didn't agree to that!" They would insist on having the words retranslated, in some instances several times, until they gave their approval. The drawn-out process often stretched the patience of Lee and his team to the breaking point.

Another stumbling block occurred when they reached an agreement on a point after negotiating for several days and everyone was satisfied. But when Jim and the others wanted to start the next session where they'd left off, the Arab team would insist on renegotiating the earlier point. The first time it happened, most of the American attorneys felt that it was deliberate and intended to mock them.

They were fortunate to have Jerry Skinner on their team. Having represented Nazir Jafaar, the father of the young Arab-American killed on Flight 103, he had learned that the practice of renegotiating an earlier agreement had historical roots. It went all the way back to the Prophet Muhammad, who counseled that when you're weak, you agree to anything. Later, when your situation improves, you renegotiate.

Skinner pointed out other differences between Arab and Western cultures as well. Unlike goal-oriented Americans who want to reach their objectives as quickly as possible, Mideasterners delighted in drawn-out arguments. They loved to haggle and barter. Skinner's explanations helped his fellow attorneys avoid losing their cool.

Although many of these meetings and follow-up phone calls to Tripoli proved unproductive, Lee did not lose heart. He was used to opponents posturing. In the strategy session with the Plaintiffs Committee, he pointed out, "Such face-saving measures are par for the course everywhere."

Toward the beginning of September, the meetings became more promising. The U.S. Congress overwhelmingly approving to extend the sanctions against Libya for another five years, and President George W. Bush signing them into law, was probably a contributing factor. Anna Sefrioui replacing her husband was a positive development too because her English was better. In any case, the discussions became less combative.

Although they were still far apart on damage awards, the Libyans acknowledged that compensation of several million dollars was not unreasonable. Agreement that the money needed to be tied to some mechanism that guaranteed Libya some relief from the crushing sanctions also changed the tenor of the talks.

Back in New York, Lee reported their progress to Judge Platt and the State Department. The judge was pleased and told him to continue. Lee and his team were happy that he allowed them to chart their own course. U.S. government officials were guardedly optimistic but reaffirmed their hands-off policy. Everyone was looking forward to the next negotiating session.

Then came September 11. The shocking terrorist attack on the United States put all discussions with Libya on hold. Lee and the Committee met with the State Department and CIA representatives several times, who urged restraint and patience.

With the negotiations suspended, Lee and his firm took on hundreds of cases for the families of victims of the World Trade Center attack.

Settlement discussions with Libya did not resume until February 2002, when the two sides reconvened in Paris. They met at the Royal Monceau Hotel, a splendid Art Nouveau edifice, within a stone's throw of the Champs-Élysées. The Arc de Triomphe was visible from the balcony of his room facing Avenue Hoche, but Lee rarely had the time to enjoy the view.

Libya Again

Once again, a new group of negotiators arrived. Their leader was a banker and businessman named Mohammed Abdul Jawad. A childhood friend of Muammar Gaddafi, he had lived for some time in New York City and had a more sophisticated understanding of American culture than his many of his predecessors. Two other important delegation members were Azzam Eddeeb, a justice on the Libyan supreme court, and Ali Dawi, a university professor.

Lee flew to Paris ahead of the meeting to get ready, and Ruth joined him a day later. Ever since his TIA, she was very concerned about his health. She quickly realized how much pressure the negotiations put on her husband and tried to help him relax in the evenings as best she could.

Although the initial discussions began with the usual tension and suspicion, Jawad seemed committed to a settlement. He approached things from a strictly economic perspective and expressed no interest when Lee raised the emotional aspects of the Lockerbie bombing and the impact on the victim's families. Jawad wanted to calculate the cost of the sanctions to the Libyan economy over five years and reduce that number to a present-day value. Based on that figure, he could recommend a settlement that would be less than the financial losses Libya would incur in the future.

He and his team also had questions: What would happen if some families accepted the money and others did not? How could they be sure sanctions would be lifted even if Libya paid a vast sum? Would an out-of-court settlement even work?

These were legitimate concerns, and Lee, Jim, and the others worked hard to come up with suitable proposals to address them. They suggested including a provision in the agreement that at least 90% of the families had to accept the payout. If Judge Platt approved the deal, and there was no reason to imagine he wouldn't, it was as good as law.

At first, Jawad was not satisfied. He insisted on 100% of the families agreeing to the settlement.

After some back-and-forth wrangling, Lee asked pointedly, "Muhammad, do you really want to scuttle the settlement if only one or two families balk?"

Jawad yielded to reason.

The most significant development was both sides agreed to an installment concept for damage compensation. There would be preconditions, or "trigger events"—lifting the sanctions and taking Libya off the state-sponsors-of-terror list—for the release of a portion of the settlement money. That way, Libya would not have to guarantee the whole amount before seeing progress in its bid to become a member of good standing in the world community again. After the Plaintiffs Committee proposed the plan, the atmosphere during the negotiations became more relaxed.

Still, the discussions went on for days with no significant progress on the dollar amount, and Libyan representatives continued to insist that their country had nothing to do with the Lockerbie bombing. A settlement with the families would not be an admission of guilt.

Lee spent many sleepless nights mulling over how to proceed. He was glad Ruth was there for the duration as a sounding board and partner willing to share his worries.

While Jim continued to take the lead in the discussions, Lee directed tactics and strategy. It helped that he was the oldest person in the room. The Libyan negotiators considered him the elder statesman of the American delegation. Coming from a traditional Arab society, they accorded Lee a high status and treated him with the utmost respect. When he spoke, they listened more intently.

Lee knew that, despite Jawad's cold, calculated economic approach, the Lockerbie case was fraught with emotion, hatred, and suspicion on both sides. He understood that personal relations and trust were as important in reaching an agreement as facts and figures. Experience had taught him that they mattered and could make the difference.

When he learned that Jawad's house had been hit as the U.S. Air Force bombed Libya in 1986 in retaliation for its terror attack it had mounted on a West Berlin disco frequented by American serviceman, threatening his family's safety, Lee approached him man to man. Speaking on behalf of his delegation, he said, "We didn't know that happened to you. We are very sorry, Mohammed. It must have been very frightening."

For the first time in their encounters, Jawad took note, and his impassive, self-controlled demeanor lapsed for a moment. After giving Lee a searching look, he bowed slightly and said, "It was. Thank you."

One Friday afternoon, during a particularly grueling and fruitless week of negotiations, Lee leaned back from the conference table and looked at the ceiling. He reached a decision and said to the Libyan delegation, "Why don't you come to dinner with us? We promise we won't talk about the case. We want to know more about you and your families."

He reserved a dining room large enough for both delegations and provided wine and liquor. He knew from experience that many Arabs, when away from their country, enjoyed drinking alcohol, which was banned in their homeland. Ruth joined them for the occasion, and everyone kept the conversation to personal matters. Lee and his team members asked their Libyan counterparts about themselves, their homes, their families and children, and what mattered to them. After a while, everyone around the table relaxed and talked more amiably. The Libyans seemed to realize that their opponents weren't sharks or American devils but ordinary people with worries about their families and hopes for a better future.

At some point, Jawad stepped out to make a telephone call. Lee could hear him speak softly in Arabic but didn't think anything of it.

After the dinner, the quality of the negotiations changed. The body language in the meeting room on both sides was more casual, less stiff and posturing. The exchanges became friendlier, with occasional joking and laughter.

Still, things did not advance toward a settlement. By early May, talks went on for days with little progress. Everyone was exhausted. Some participants were so tired they often leaned back in their chairs with eyes closed. It was clear people wanted to go home. At some point, looking around the room, Lee suggested they take a break. People on both sides of the table yawned openly and nodded their agreement. Most of the Libyans got up to go to the restroom and smoke. A few put their heads down to rest.

As everyone trickled back into the room to take their seats, Lee approached Jawad and said, "Mohammad, let's talk outside."

They went into the hall and sat down on a sofa in an alcove. Jawad lit a cigarette, took a drag, leaned back, and closed his eyes Then, he exhaled through his nostrils and turned to Lee, keeping the cigarette away from him.

"So, where are we?" Lee asked.

Mohammad said, "I am willing to consider terms, but I need guarantees."

For the next 20 minutes, Lee listened carefully and suggested several options. As they went back and forth, their conversation became more animated.

When they returned to the meeting room, the others around the table looked up at them expectantly.

Lee turned to Jawad and said, "Mohammed, you tell them."

Mohammed shook his head and said, "No, Lee, you did it. You tell them."

A magnificent smile broke out on Lee's face as he announced, "We have reached a deal! We have an understanding."

The room erupted in cheers. Jim and Steve Pounian gave each other high fives.

Later, Jawad revealed how their dinner together contributed to breaking the impasse. When he stepped out of the room, he called his childhood friend Muammar Gadaffi. "You'll never guess where I am," he said. "I'm at the hotel, and we're having a pleasant dinner with the plaintiffs' lawyers. If we can do that with them, our country can change dramatically. We can reestablish relations with the United States."

Gaddafi told him to go ahead and make a deal.

On May 29, 2002, Lee held a press conference in New York and announced the settlement with Libya, using the exact words as in Paris: "We have reached a deal. We have an understanding."

Libya agreed to compensation of $2.7 billion, $10 million per passenger, the largest settlement in the history of American mass disasters. Every victim's family would be paid the same amount, regardless of economic loss or nationality. Lee and his team felt that giving less compensation to the European, African, and South American families would have dishonored them.

The following day, through its state-run news agency, Libya denied any official offer of compensation, giving Gaddafi cover if the agreement fell apart later. But some government members let on that a "non-governmental" negotiator might have made an unofficial offer.

Lee told the news media, "I have confirmed with my counterpart in Libya that we are still very much in business, and we are proceeding according to plan."

The reactions from the Lockerbie victims' families were mixed.

Some were pleased with the outcome and happy with the financial settlement. "Gadaffi's been trying to get under and around this," said Helen Engelhardt, whose husband died in the bomb attack. "The way it seems to be set up right now is excellent. Of course, I'm delighted."

Others were outraged.

One of the most vocal dissenters was Susan Cohn who gave several interviews. "It's absolutely disgusting," she said in one of them. "They're simply trying to buy their way off the terrorism list. I will fight as hard as I can to keep them on it." In another, she declared, "I don't care by how much they try to bribe us. They could give me $50 million. Do you think I'm going to betray my kid's memory and suddenly become a cheering section for the Libyans?"

Kathleen Flynn, who lost her 21-year-old son, John Patrick, in the disaster, was just as offended. "No amount of money will ever compensate me for the loss of my child," she said.

Lee understood the depths of their fury and hoped they would see things differently in time. He could not imagine Libya agreeing to such a large settlement without taking the other steps necessary to get out from under the sanctions, including accepting responsibility for the bombing and renouncing terrorism.

"We are acting on behalf of the victims to put an end to a lasting tragedy," Lee told a reporter. "We are also acting to avoid future terrorist attacks. If you make it sufficiently expensive, you will deter terrorism."

Further meetings in Paris with the Libyan delegation over the summer and early fall nailed down the timing and sequence of actions by Libya, the U.N., and the U.S. government that would trigger the release of the payments.

Libya would deposit the money into an escrow account at the Bank of International Settlements in Basel, Switzerland. Families would receive $4 million each after U.N. sanctions were lifted, another $4 million when U.S. commercial sanctions were lifted and frozen Libyan assets released. The final $2 million would come when the U.S. State Department took Libya off the terrorist nations list.

* * *

On October 23, 2002, all major negotiation participants signed a memorandum of understanding. For the Libyan side: attorneys Robert Mirone and Anne Sefrioui, Mohammed Abdul Jawad, Azzam Eddeeb, and Ali Dawi. For the victims' families: Lee and Jim Kreindler, Mitch Baumeister, Frank Granito Jr, Frank Granito III, Read Caffrey, and Jerry Skinner.

Afterward, Lee and the other plaintiffs' attorneys went out to dinner to celebrate. Nearly 14 years after the Lockerbie disaster, they had achieved the near-impossible. It had taken 18 face-to-face meetings and numerous telephone conferences with Tripoli to finally reach an agreement.

At 78, Lee felt vindicated and pleased, for himself and his firm. But most of all, he was happy for the relatives of the victims who had perished in the crash. The money would not bring their loved ones back, but at least they and their children would be taken care of financially.

36

AFTERMATH

2002 - 2008

Following the U.S. invasion of Iraq and the bombing of Baghdad in April of 2003 in retaliation for the September 11 attacks, Jawad called the Plaintiffs Committee. He and his two colleagues were no longer directly involved with the negotiating process, and the signed agreement was meeting with opposition in Tripoli. But the new delegation, led by two high-ranking ambassadors, invited the team to meet with them in London on May 22 to discuss compensation and acceptance of responsibility for the Lockerbie disaster.

A month earlier, Libyan officials had met with representatives of the U.S. and British governments to work out a statement with language acceptable to all sides regarding Libyan acknowledgment of its accountability. In a press conference, participants deemed the talks "promising" but kept the successful outcome secret.

It took another flurry of meetings over the summer between the Plaintiffs Committee and the Libyan delegation before the final escrow agreement was signed on August 13, 2003.

In the past, referring to the "Lockerbie curse," Jim Kreindler had joked that the number 13 seemed to play a notable role in the case. The trial against Pan Am in 1992 lasted 13 weeks, the bag containing the bomb had been number 13 to be screened in Frankfurt, and the first appeal trial occurred on May 13, 1993. Now, Read McCaffrey pointed out to him that 13 members of the Libyan delegation were seated across the table when the final agreement was reached.

Jim smiled, amused at the coincidence. He was not a superstitious man.

On August 15, Libya submitted a letter to the U.N. Security Council, acknowledging responsibility for the bombing of Pan Am Flight 103. The carefully crafted words said that Libya, as a "sovereign state, accepted responsibility for the actions of its officials." That tied its legal responsibility to the employment of Megrahi, not to an admission of any government involvement.

A week later, the European bank received $2.7 billion in an escrow account. The following month, on September 22, an initial deposit of $1.068 billion—$4 million per victim—arrived in the Plaintiffs Committee's New York Trust account. Conferences with Judge Platt about the dispersal began.

Eventually, all but one of the victim's families agreed to the settlement, following a lengthy procedure of affidavits, letters testamentary, due diligence, and additional orders from Judge Platt concerning payment and distribution of the funds. Only Susan Cohn and her husband refused to accept all three settlement provisions. They balked at the third "trigger," wanting to keep Libya on the international terrorist nations list.

By mid-January 2004, most families and the various law firms involved had received their portion of the initial payment.

On October 7, 2004, after commercial sanctions against Libya were lifted and its assets "unfrozen," the second payment was transferred and quickly deposited in the various accounts of the families and law firms.

The third "trigger" required removing Libya from the State Department's list of countries that sponsor terrorism. Unfortunately, that did not happen in a timely fashion, and the escrow agreement deadline expired. The remaining funds were returned to Libya.

The final payout did not happen until the end of 2008 after the U. S. Congress unanimously passed the Libyan Claims Resolution Act. Originating in the Senate, with the help of then-Senator Joseph Biden, it included provisions for settling all remaining monetary claims against Libya. In return, Libya was readmitted to the international community and received guarantees for the restoration and protection of its assets.

Twenty years after the fateful bombing, the civil case was finally settled for good, and the families received their final payment.

* * *

Lee never dealt with any of these maneuvers, participated in any further discussions, or saw the fruits of his labors. Like Moses, who guided his people through the desert, he'd shepherded his fellow attorneys and the victims' families through legal quicksand, prolonged dry spells, and seemingly endless negotiations to ultimate success. But he did not get to enter the promised land. He only caught a glimpse of it when he signed the memorandum of understanding in October 2002.

A month and a half later, on December 8, Lee suffered a massive stroke at his home in Chappaqua. It came as a shock to everyone. No one expected it. At 78, Lee had seemed healthy, vigorous, and active. It turned out that, despite taking blood thinners, he had suffered several small undetected TIAs after the initial one.

Lee spent the next month in Northern Westchester Hospital in Mount Kisco, lingering in a semi-conscious state. Ruth rarely left his side, holding his hand and talking to him. Then, he was transferred to New York University Hospital in Manhattan for further expert care.

During one of the visits to his father's bedside, Jim had the strong feeling that Lee could hear and understand him. Referring to Lockerbie, he told him, "Don't worry, Dad, I'm going to finish this."

A month later, on February 18, Lee died.

Nearly 1,000 letters of condolence poured in, some typed, many hand-written. They came from clients, friends, other attorneys, and people who had worked at the law firm. They remembered Lee for his kindness, brilliance, and compassion and thanked him for his help in their careers and the difference he'd made in their lives.

The funeral was held at Temple Beth El in Chappaqua. Hundreds of people attended the service, including men and women from the aviation accident and insurance world, judges, other attorneys, partners and staff of Kreindler & Kreindler, and numerous friends and acquaintances. After the ceremony, Lee was interred in nearby Mount Pleasant Cemetery.

Ruth found a bagpiper to play at the gravesite. The plaintive, haunting sounds reminded everyone of the Lockerbie case in Scotland, which Lee had pursued with tenacious determination in the autumn of his life and had become an indelible part of his own heritage. At some point, a flock of birds roused from the nearby trees took to the air. Coincidentally, four Air Force fighter jets flew overhead, as if in salute. Ruth looked up and, for a moment, felt at peace.

EPILOGUE

In 2006, Dona Bainbridge and her son, who had turned 18 two weeks earlier, visited Jim Kreindler at the law firm office in New York. Harry Jr was almost as tall as Jim and had light brown hair and an outgoing smile. He reminded Jim of photographs of his father that Dona had shown him.

Now in her early 50s, Dona seemed relaxed and content. "I showed Harry the transcript of the trials," she said, "and he wanted to meet you in person."

Harry took a step toward Jim, held out his hand, and said, with a slight smile, "Mr. Kreindler, thank you."

They shook hands. Jim noticed that Harry had a firm grip.

It was a quick meeting, but it meant the world to Jim to see the impact of the protracted Lockerbie litigation on one family.

A year later, he participated in a seminar at Duke University School of Law: "From Pan Am to Gaddafi." He shared the stage with fellow Plaintiffs Committee member Jerry Skinner and with Robert Mirone, who had represented the Libyan government during settlement negotiations. Although Jim and Mirone had been on opposite sides of the case, their comments and exchanges were collegial.

Speaking about the enormous risks taken by his father and the law firms involved, Jim said, "The Pan Am battle was a fight to the death. It was an enormously expensive litigation. We invested our personal money and devoted two-thirds of our firm's resources for years in an extraordinarily difficult case. It's not an exaggeration to say that probably none of our law firms could have survived losing the Pan Am 103 case."

Mirone, describing the negotiations that led to the $2.7 billion settlement with Libya, said, "You always have to trust the attorneys on the other side until they prove you wrong. Lee Kreindler was the father of us in all of that."

A year later, after the terms to trigger the third Libyan payment were fulfilled and the sums of money were on their way to the accounts of the victims' families, Jim Kreindler sent an invite to the law firm's Lockerbie clients. More than 500 people came to the 20th-anniversary luncheon to commemorate the downing of Pan Am's Flight 103. An international audio transmission hookup allowed people on the West Coast and in Europe to listen to the event.

The luncheon took place at Cipriani's in New York City. Located on 42nd Street between Park and Lexington Avenues, the world-famous restaurant was situated in what had been a bank building and used its largest banquet hall to accommodate all the attendees. Ruth was an honored guest.

Parents of the Syracuse students who died aboard the plane came. All the members of Victims of Pan Am Flight 103 showed up. Other attendees included many children of passengers who perished in the disaster. They had successful careers by then. Some had families of their own.

Jim and Steve Pounian spoke about the litigation efforts and Lee's pivotal role in all aspects of the Pan Am trial and negotiations with Libya. Several younger participants told stories of how they and their surviving mother or father could keep their homes and how they went to college thanks to Lee's tireless efforts on their behalf.

They gave Ruth a plaque and flowers to express their gratitude for the difference she and Lee had made in their lives.

* * *

Epilogue

In 2010, having been diagnosed with terminal pancreatic cancer, Megrahi was pardoned in Scotland. The decision outraged many Lockerbie families. The terrorist was allowed to return home to Libya and died there two years later.

Thirty-four years after the terrorist attack, the maker of the bomb, Abu Agila Masud, was finally arrested. He was arraigned on December 22, 2022, and is awaiting trial in the United States, as of this writing.

The Victims of Pan Am Flight103 remain an active voice as new developments occur.

There are memorials honoring the Victims of Pan Am Flight 103 in Arlington National Cemetery, at Syracuse University, at the Tundergarth Parish Church two miles east of Lockerbie, and at the Dryfesdale Cemetery & Garden of Remembrance just outside the town.

A poem by Karen Lee Hunt, one of the Syracuse students who died in the crash on December 21, 1988, is inscribed on a gravestone at Dryfesdale:

> *Something has happened*
> *To keep us apart*
> *But always and forever*
> *You're in my heart.*
>
> *Someday soon*
> *From now till forever*
> *I'll meet you again*
> *And we'll be together.*
>
> *I'm not sure how*
> *And I'm not sure when,*
> *Together, Forever,*
> *Somewhere, my friend.*

Ruth was deeply moved when she first read the words. Recalling them later, they beautifully expressed her feelings for Lee, too.

AFTERWORD

After the Pan Am trial was settled, Lee Kreindler wanted to write a book about the case. He created two drafts in outline, first-person accounts with some parts filled in. For the first, he used pseudonyms for many of the victims' families, presumably to preserve their privacy. In the second, he reverted to their real names. Because the Libya suit and negotiations and other air disaster cases kept him busy, he tabled the project.

This book, based on Lee's and Ruth's recollections, is a creative history that tells the story mostly from his perspective. Taking as models third-person, literary journalistic accounts like *All the Presidents' Men*, Norman Mailer's *The Armies of the Night*, and *Schindler's List*, we have kept to what happened as much as possible, but we have streamlined some events and dramatized others. In keeping with his second draft, we have used individuals' real names, but we have taken liberties with some descriptions, portraits of participants, and occurrences.

Many books and articles have been written about the criminal investigation and trial of the Lockerbie bombing, including conspiracy theories questioning the established narrative regarding what happened. Other bogus accounts continue to circulate on the internet and on YouTube. We have avoided them, relying on publications that recognize the chain of events of what led to the terrorist bombing as determined by the Scottish inquiry and by Lee and his team and presented at the criminal and civil trials.

THE FIGHT FOR JUSTICE

No story like this can be told without the help of others. We have used a number of online documentaries and articles written by journalists, participants in the trial, and members of the victims' families. We want to thank them all for their analyses and recollections.

ACKNOWLEDGMENTS

I owe immense gratitude to my son, Jim Kreindler, and my daughter, Laurie Kreindler. Night after night, they quietly and respectfully listened as their father recounted the day's events at trials throughout his career.

For this book, Jim, with his unmatched experience plus memory for names and dates kept everything factually correct. Laurie encouraged me from day one to write it. They provided unwavering support throughout.

I would also like to thank William and Laurence Weinbaum for helping me come out of my shell and encouraging me to live fully. Special thanks to Laurence for checking the manuscript with a fine-tooth comb.

My heart goes out to those who have lost loved ones. May they find peace.

—Ruth Kreindler

I especially want to thank Jim Kreindler, who participated in all aspects of the Pan Am trial and the Libya negotiations as a member of the Plaintiffs Committee. He generously shared the trial transcript, his knowledge of legal details and practices, and his memories. We could not have written the book without his expert help.

I want to thank Nancy Roucher for bringing Ruth and me together.

Daniel Rubin, Ed Linehan, and my wife, Susan Angermann, read the manuscript at various stages. I can't thank them enough for providing valuable feedback regarding legal procedures, structure, and narrative flow to make the book more accurate and dramatic.

—Chris Angermann

BIOGRAPHIES

Ruth Kreindler graduated from New York University as a pre-law major and studied architecture at Columbia University. She and her husband Lee became partners in every sense of the word. Whether it concerned their family or the Kreindler law firm, they were strategists, confidants, and each other's sounding boards. Ruth was often at Lee's side—traveling to international legal conferences, attending all his speeches and important trials, and hosting events at their home in Chappaqua for lawyers, judges, and local, state, national and world political leaders.

Passionate about innovation and technology, Ruth designed their Frank Lloyd Wright inspired home herself and oversaw its construction. She also contributed to the expansion and modernization of the Westchester County Airport and invented the "AdjusTABLE," (mentioned in this book), for which she holds the patent.

As president of The Lee S. Kreindler Foundation, Ruth has continued to carry on Lee's legacy including overseeing the creation of:

- The Kreindler Conference Hall, Room 41, Haldeman at Dartmouth College, a dynamic symposium venue designed to encourage dialogue between students around the world.

- The Endowment of the Lee S. Kreindler Professorship of Law chair at Harvard Law School focused on torts, class actions, criminal procedure, labor law, the federal courts and professional responsibility.

- The International Academy of Trial Lawyers Lee S. Kreindler Award given to outstanding members of the legal community, including William Guillimie, Chief Justice, International Court of Justice; then-Senator Joe Biden; George Tompkins; and Senator Kirsten Gillibrand.
- The Kreindler Website housing family archives.
- The publication of The Fight for Justice.

Chris Angermann earned a BA degree in English and German literature from Yale University and an MFA from the Yale School of Drama. He has worked as a professional theater and opera director, journalist, writer, and editor, and helps other writers publish their works under the imprint Bardolf & Company. Over the past decade, he has produced more than 100 titles, many of which have won national awards, including his own books *Dramatic Measures: Lesson from a Life in the Theater* and *How to Mess with Others for Their Own Good*. He lives with his wife Susan in Sarasota, Florida.

Dive Deeper:

For resources—including photographs, videos, and print materials on Pan Am 103 and Lee Kreindler— please visit:

www.FightForJusticeTeam.com

www.ingramcontent.com/pod-product-compliance
Lightning Source LLC
Chambersburg PA
CBHW030454100526
44580CB00009B/121/J